HIGH COURT CASE SUMMARIES

CIVIL PROCEDURE

Keyed to Yeazell's Casebook on Civil Procedure, 8th Edition

Mat #41549524

© West, a Thomson business, 2005
© 2009 Thomson Reuters
© 2014 LEG, Inc. d/b/a West Academic
    444 Cedar Street, Suite 700
    St. Paul, MN 55101
    1-877-888-1330

West, West Academic Publishing, and West Academic are trademarks of West Publishing Corporation, used under license.

Printed in the United States of America

ISBN: 978–0–314–29063–2

Table of Contents

Alphabetical Table of Cases

CHAPTER 1

An Overview of Procedure

Hawkins v. Masters Farms, Inc.

Instant Facts: Hawkins (P), on behalf of the estate of James Creal, sued the defendants in Kansas federal court alleging diversity of citizenship.

Black Letter Rule: A party's domicile is that place in which the party has established a physical presence with the intent to remain there.

Bridges v. Diesel Service, Inc.

Instant Facts: An attorney representing a plaintiff in an employment discrimination case violates Rule 11(b) because she does not perform a competent level of legal research in preparing the complaint, but the court determines that Rule 11 sanctions are not appropriate under the circumstances.

Black Letter Rule: Rule 11 sanctions are designed to deter improper conduct and will only be applied in exceptional circumstances where the claim is patently frivolous. Procedural errors likely will not result in sanctions.

Bell v. Novick Transfer Co.

Instant Facts: A minor child injured when a tractor-trailer truck crashed into the car in which he was a passenger sues the truck driver and his employer in federal court; and although the court applies state substantive law, it decides to apply federal procedural rules.

Black Letter Rule: A federal court is not required to apply a state "well-pleaded complaint" rule even when the case originated in state court under state substantive law.

Larson v. American Family Mutual Ins. Co.

Instant Facts: The plaintiffs sought to add a new defendant to their case against their insurer, which had removed the case to federal court on the basis of diversity, and which diversity would be destroyed by the amendment, so the insurer objected.

Black Letter Rule: Under 28 U.S.C. § 1447(e), if, after removal to federal court, the plaintiff seeks to join additional defendants whose joinder would destroy subject matter jurisdiction, the court may either (1) deny joinder or (2) permit joinder and remand the action back to the state court.

Butler v. Rigsby

Instant Facts: The defendant in a lawsuit arising from a car accident requested information from the plaintiffs' health care providers and the providers objected on the grounds that the information was confidential.

Black Letter Rule: A legal privilege can be used to protect information from discovery under Rule 26.

Houchens v. American Home Assurance Co.

Instant Facts: A widow sues an insurance company for breach of contract when the insurance company refused to pay on her husband's accidental death claims after her husband had been declared legally dead.

Black Letter Rule: A legal presumption cannot be used to defeat a motion for summary judgment made on the grounds that a party does not have enough evidence to meet his burden of proof.

Norton v. Snapper Power Equipment

Instant Facts: A judge granted a judgment notwithstanding the verdict in a strict liability case involving a man who lost four fingers after a lawnmower accident.

Black Letter Rule: A judgment notwithstanding the verdict cannot be granted after a motion for a directed verdict has been denied based on the same facts.

Rush v. City of Maple Heights

Instant Facts: One judge limited Rush's recovery from the City for her injuries from an accident to $100, and another judge ordered the County to pay more.

Black Letter Rule: Whether or not injuries to both person and property resulting from the same wrongful act are to be treated as injuries to separate rights or as separate items of damage, a plaintiff may maintain only one action to enforce his rights existing at the time such action is commenced.

Apex Hosiery Co. v. Leader

Instant Facts: A hosiery company sues a labor union for treble damages under the Sherman Antitrust Act and when the hosiery company requests information from the union during discovery, the union objects, is denied, and appeals.

Black Letter Rule: An order to produce information under Rule 34 cannot be appealed.

(Personal Representative) v. (Alleged Tortfeasor)

2003 WL 21555767 (D. Kan. 2003)

MINOR CONNECTIONS TO A STATE ARE INSUFFICIENT TO ESTABLISH CITIZENSHIP

■ **INSTANT FACTS** Hawkins (P), on behalf of the estate of James Creal, sued the defendants in Kansas federal court alleging diversity of citizenship.

■ **BLACK LETTER RULE** A party's domicile is that place in which the party has established a physical presence with the intent to remain there.

■ **PROCEDURAL BASIS**

On consideration of the defendant's motion to dismiss for lack of subject matter jurisdiction.

■ **FACTS**

In December 2000, James Creal was killed when the vehicle he was driving collided with a vehicle driven by a representative of Master Farms, Inc. (D), a Kansas citizen. On behalf of Creal's estate, Hawkins (P) sued Master Farms (D) in federal court, asserting the defendants' negligence was the cause of Creal's death. The defendants filed a motion to dismiss under Federal Rule of Civil Procedure 12(b)(1), arguing that the complaint failed to establish complete diversity as needed to confer jurisdiction upon the court.

Creal met his wife in 1999 in Missouri, where he lived with his mother. Beginning in 2000, Creal began to spend nights at his wife's Kansas apartment with her children. He gradually moved his clothing and belongings into the apartment, slept each night in the apartment, and paid a portion of the utilities and groceries. Two weeks before his death, Creal and his wife purchased a home in Kansas. However, Creal had registered his motor vehicles in Missouri, maintained a Missouri driver's license, and continued to receive mail at his mother's Missouri home. Additionally, Creal's estate was opened in a Missouri court, indicating his mother's Missouri address as his permanent residence.

■ **ISSUE**

Was Creal a citizen of Kansas at the time of his death, notwithstanding that his vehicles were registered in Missouri, he possessed a Missouri driver's license, and he continued to receive mail in Missouri?

■ **DECISION AND RATIONALE**

(Van Bebber, J.) Yes. Federal diversity jurisdiction exists only when the case involves parties with complete diversity of citizenship. Citizenship is established by the state in which a party is domiciled. In turn, a party's domicile is that place in which the party has "established a physical presence" with the "intent to remain there." In considering a motion to dismiss for lack of subject matter jurisdiction, a party may either challenge the sufficiency of the plaintiff's allegations of jurisdiction in the complaint or challenge the facts underlying those allegations. Here, Masters Farms (D) challenges plaintiff's factual assertion that Creal was a citizen of Missouri at the time of his death. Although Creal had some connection to the state of Missouri, those connections are too insignificant to establish citizenship. Creal had been living with his wife and two children in Kansas, moved his belongings into the home, and contributed to the household expenses. Shortly before his death, Creal purchased a new home in Kansas.

Although Creal gave some consideration to moving back to Missouri to be closer to his place of employment, no evidence suggests that he acted upon that possibility to demonstrate an intention not to remain in Kansas. Because Creal had established a physical presence in Kansas with the intention to remain there, Creal is a Kansas citizen. Because the defendants are also Kansas citizens, there is not complete diversity of citizenship and the court lacks subject matter jurisdiction. Motion granted.

Analysis:

Domicile has both a physical and a mental component. On the one hand, domicile is where a person maintains a physical presence, although he or she may not be physically situated in that domicile at a given time. On the other hand, physical presence must be accompanied with the intent to remain there. Thus, a law student attending an out-of-state university may not change his domicile if he intends to return to his home state to practice law.

■ **CASE VOCABULARY**

COMPLETE DIVERSITY: In a multiparty case, diversity between both sides to the lawsuit so that all plaintiffs have different citizenship from all defendants.

DIVERSITY JURISDICTION: A federal court's exercise of authority over a case involving parties from different states and an amount in controversy greater than a statutory minimum.

DIVERSITY OF CITIZENSHIP: A basis for federal-court jurisdiction that exists when (1) a case is between citizens of different states, or between a citizen of a state and an alien, and (2) the matter in controversy exceeds a specific value.

DOMICILE: The place at which a person is physically present and that the person regards as home; a person's true, fixed, principal, and permanent home, to which that person intends to return and remain even though currently residing elsewhere.

Bridges v. Diesel Service, Inc.

(Disabled Man) v. (Former Employer)

1994 WL 369508 (E.D. Pa. 1994)

ATTORNEY'S INCOMPETENCE FAILS TO INCUR RULE 11 SANCTIONS

■ **INSTANT FACTS** An attorney representing a plaintiff in an employment discrimination case violates Rule 11(b) because she does not perform a competent level of legal research in preparing the complaint, but the court determines that Rule 11 sanctions are not appropriate under the circumstances.

■ **BLACK LETTER RULE** Rule 11 sanctions are designed to deter improper conduct and will only be applied in exceptional circumstances where the claim is patently frivolous. Procedural errors likely will not result in sanctions.

■ **PROCEDURAL BASIS**

Defendant's motion for sanctions for plaintiff's violation of Rule 11(b).

■ **FACTS**

James Bridges (P) sued Diesel Services, Inc. ("Diesel") (D), his former employer on the grounds that Diesel had terminated his employment because of his disability in violation of the Americans with Disabilities Act ("ADA"). The ADA requires that all administrative action be exhausted before a discrimination suit can be brought. Bridges' (P) attorney did not exhaust all administrative remedies before filing the complaint. She failed to file a charge with the Equal Employment Opportunity Commission ("EEOC") as required by the ADA. The court dismissed Bridges complaint for failure to exhaust administrative remedies. Diesel (D) moved for sanctions under Rule 11(c) of the Federal Rules of Civil Procedure, claiming that Bridges had violated Rule 11(b)(2)'s provision that by presenting a complaint to the court, an attorney is certifying that to the best of his knowledge, information, and belief, formed after a reasonable inquiry, that the claims in the complaint are warranted by existing law. Rule 11(c) allows the court to award sanctions for violations of Rule 11. The court can order the violator to pay the moving party's legal expenses.

■ **ISSUE**

Is the court obligated to impose sanctions under Rule 11(c) for any violation of Rule 11(b)?

■ **DECISION AND RATIONALE**

(Huyett, J.) No. The court is not obligated to impose sanctions for every violation of Rule 11(b). Rule 11(b) requires counsel to " 'Stop, Think, Investigate and Research' " before filing a complaint. An attorney violates Rule 11(b) if signing the complaint is objectively unreasonable under the circumstances. An attorney's signature is a certification that the pleading is supported by a reasonable amount of factual investigation and a competent level of legal research. In this case, Bridges' (P) attorney did not demonstrate a competent level of research because she would have discovered the EEOC filing requirement after even a cursory examination of the ADA case law. However, although there is precedent for awarding Rule 11 sanctions for failure to exhaust administrative remedies, sanctions are not appropriate in this case. Rule 11 is designed to deter improper conduct and in this case there is no evidence that sanctions are necessary to deter future improper conduct by Bridges' (P) attorney. Bridges'

(P) attorney acknowledges her error and filed the charge with the EEOC. Bridges' (P) complaint was dismissed and can be re-filed once the administrative remedies are finally exhausted. Rule 11(c) sanctions are only appropriate in exceptional circumstances, where the claim is patently frivolous. In this case, the attorney's mistake was not substantive, but procedural and possibly caused by a mistaken interpretation of a Supreme Court ruling on a matter involving an EEOC filing requirement. There is also a policy rationale for denying sanctions in cases such as this one: the possibility that plaintiffs would have to pay defendant's legal fees if the plaintiff's attorneys make procedural mistakes in filing pleadings would have a chilling effect on discrimination litigation. Motion for sanctions denied.

Analysis:

Rule 11(c) states that the court may impose sanctions for violations of Rule 11(b). Courts have discretion in deciding under what circumstances they will impose sanctions. In this case, the court decided that it would not impose sanctions where the defect in the complaint was minor and merely procedural rather than substantive. The defect was easy to cure, and Bridges' (P) attorney did so promptly. The court advances an important policy reason for not imposing sanctions for minor violations in discrimination cases. The court balances the need to avoid chilling Title VII litigation with the need to deter future violations of Rule 11 by naming Bridges' (P) attorney in the opinion and questioning her professional competence.

■ **CASE VOCABULARY**

CONDITION PRECEDENT: The condition that must be performed or event that must occur before a party can perform an obligation.

Bell v. Novick Transfer Co.

(Injured Automobile Passenger) v. (Owner of Tractor-Trailer Truck)

17 F.R.D. 279 (D. Md. 1955)

PLEADING A DETAILED AND SPECIFIC CLAIM IS NOT NECESSARY TO SURVIVE MOTION TO DISMISS IN FEDERAL COURT

■ **INSTANT FACTS** A minor child injured when a tractor-trailer truck crashed into the car in which he was a passenger sues the truck driver and his employer in federal court; and although the court applies state substantive law, it decides to apply federal procedural rules.

■ **BLACK LETTER RULE** A federal court is not required to apply a state "well-pleaded complaint" rule even when the case originated in state court under state substantive law.

■ **PROCEDURAL BASIS**

Motion to dismiss for failure to state a compensable claim in a negligence action for damages.

■ **FACTS**

Ronald Bell (P), a minor, was injured after the car he was riding in was hit from the side by a tractor-trailer truck. The truck was owned by Novick Transfer Company ("Novick") (D) and Katie Marie Parsons (D) and was operated by Morris Jarrett Coburn, III (D). Bell (P) filed a negligence claim in Maryland state court. The case was removed to federal court on Novick's (D) motion under 28 U.S.C. §§1441 and 1446. Novick (D) then moved to dismiss the case because Bell's (P) complaint failed to state a claim under which relief could be granted. Novick (P) argued that the complaint failed to state a compensable claim under Maryland rules of civil procedure because it did not allege any specific act of negligence that resulted in an injury to Bell (P). The complaint alleged that on August 14, 1954, Bell (P) was riding in a car on Race Road in Baltimore County, Maryland when, at the intersection of Race Road and Pulaski Highway, the car was struck on the passenger side by a tractor-trailer truck owned by Novick (D) and Parsons (D) and operated by Coburn (D). Coburn had been driving the truck in a reckless and negligent manner. The complaint listed Bell's (P) injuries and damages and asserted that they were caused by Novick's negligence.

■ **ISSUE**

Is a federal court required to apply a state "well-pleaded complaint" rule when the case originated in state court under state substantive law?

■ **DECISION AND RATIONALE**

(Thompsen, J.) No. A federal court is not required to apply a state "well-pleaded complaint" rule, even though the case originated in state court under state substantive law. Rule 8 of the Federal Rules of Civil Procedure requires only that a complaint be "a short and plain statement of the claim showing that the pleader is entitled to relief." Bell's (P) complaint satisfies this requirement by alleging negligence on Novick's (D) part and asserting that this negligence caused Bell's (P) injuries. Novick (D) also is not entitled to a "more definite statement" under Rule 12(e), because the information that Bell (P) would have to provide can be obtained during the discovery phase of the litigation. In this case, a more definite statement is not necessary to enable Novick (D) to form an adequate response to the complaint. Motion to dismiss denied.

Analysis:

This case highlights a difficult problem in civil procedure: how specific should a plaintiff's complaint be in order to survive a motion to dismiss for failure to state a compensable claim? The injured party is not always in a position to know all the facts relating to his cause of action. The factual development happens during discovery. The discovery phase of litigation is where the parties spend most of their time and money. At the complaint stage, the plaintiff will have very little evidence—he may only have suspicions and theories. But it may not be fair to slap the defendant with a lawsuit, forcing him to hire a lawyer and incur fees and expenses, on the basis of suspicions and theories with little factual support. This case shows how different the federal approach to pleading can be from the state approach. Maryland rules of procedure require plaintiffs to do at least some factual development before filing a complaint. Rule 8 requires only a short and simple statement of the claim under which the plaintiff is entitled to relief. Bell's complaint satisfies this requirement.

■ CASE VOCABULARY

DECLARATION: Usually a statement under penalty of perjury; document which sets forth the plaintiff's cause of action and facts which sustain the cause of action, which advise defendant of the grounds upon which he is being sued.

DISCOVERY: The process through which both parties obtain the information that they intend to use as evidence at trial or to use in preparing their cases.

INTERROGATORY: Questions submitted by one party to the other party; interrogatories can be written, or they can be oral, in which case they take place during depositions.

Larson v. American Family Mutual Ins. Co.

(Insured) v. (Insurer)

2007 WL 1686747 (D. Colo. 2007)

AN ATTORNEY'S FAILURE TO SUE AN INSURANCE COMPANY BECAUSE HE WANTED
TO WORK THERE LANDED HIM IN THE SAME LAWSUIT

■ **INSTANT FACTS** The plaintiffs sought to add a new defendant to their case against their insurer, which had removed the case to federal court on the basis of diversity, and which diversity would be destroyed by the amendment, so the insurer objected.

■ **BLACK LETTER RULE** Under 28 U.S.C. § 1447(e), if, after removal to federal court, the plaintiff seeks to join additional defendants whose joinder would destroy subject matter jurisdiction, the court may either (1) deny joinder or (2) permit joinder and remand the action back to the state court.

■ **PROCEDURAL BASIS**

Federal district court consideration of the plaintiffs' motion to amend to add a new defendant.

■ **FACTS**

The plaintiffs hired attorney Ross-Shannon to represent them in a case against American Family (D) for failure to pay their house fire claim. Ross-Shannon failed to file the Larsons' (P) claim, however, because he was seeking to be hired by American Family (D). The Larsons (P) obtained a new lawyer, who filed suit in state court, but American Family (D) removed the case to federal court based on diversity of citizenship. The Larsons (P) later sought to amend their complaint to add claims against Ross-Shannon, which would have destroyed the diversity, and American Family (D) objected. The insurance company argued that the motion to amend was too late, and that the claims against Ross-Shannon did not arise out of the same transaction or occurrence.

■ **ISSUE**

Could the plaintiffs amend their complaint to add as a defendant the attorney who failed to file their claim against the defendant insurance company?

■ **DECISION AND RATIONALE**

(Figa, J.) Yes. Under 28 U.S.C. § 1447(e), if, after removal to federal court, the plaintiff seeks to join additional defendants whose joinder would destroy subject matter jurisdiction, the court may either (1) deny joinder or (2) permit joinder and remand the action back to the state court. Here, American Family (D) argues that the amendment to add a new defendant was sought too late, and that the claims against Ross-Shannon did not arise out of the same transaction or occurrence as their claims against the insurer. We reject both contentions. The plaintiffs were not aware of the existence of evidence to support their possible claims against their first attorney until American Family (D) responded to discovery requests served by their second attorney. Moreover, the Larsons (P) would be prejudiced if they were denied the opportunity to amend their complaint to add Ross-Shannon as a defendant, because then they would have to bring a separate, somewhat duplicative case in state court. In addition, this is

---

not a case of fraudulent joinder, in which a party seeks to add another party to a lawsuit merely to destroy diversity.

As for whether the claims against Ross-Shannon arise out of the same transaction or occurrence as the claims against American Family (D), Fed. R. Civ. P. 20(a)(2)(A) provides that all persons may be joined as parties if there is any asserted right to relief against them arising out of the same transaction or occurrence or series of transactions or occurrences. Although the alleged duties of the defendants may be different in this case, the breaches of those duties arose out of the same transaction or occurrence or series of transactions or occurrences. It would be inefficient to require the plaintiffs to bring two separate lawsuits in two separate courts. Joinder should be permitted, and thus the case must be remanded to state court.

Analysis:

Complete diversity must exist in order for a federal court to have diversity jurisdiction over the case. The rule of complete diversity was first laid down by Chief Justice Marshall in *Strawbridge v. Curtiss*, 7 U.S. (3 Cranch) 267 (1806). As this case demonstrates, however, complete diversity may be destroyed by joinder of a non-diverse party. Joinder is more likely to be allowed, despite its effect on diversity, when it is deemed "compulsory." Joinder is deemed compulsory when (1) those already involved in the lawsuit cannot receive complete relief in the absence of joinder; or (2) the party sought to be joined claims an interest in the subject of the action, such that failure to join might impair that interest or subject another party to multiple or inconsistent obligations. *See* Fed. R. Civ. P. 19(a). Permissive joinder, by contrast, is optional, and occurs when (1) the parties' claims or the claims asserted against them are asserted jointly, severally, or in respect to the same transaction or occurrence; and (2) any legal or factual question common to all of them will arise. *See* Fed. R. Civ. P. 20.

■ CASE VOCABULARY

DIVERSITY: A basis for federal-court jurisdiction that exists when (1) a case is between citizens of different states, or between a citizen of a state and an alien, and (2) the matter in controversy exceeds a specific value (now $75,000). 28 U.S.C.A. § 1332. For purposes of diversity jurisdiction, a corporation is considered a citizen of both the state of incorporation and the state of its principal place of business. An unincorporated association, such as a partnership, is considered a citizen of each state where at least one of its members is a citizen.

JOINDER: The uniting of parties or claims in a single lawsuit.

REMAND: To send (a case or claim) back to the court or tribunal from which it came for some further action.

REMOVAL: The transfer of an action from state to federal court. In removing a case to federal court, a litigant must timely file the removal papers and must show a valid basis for federal-court jurisdiction. 28 U.S.C.A. § 1441.

(Automobile Accident Victims) v. (Negligent Party)

1998 WL 164857 (E.D.La. 1998)

COURT PREVENTS DISCOVERY OF INFORMATION PROTECTED BY DOCTOR-PATIENT PRIVILEGE

■ **INSTANT FACTS** The defendant in a lawsuit arising from a car accident requested information from the plaintiffs' health care providers and the providers objected on the grounds that the information was confidential.

■ **BLACK LETTER RULE** A legal privilege can be used to protect information from discovery under Rule 26.

■ **PROCEDURAL BASIS**

Appeal of Magistrate Judge's denial of expert witnesses' motion for a protective order under Rule 26(c).

■ **FACTS**

The lawsuit arose from an automobile accident. Butler and the other plaintiffs in the case (P) received medical treatment from the American Medical Group ("AMG") and from Midtown Health Center ("MHC"). Rigsby (D) served AMG and MHC with notices of depositions requesting documents and other information. Rigsby (D) asked AMG and MHC to provide any documents and other evidence that reflect: a listing of the total number of patients treated by AMG and MHC since 1992 that are now involved in the lawsuit and a list of patients referred to AMG and MHC by specific personal-injury lawyers. Rule 26(c) allows individuals from whom discovery is sought to move for a protective order even if they are not parties to the suit. Rule 26(b)(1) allows parties to obtain discovery "regarding any matter, not privileged, which is relevant to the subject matter involved in the pending action." Rule 26(b)(2) allows courts to restrict discovery if "the burden or expense of the proposed discovery outweighs its likely benefit." AMG and MHC moved for a protective order prohibiting Rigsby's (D) discovery on the grounds that the list of patients referred by certain personal-injury lawyers was not relevant to the lawsuit under Rule 26(b)(1), that the listing of the number of current AMG and MHC patients was protected by the doctor-patient privilege, and that the request for information was unduly burdensome under Rule 26(b)(2) and (c). Rigsby (D) argued that the listing of patients referred to AMG and MHC by specific personal-injury lawyers was relevant because it would show that AMG and MHC receive income from the lawyers who had originally represented Butler (P). The magistrate judge denied AMG's and MHC's motion.

■ **ISSUE**

Can a privilege, such as the doctor-patient privilege, protect certain information from discovery even when that information is relevant to the case under Rule 26(b)(1) and the request is not unduly burdensome under Rule 26(b)(2)?

■ **DECISION AND RATIONALE**

(Sarah Vance, J.) Yes. A privilege, such as the doctor-patient privilege, can protect certain information from discovery, even when the information is relevant to the subject of the lawsuit under Rule 26(b)(1) and the request was not unduly burdensome under Rule 26(b)(2). Rule

---

26 authorizes a broad definition of relevance. However, discovery can be limited when the request for information is unreasonably cumulative or duplicative or where the burden imposed outweighs the likely benefit of obtaining the information. AMG and MHC argued that the listing of all patients referred by certain personal-injury lawyers was both irrelevant and burdensome. Rigsby (D) argued that the information was necessary to establish that AMG and MHC had received substantial income from attorneys who had represented Butler, et al. (P) and that AMG and MHC were biased as a result. Evidence of a "special relationship" between an attorney and his expert witness is relevant to establishing bias. Discovery that is designed to produce such evidence is allowed when the request for information is not too burdensome. In this case, the burden imposed on AMG and MHC does not outweigh the likely benefit to Rigsby (D). However, because AMG and MHC will be put to considerable expense to provide lists of patients, and research the source of their referrals, Rigsby (D) will have to pay half of AMG and MHC's costs. The listing of patients treated by AMG and MHC since 1992 would include a list of both current and past patients. The identities of a health care provider's past and current patients are protected under Louisiana case law by the doctor-patient privilege and are therefore not discoverable under Rule 26(b)(1). As an additional matter, it is unclear whether a list of past and current patients would be relevant to the subject matter of the lawsuit. Affirmed in part and reversed in part.

Analysis:

Why has Congress given protection from discovery to certain legally recognized types of privileged communications when other types of inadmissible evidence are not protected from discovery? Congress and the courts may want to encourage Individuals to make these kinds of communications. Society has an interest in encouraging individuals to disclose their identities and the nature of their Injuries to doctors. Patients might be less inclined to discuss their medical problems with their doctors if they knew that their discussion was not absolutely confidential. To allow doctors to reveal confidential information in a room full of lawyers during a deposition might undermine patients' trust in their doctors—especially in cases such as this one, where the patients had suffered injuries in an automobile accident and were planning to sue for damages.

■ CASE VOCABULARY

AFFIDAVIT: a written statement that has been signed and notarized.

Houchens v. American Home Assurance Co.

(Widow) v. (Insurance Company)

927 F.2d 163 (4th Cir. 1991)

PRESUMPTION THAT MAN IS DEAD NOT ENOUGH TO CONVINCE JURY THAT HE DIED BY ACCIDENT

■ **INSTANT FACTS** A widow sues an insurance company for breach of contract when the insurance company refused to pay on her husband's accidental death claims after her husband had been declared legally dead.

■ **BLACK LETTER RULE** A legal presumption cannot be used to defeat a motion for summary judgment made on the grounds that a party does not have enough evidence to meet his burden of proof.

■ **PROCEDURAL BASIS**

Appeal of district court's granting motion for summary judgment.

■ **FACTS**

In 1980, Coulter Houchens disappeared while on vacation in Thailand. According to Thai immigration records, Mr. Houchens arrived in Bangkok on August 15, 1980 and his entry permit was valid until August 29. No one has heard from Mr. Houchens since his arrival in Thailand. The State Department, FBI, ICAO, Red Cross, and Mrs. Houchens (P) all searched for Mr. Houchens, unsuccessfully. In 1988 a Virginia court issued an order declaring that Mr. Houchens was legally dead under Virginia law. Mrs. Houchens (P) then filed a claim with American Home Assurance Company ("American") (D), the provider of Mr. Houchens' two accidental death policies. American (D) refused to pay under these policies because there was no evidence that Mr. Houchens had died by accident. Mrs. Houchens (P) sued for breach of contract, and American (D) moved for summary judgment. The district court granted the motion on the grounds that Mrs. Houchens (P) did not have sufficient evidence that would allow a jury reasonably to find that Mr. Houchens was dead and that his death resulted from an accident.

■ **ISSUE**

Can a legal presumption be used to defeat a motion for summary judgment made on the grounds that the plaintiff cannot meet the burden of proof?

■ **DECISION AND RATIONALE**

(Ervin, C.J.) No. A legal presumption of death cannot be used to defeat a motion for summary judgment made on the grounds that the plaintiff cannot meet her burden of proving that there was a death by accident. Under Virginia law, a person who has been missing for seven years is presumed to be dead. But in order to recover under American's (D) insurance policies, Mrs. Houchens (P) must prove that Mr. Houchens' death was caused by accident. The district court applied the standard for granting summary judgment developed by the Supreme Court. Under the Supreme Court standard, the court should grant a motion for summary judgment against a party "who fails to make a showing sufficient to establish the existence of an element essential to that party's case." Under the 4th Circuit's summary judgment jurisprudence, the court will reverse a grant of summary judgment made by a district court if the record shows that there is

---

"an unresolved issue of material fact." The 4th Circuit will examine the evidence presented in the light most favorable to the party opposing the motion. Mrs. Houchens (P) argued that the presumption that Mr. Houchens is dead was enough to meet her burden of proving that Mr. Houchens died accidentally. She based her argument on three cases decided outside the 4th Circuit. In one case, the court applied the rule that a jury is not allowed to reach a conclusion by piling inferences upon inferences. In other words, "a jury will not be permitted to extrapolate conjecturally beyond a legal conclusion which is itself arrived at circumstantially by inference from a proven fact." That court went on to find that the evidence that the deceased man had last been seen alive while asking for directions in the American River Ridge, where he had been hunting elk without the aid of a compass, was enough to give rise to two separate inferences: that the man had died, and that he had died by accident. Because a jury could reasonably have decided that the evidence supported either or both of those conclusions, the plaintiff in that case had not "piled inferences on inferences." In this case, however, there is only evidence of a disappearance, not of a death or an accident. A jury could conclude that Mr. Houchens disappeared, and presume that he died under Virginia law, but there is no evidence that would allow a jury to conclude that Mr. Houchens died as a result of an accident. To conclude that Mr. Houchens had died by accident based on Virginia's presumption that he was dead, which itself was based not on the fact that he had died but on the fact that he had disappeared, would be to pile inference upon inference. Affirmed.

Analysis:

Under Rule 56, the judge must decide on the basis of the documents presented to him whether a reasonable juror could conclude that the nonmoving party had enough evidence to meet his burden of proof and win the case. The jury's role is to decide between issues of conflicting material facts. If one party's assertions are unsupported by the evidence, there is no issue for the jury to decide. However, if the parties are able to present witnesses that contradict each other, or documentary evidence that can be disputed, then the judge will not take the case away from the jury. Summary judgment reduces the administrative burden that an excessive number of trials would impose on the court system. It prevents juries from hypothesizing a plausible set of circumstances to support assertions made in the absence of evidence, as in this case. And it prevents defendants from having to go to the expense of defending themselves from a frivolous claim that is not supported by evidence.

■ **CASE VOCABULARY**

INFERENCE: A permissible conclusion drawn from the evidence presented.

PRESUMPTION: A mandatory conclusion that has the effect of shifting to the opposing party the burden of disproving it.

Norton v. Snapper Power Equipment

(Lawnmower Accident Victim) v. (Lawnmower Manufacturer)

806 F.2d 1545 (11th Cir. 1987)

COURT TRIES UNSUCCESSFULLY TO GRANT A JUDGMENT NOTWITHSTANDING THE VERDICT AFTER DENYING A MOTION FOR A DIRECTED VERDICT

■ **INSTANT FACTS** A judge granted a judgment notwithstanding the verdict in a strict liability case involving a man who lost four fingers after a lawnmower accident.

■ **BLACK LETTER RULE** A judgment notwithstanding the verdict cannot be granted after a motion for a directed verdict has been denied based on the same facts.

■ **PROCEDURAL BASIS**

Appeal from district court's entering of a judgment notwithstanding the verdict to the defendant in a strict liability action for damages.

■ **FACTS**

James L. Norton (P) was in the commercial lawn mowing business. He bought a riding mower manufactured by Snapper Power Equipment ("Snapper") (D) in 1981. In 1983 Norton (P) was using the riding mower to clear leaves from a yard. He drove the mower up an incline away from a creek. When he reached the top of the incline, the mower began to reverse toward the creek. The mower did not respond when Norton (P) tried to brake, and eventually the mower crashed into the creek. Norton (P) caught his hand in the mower's blades and lost four of his fingers [yipes!]. After Norton (P) had presented his case, Snapper (D) moved for a directed verdict on all counts. The court dismissed all of Norton's claims but the strict liability claim. Norton's (P) strict liability claim was that Snapper's (D) failure to install a safety device called a "dead man" device in the mower rendered the mower defective and that this defect was the cause of his injury. The jury found for Norton (P) on the strict liability claim, and the court decided to enter a judgment notwithstanding the verdict. The court decided that the jury could not reasonably have found that a Snapper mower used in the normal course of use for which it had been designed could have had a defect that was the cause of Norton's (P) injury because Norton (P) did not present sufficient evidence that there was a defect in the mower at the time he bought it.

■ **ISSUE**

Can a court grant a judgment notwithstanding the verdict on an issue on which it has already decided not to grant a motion for a directed verdict based on the same facts?

■ **DECISION AND RATIONALE**

(Clark, J.) No. A court cannot grant a judgment notwithstanding the verdict on an issue on which it has already denied a motion for a directed verdict based on the same facts. The test for a judgment notwithstanding the verdict is the same as the test for a directed verdict. The court must consider the evidence presented in the light most favorable to the nonmoving party and should grant the judgment only when the evidence points so strongly in favor of the moving party that a reasonable jury could not arrive at a contrary verdict. Snapper (D) argued that because Norton (P) did not know exactly how his hand got caught in the mower's blades,

---

the jury could not have determined that Snapper's (D) failure to install the "dead man" safety device was the cause of Norton's (P) injury. The 11th Circuit applies the rule that plaintiffs "are not entitled to a verdict based on speculation and conjecture." Juries are allowed to decide on the facts by drawing inference upon inference. In the 5th Circuit case of *Fenner v. General Motors Corp.*, the district court had granted a judgment notwithstanding the verdict in a case where the plaintiff argued that his injuries were caused when a defective steering mechanism caused his car to swerve off the highway after a stone lodged itself in the mechanism. In that case, the plaintiff had not allowed experts to examine his car to verify his claim. Because the experts could only testify that theoretically it was possible that a stone had been lodged in the plaintiff's steering mechanism, the court entered a judgment notwithstanding the verdict. In this case however, the causation evidence is much stronger. Norton (P) testified that his mower reversed into the creek and expert testimony verified that a "dead man" safety device would have stopped the blades in less than a second. The blades in Norton's (P) mower took two or three seconds to stop. A reasonable jury could have concluded that a "dead man" device could have prevented Norton's (P) injury.

Analysis:

When it reversed the jury's verdict, the trial court was saying that it thought this jury unreasonable, because no reasonable jury could have decided that Snapper (D) was liable for Norton's (P) injuries on the basis of the facts presented. But why allow the jury to enter a verdict at all? Why did the court not dispose of the case by granting Snapper's (D) motion for a directed verdict? The court wanted a jury verdict on record in case its decision to issue a judgment notwithstanding the verdict was reversed on appeal. Having a jury verdict on record prevented the court and the parties from re-trying the case with a new jury. This saved the parties money and the court time.

■ CASE VOCABULARY

DIRECTED VERDICT: A verdict that the jury issues after the court tells it exactly which verdict to issue.

(Motorcycle Rider) v. (City)

167 Ohio St. 221, 147 N.E.2d 599 (1958)

A PLAINTIFF MAY MAINTAIN ONLY ONE ACTION TO ENFORCE HIS OR HER RIGHTS EXISTING AT THE TIME SUCH ACTION IS COMMENCED

■ **INSTANT FACTS** One judge limited Rush's recovery from the City for her injuries from an accident to $100, and another judge ordered the County to pay more.

■ **BLACK LETTER RULE** Whether or not injuries to both person and property resulting from the same wrongful act are to be treated as injuries to separate rights or as separate items of damage, a plaintiff may maintain only one action to enforce his rights existing at the time such action is commenced.

■ **PROCEDURAL BASIS**

Appeal from judgment in negligence action for damages.

■ **FACTS**

Rush (P) was injured in a motorcycle accident. She (P) sued the City of Maple Heights (D) in the Municipal Court of Cleveland. Rush (P) claimed the City (D) was negligent in maintaining the street and this negligence was the proximate cause of her (P's) damages. The trial court ruled for Rush (P), and damages were fixed at $100. The City (P) appealed, but the judgment was affirmed by the Ohio Court of Appeals and Supreme Court. Rush (P) also brought this action in the Court of Common Pleas of Cuyahoga. Rush (P) sought recovery for personal injuries she suffered in the same accident. She (P) moved to set trial on the issue of damages alone. The court granted this motion on the ground that the issue of negligence was res judicata because of the Municipal Court action. The Cuyahoga court entered judgment on a verdict for $12,000 for Rush (P). The Court of Appeals affirmed.

■ **ISSUE**

Can a plaintiff maintain more than one action for injuries to his or her rights resulting from one accident?

■ **DECISION AND RATIONALE**

(Herbert) No. Whether or not injuries to both person and property resulting from the same wrongful act are to be treated as injuries to separate rights or as separate items of damage, a plaintiff may maintain only one action to enforce his rights existing at the time such action is commenced. The rule presented in *Vasu v. Kohlers* [recovery or denial of recovery of compensation for damages to property is no bar to subsequent action for personal injury from same wrongful act unless an adverse judgment in first action would affect issue in second action] should not be followed because it is in conflict with the great weight of authority in this country. Generally, injuries to person and property amount to several effects of a single, wrongful act. A single tort can be the basis of but one action. Otherwise, multiple suits will arise, leading to significant delays and costs for all parties concerned. Allowing more than one action to arise from a single tort would allow, as Lord Coleridge stated in his dissent in

Brunsden v. Humphrey, a man to bring two actions "if besides his arm and leg being injured, his trousers, which contain his leg, and his coat-sleeve, which contains his arm, have been torn." Judgment reversed, and final judgment for the City (D).

■ CONCURRENCE

(Stewart) The discussion in *Vasu* as to whether a single or double cause of action arises from one tort nor the language of the syllabus of the lower court in *Vasu* were necessary to decide this case. Neither are appropriate to the question presented in this case.

■ DISSENT

(Zimmerman) Without changing conditions to compel upsetting prior decisions of this court, established law should remain undisturbed. There should be some kind of stability that the lower courts and other members of the legal profession can rely on.

Analysis:

The limits on the scope of claim preclusion have developed greatly since the turn of the century. As the Restatement (Second) of Judgments explains, the courts used to associate the word "claim" with a plaintiff's single theory of recovery. This meant that a plaintiff would have as many claims as there were theories of substantive law that he could use to gain relief from the defendant. Thus, a plaintiff could raise several claims from just one injury-causing act or event. Other courts held that if certain evidence were used in an earlier claim, a second action on the same evidence was precluded. At times, this evidence test was used as the sole test; at other times, courts used it as just one test out of many. Today, the courts generally see claims in factual terms and make the underlying transaction the basis of the litigation. In other words, the scope of claim preclusion is tied to the transaction, and not the number of theories, the number of primary rights, or the body of evidence.

■ CASE VOCABULARY

VEXATIOUS: Distressing, troubling.

Apex Hosiery Co. v. Leader

(Hosiery Company) v. (Labor Union)

102 F.2d 702 (3rd Cir. 1939)

PARTIES ARE NOT ALLOWED TO APPEAL DISCOVERY ORDERS

■ **INSTANT FACTS** A hosiery company sues a labor union for treble damages under the Sherman Antitrust Act and when the hosiery company requests information from the union during discovery, the union objects, is denied, and appeals.

■ **BLACK LETTER RULE** An order to produce information under Rule 34 cannot be appealed.

■ **PROCEDURAL BASIS**

Appeal from a Rule 34 order to produce documents for discovery purposes in a case for treble damages arising under the Sherman Antitrust Act.

■ **FACTS**

Apex Hosiery Co. ("Apex Hosiery") (P) is the plaintiff in an antitrust action. During discovery, Apex Hosiery (P) requested that Leader (D) (a labor union) produce documents for its inspection, copying, and photographing under Rule 34. Leader (D) objected, and the court issued an order requiring that Leader (D) produce the documents. Leader (D) appealed.

■ **ISSUE**

Can a party appeal a federal court order to produce documents under Rule 34?

■ **DECISION AND RATIONALE**

(Per Curiam) No. An order to produce documents for the inspection, copying, and photographing of the opposing party is an interlocutory order and cannot be appealed. This is the rule developed by the Supreme Court in *Cogen v. United States*. Only orders that have the effect of ending the case in favor of one party or the other can be appealed. The only exception is for orders that punish parties criminally for contempt: these orders do not effectively end the trial, but can be appealed. The order to produce documents will not cause the final disposition of the case in favor of Apex Hosiery (P) or Leader (D), and is therefore not appealable under *Cogen*. It is also clear that in this case the district court drafted the order carefully enough so that the document production will not unduly burden Leader (D).

Analysis:

The final judgment rule has two important effects: prohibiting parties from appealing non-final orders, such as the discovery order in this case; and encouraging parties to settle. Defendants, who usually have been dragged into expensive litigation against their will, have an incentive to settle cases as soon as possible in order to avoid the expense of discovery and the further expense of a trial. The process of discovery influences settlement terms. If a plaintiff is unable to obtain information to convince a jury to award him damages, and the court will not issue a discovery order, he may be tempted to settle with the defendant. If the court does issue an order, the defendant may be encouraged to make a settlement offer to the plaintiff in order to avoid going to the expense of document production. Thus, the appellate court need only review a case once. Two things should be noted. First, just because a discovery order is not appealable when it is made, does not mean that it cannot be appealed after a final judgment is entered. After final judgment is entered, any error of the trial court can be appealed, including a discovery order. Second, discovery orders are often reviewable by extraordinary writ (which is not the same as an appeal).

■ **CASE VOCABULARY**

INTERLOCUTORY ORDER: an order that is related to the action, but whose resolution will not determine the final outcome of the action.

SUBPOENA DUCES TECUM: a subpoena that both requires a witness to appear in court to testify and requires the witness to produce documents or other evidence.

CHAPTER 2

Personal Jurisdiction

Pennoyer v. Neff

Instant Facts: Neff (P) sought to recover possession of land which had been seized and sold to pay off a default judgment against him, claiming that the judgment was invalid, as the court involved had not had personal jurisdiction over him.

Black Letter Rule: Every state possesses exclusive jurisdiction and sovereignty over persons and property within its territory; therefore, the courts of that state may enter a binding judgment against a non-resident only if he is personally served with process while within the state, or, if he has property within the state, if that property is attached before litigation begins.

International Shoe Co. v. Washington

Instant Facts: A shoe company with salesmen in Washington State claimed not to be subject to Washington's jurisdiction when the state tried to collect unemployment taxes.

Black Letter Rule: A corporation will be subject to the jurisdiction of any state with which it has "minimum contacts" that make the exercise of jurisdiction consistent with "traditional notions of fair play and substantial justice."

McGee v. International Life Insurance Co.

Instant Facts: McGee (P), the beneficiary of a life insurance policy held by International Life (D), a Texas company, brought suit in California when International Life (D) refused to pay.

Black Letter Rule: A state may exercise jurisdiction over a defendant whose contacts with that state consist of only a single act, provided that that act is what gave rise to the claim for which jurisdiction is being sought, and was deliberately directed toward the state.

Hanson v. Denckla

Instant Facts: Various claimants to a Delaware trust filed suit against the trustee in Florida, claiming that the trust was invalid under Florida law.

Black Letter Rule: A state may not exercise jurisdiction over a defendant if the defendant's contacts with the state are negligible and non-deliberate, and the claim does not arise from those contacts.

Shaffer v. Heitner

Instant Facts: Heitner (P) brought a shareholder's derivative suit against several officers and directors of Greyhound, a Delaware corporation, gaining in rem jurisdiction by attaching their stock in Greyhound.

Black Letter Rule: Minimum contacts must exist in order for in rem jurisdiction to attach.

World-Wide Volkswagen v. Woodson

Instant Facts: A New York family passing through Oklahoma was in a car accident, and tried to bring suit there against the dealer who sold them the car in New York.

Black Letter Rule: In order to be subject to a state's jurisdiction, a defendant must have chosen to have some contact with that state; considerations of fairness, convenience, and the interests of the state in overseeing the litigation are otherwise irrelevant.

Burger King Corp. v. Rudzewicz

Instant Facts: Rudzewicz (D) contracted with Burger King (D), a Florida corporation, to operate a Burger King restaurant in Michigan, then defaulted on payments, so Burger King (P) sued him in Florida.

Black Letter Rule: Once it has been established that the defendant has minimum contacts with a state, it is up to the defendant to prove that being required to defend a suit there would be "fundamentally unfair."

Pavlovich v. Superior Court

Instant Facts: A Texas resident who posted information infringing upon the licensing rights of a California business on a Web site created in Indiana was sued in California state court for misappropriation of trade secrets.

Black Letter Rule: A court may exercise personal jurisdiction over a nonresident defendant only if the defendant has purposefully availed himself of the benefits of the forum state, the action relates to the defendant's contacts with the forum state, and jurisdiction would not offend notions of fair play and substantial justice.

J. McIntyre Machinery, Ltd. v. Nicastro

Instant Facts: Nicastro (P) sued J. McIntyre Machinery (D) in New Jersey for injuries caused by a machine manufactured by McIntyre (D), but McIntyre (D) had no contacts with New Jersey.

Black Letter Rule: Personal jurisdiction over an out-of-state defendant requires some showing that the defendant purposefully availed itself of the privilege of conducting activities within the state.

Goodyear Dunlop Tire Operations, S.A. v. Brown

Instant Facts: The sons of Brown (P) and Helms (P) were killed in a bus accident, allegedly because of tires manufactured by a foreign subsidiary of Goodyear (D), and the subsidiaries (D) claimed that the state court did not have jurisdiction.

Black Letter Rule: Sale of an out-of-state manufacturer's products in a forum state will justify the exercise of specific jurisdiction only with regard to the product that was sold in the state.

Burnham v. Superior Court

Instant Facts: While visiting California for business and vacation, Dennis Burnham (D) was served with process for a divorce proceeding, and Burnham (D) contends that California jurisdiction violates due process.

Black Letter Rule: Jurisdiction based on physical presence comports with due process, regardless of the defendant's contacts with the forum State.

Carnival Cruise Lines v. Schute

Instant Facts: In response to a suit for injuries occurring on one of its cruise ships, Carnival Cruise Lines (D) argued that the forum selection clause contained on the ticket should establish jurisdiction.

Black Letter Rule: Reasonable forum selection clauses are effective in imposing jurisdiction.

Mullane v. Central Hanover Bank & Trust Co.

Instant Facts: Central Hanover Bank and Trust Company (P) petitioned for a judicial settlement of a trust and provided notice by publication to all of the beneficiaries.

Black Letter Rule: Notice by publication fails to comply with due process where the names and addresses of the parties are known.

Gibbons v. Brown

Instant Facts: Passenger versus passenger lawsuit where personal jurisdiction was asserted based upon non-resident Brown (D) having filed a lawsuit in the state two years prior against a non-party driver.

Black Letter Rule: Jurisdiction over a non-resident defendant is not proper where the only contact with the state was filing a lawsuit two years earlier against a defendant not a party to the current suit.

Dee-K Enterprises, Inc. v. Heveafil Sdn. Bhd.

Instant Facts: Manufacturers of rubber thread outside of the United States challenge jurisdiction and venue to sue them in federal district court.

Black Letter Rule: General federal venue statute subjecting alien corporations to suit in any judicial district overrides other federal statutes that may contain specific venue provisions.

Piper Aircraft Co. v. Reyno

Instant Facts: The Scottish heirs of plane crash victims in Scotland try to sue for wrongful death in an American court because American courts recognize wrongful death as a cause of action and are known generally to be more favorable to plaintiffs than the courts in Scotland.

Black Letter Rule: The fact of a substantive law being less favorable to plaintiffs in an alternative forum should not be given conclusive or even substantial weight in applying the doctrine of forum non conveniens.

Pennoyer v. Neff

(Current Occupier of Land) v. (Rightful Owner of Land)

95 U.S. (5 Otto) 714 (1877)

SUPREME COURT SPELLS OUT THEORY OF PERSONAL JURISDICTION

■ **INSTANT FACTS** Neff (P) sought to recover possession of land which had been seized and sold to pay off a default judgment against him, claiming that the judgment was invalid, as the court involved had not had personal jurisdiction over him.

■ **BLACK LETTER RULE** Every state possesses exclusive jurisdiction and sovereignty over persons and property within its territory; therefore, the courts of that state may enter a binding judgment against a non-resident only if he is personally served with process while within the state, or, if he has property within the state, if that property is attached before litigation begins.

■ **PROCEDURAL BASIS**

Writ of Error to the Circuit Court of the United States for the District of Oregon, for its judgment in action to recover the possession of land.

■ **FACTS**

In the years prior to the Civil War, as America pursued its Manifest Destiny ever Westward, a young man named Marcus Neff (P) set out for the Oregon frontier—thus setting in motion a chain of events that would eventually culminate in one of the most famous Supreme Court cases ever—as well as the bane of law students everywhere for more than a hundred years. Neff (P) staked a claim for land from the federal government and in 1862 sought advice from a well-known Portland attorney (and future U.S. Senator) named John Mitchell, who specialized in land litigation. Whatever Mitchell did for Neff (P), Neff (P) apparently never paid him for it. Mitchell waited until late 1865, and then brought suit against Neff (P) in Oregon state court to recover the unpaid legal fees. As was totally proper under Oregon law at the time, Mitchell did not serve Neff (P) personally with notice of the suit, but published notice in a local newspaper (so-called "service by publication"). Neff (P), not being an Oregon resident at the time, somehow failed to see this notice, and did not show up to defend his rights in court. Mitchell thus easily obtained a default judgment against Neff (P) in 1866. Coincidentally enough, this happened to be the same year that Neff's (P) land patent arrived, which enabled Mitchell to have the land seized and sold at auction by the local sheriff to satisfy the judgment. At the auction, Mitchell himself was the lucky bidder. One can only assume that he got a fair price from himself for the land! Anyway, a few days after the auction Mitchell assigned the land to Sylvester Pennoyer (D), future Mayor of Portland and Governor of Oregon. Pennoyer (D) spent nine years and quite a bit of money improving the property, only to have Neff (P) show back up, claiming the land was still his. Neff (P) then sued Pennoyer (D) in federal court for possession of the property, claiming that the original judgment against him had not been valid, because the Oregon court had not had jurisdiction over him or the land. The Federal Circuit Court agreed that the other judgment was invalid and that the land really did belong to Neff (P), although not for the reasons that the Supreme Court later found

---

persuasive. Apparently, the Circuit Court's decision was based on some technicality related to how the notice had been published. Of course, it's possible to suspect ulterior motives for the Circuit Court's judgment, since Judge Deady, the judge involved, seemed to be just as immersed in local politics as Mitchell and Pennoyer (D). In fact, Deady was later instrumental in exposing Mitchell for the lying, bigamous, adulterer that he was. (Not that this had a negative impact on his career as a Senator) Pennoyer (D) appealed Deady's decision to the Supreme Court, but lost there too. So Neff (P) got his land back, and the country got a new-and-improved theory of personal jurisdiction. Well, the personal jurisdiction theory lived on for years, but Mitchell's career was eventually brought to a halt, when he was indicted and convicted for—of all things—land fraud in Alaska.

■ ISSUE

Can a state court exercise personal jurisdiction over a non-resident who has not been personally served with process while within the state, and whose property within the state was not attached before the litigation began?

■ DECISION AND RATIONALE

(Field) No. A state can obtain *in personam* jurisdiction over a non-resident only if that non-resident is personally served with process while within the territory of the state. *In rem* jurisdiction can be obtained if the non-resident owns property within the state, and that property is attached at the very outset of the trial. *In personam* jurisdiction means that the state has complete power over an individual, and stems from the notion that a state has exclusive control over all people within its borders; *in rem* jurisdiction stems from the idea that a state has exclusive control over all land within its territory, and means that the state can adjudicate disputes over the status of such property, but only up to the value of the property. In the case before us, the original action was initiated by publication of service. The Oregon state court which heard that case did not exercise either *in personam* or *in rem* jurisdiction—nor could it have. Neff (P), the defendant in that action, was not within the state of Oregon at the time, and so could not be personally served with process. Service of process is basically a command by a court to appear before it, or suffer the consequences. It dates back to a time when lawsuits were initiated not by a command to appear before the court, but by the sheriff actually taking the defendant into custody and physically bringing him before the court. But an Oregon sheriff could not go into another state—say California—and start hauling California residents back to Oregon to appear before an Oregon court. This would be an infringement of California's sovereignty. Thus, those same California residents could not be commanded to appear before an Oregon court either—unless, of course, they came into Oregon, in which case they came under Oregon's power, and could be seized or served with process while there. As Neff (P) was not within Oregon, he was not within Oregon's power, and could not be made to appear before an Oregon court. Period. Certainly not by publication in some obscure local newspaper, but not even if he had been tracked down and served with process personally wherever he was at the time. If he had come into Oregon and been served with process while there, then the Oregon courts would have had *in personam* jurisdiction over him. But he did not, and they did not. End of (*in personam*) story. *In rem,* however, still remains to be dealt with. While Oregon courts cannot exercise power over non-residents not found within the state, they do have power over any property the non-residents might own within Oregon. Originally, "property" in this context meant land, and dated back to the idea that a state should and did have ultimate power over all land within its borders. If there is a dispute over land, it makes sense that the state where that land is located should be able to mediate and resolve the dispute. And it also makes some sense that anyone who claims an interest in that particular piece of land should keep an eye on it—or at least check on it every so often. Ideally, an out-of-state landowner will appoint an agent of some kind to look after the land in his absence. It's not good public policy to encourage people to just abandon land for years at a time. Therefore, it is reasonable to assume that if land is attached by a court prior to a lawsuit, the owner of the land will—or should—find out about the lawsuit. (Attachment here simply means that the court forbids the land from being sold, etc., while the suit is pending.

Practically speaking, the sheriff will go out to the land and post notices announcing the suit, so anyone living there or going by to check it out will see them and know what's going on.) If the owner of that land does not check on it at least occasionally, he doesn't really deserve to own it, and it will be forfeit to the other party. While this type of proceeding was originally limited to pure *in rem* actions actually relating to the land itself, the doctrine of *quasi in rem* jurisdiction developed to allow the attachment of land as a means of initiating an action that had absolutely nothing to do with the land. But the same theory was involved—anyone really taking care of his land would find out what was going on. However, this was not done in the case at issue. If Mitchell had attached Neff's (P) land at the very beginning of his suit, then the court would have been able to issue a valid judgment in the case. However, Mitchell did not attach Neff's (P) land at the beginning of the suit. In fact, there's no way that he could have done so, since Neff (P) did not own the land at the time Mitchell instituted the action. Neff's (P) land patent did not arrive until after Mitchell had already obtained a judgment. Thus the court had no basis for exercising jurisdiction over Neff (P) at all, so the default judgment must be declared invalid. Since the sheriff therefore had no power to auction the land, Neff (P) must still legally own it. Judgment affirmed.

Analysis:

Pennoyer represents the first time that the U.S. Supreme Court enunciated a coherent, national standard for the exercise of jurisdiction by states over non-residents. The idea that a sovereign state had exclusive and complete power over everything and everyone within its borders, but not outside them, wasn't new, and was similar to how the international law worked at the time. What was different, of course, was that the various states of the United States were not independent and fully sovereign nation-states. More mobility of people could be expected between the states than between countries, which increased the chances that one state's citizen would come under the jurisdiction of another state. A standard was needed that would allow states some power over non-residents without offending the power of other states. *Pennoyer* was the Supreme Court's answer to this problem, but as it turned out, it was probably well on its way to being obsolete even at the time it was announced.

■ **CASE VOCABULARY**

EX PARTE: With the presence of one party only.

International Shoe Co. v. Washington

(Delinquent Taxpayer) v. (Tax Assessor)

326 U.S. 310, 66 S.Ct. 154 (1945)

SUPREME COURT REVOLUTIONIZES PERSONAL JURISDICTION

■ **INSTANT FACTS** A shoe company with salesmen in Washington State claimed not to be subject to Washington's jurisdiction when the state tried to collect unemployment taxes.

■ **BLACK LETTER RULE** A corporation will be subject to the jurisdiction of any state with which it has "minimum contacts" that make the exercise of jurisdiction consistent with "traditional notions of fair play and substantial justice."

■ **PROCEDURAL BASIS**

Appeal from sustaining of denial of motion to dismiss notice of assessment of unpaid unemployment contributions.

■ **FACTS**

International Shoe Co. (D) was incorporated in Delaware, and had its primary place of business in St. Louis, Missouri. It made and sold shoes in several states. In Washington State it did not maintain any offices or manufacturing facilities, but did employ some 11 to 13 salesmen during the years at issue (1937–1940). These salesmen were under the direct supervision of sales managers in St. Louis but lived and worked entirely within the state of Washington. The salesmen received samples from the company and showed these samples to potential customers to solicit orders. Sometimes the salesmen rented showrooms for the samples. Orders were filled from St. Louis, and the merchandise was sent straight to the customer, not to the salesman. The salesmen operated on commission and averaged around $31,000 per year (not bad during the Great Depression!). The State of Washington (P), in accordance with its laws on unemployment insurance, assessed International Shoe Co. (D) for its contribution and served notice both personally on one of the salesmen within the state and by mail to the St. Louis headquarters. International Shoe (D) challenged the service, claiming that the salesman was not a proper agent for service of process, and that it was not "present" or "doing business" within the state of Washington so as to be subject to that state's jurisdiction. The unemployment office, the Commissioner, the Superior Court, and the Supreme Court of Washington all held that service had been proper, and that jurisdiction did exist. International Shoe (D) appealed to the U.S. Supreme Court, claiming that its due process rights had been violated.

■ **ISSUE**

Is a corporation not chartered within a state subject to that state's jurisdiction if it has certain "minimum contacts" with the state?

■ **DECISION AND RATIONALE**

(Stone) Yes. A corporation is subject to the jurisdiction of a state so long as it has certain "minimum contacts" with that state. Many previous decisions have based jurisdiction over corporations on whether they are "present" within the state. Since it is much harder to determine whether a corporation—which is after all merely a fiction—is to be found within a

---

state's borders for exercise of its territorial power than it is with an actual human defendant, there has been a lot of debate over what it means for a corporation to be "present" within a state. Discussions of "presence" have centered around the extent of a corporation's activities within a state necessary to make subjecting it to jurisdiction there consistent with due process. Generally, systematic and continuous activities within a state have been held to be enough to subject a corporation to jurisdiction there—especially when the cause of action arises from those activities, but even in some cases where the cause of action does not arise from those activities. In some cases even a single, isolated contact with a state has been enough, when that contact gives rise to the cause of action. Obviously, a corporation that has no contacts at all with a state should not be subject to that state's jurisdiction. But a corporation that does conduct activities within a state also enjoys the benefits and protections of the state's laws and should therefore be held subject as well to those laws, and to actions brought to enforce those laws. There is no mechanical way to decide whether, in a particular case, a corporation's contacts with a state have reached the level necessary for the exercise of jurisdiction; instead, the nature and extent of those contacts must be evaluated under traditional concepts of fairness and justice to determine whether it would be reasonable to require the corporation to defend a suit in that state. In this case, International Shoe (D) has benefitted from the laws of Washington, which protected its numerous sales there. It has shipped a large volume of merchandise into Washington over the years, and has exercised continuous and systematic sales activities there. Also, the very nature of this suit arose from the company's activities there. The fact that International Shoe (D) employed salesmen within the state of Washington raised the issue of whether the company, as an employer, was required to make contributions to the state unemployment system. Therefore, the exercise of jurisdiction in this case by the courts of the state of Washington was not improper, and did not infringe International Shoe's (D) due process rights. Judgment affirmed.

■ CONCURRENCE

Jurisdiction was proper in this case. The U.S. Constitution granted to each state the right to tax and subject to suit any corporation whose activities within a state affect that state's citizens and businesses. Period. This Court should not have the power to invalidate a state's assertion of jurisdiction merely because the members of this Court have a different opinion of what is "fair" or "reasonable."

Analysis:

International Shoe essentially overturned the in personam half of *Pennoyer*, and provided the basis for the jurisdictional tests that are still used today. While *International Shoe* was originally geared to the burgeoning problem of establishing jurisdiction over corporations, which did not really fit within the *Pennoyer* categories, it did not take long for the ideas behind *Shoe* to spill over onto individuals. With regard to corporations, however, some guidance was badly needed. Since corporations are considered legal fictions that could not exist outside the state that created them, it was difficult for states to get jurisdiction over foreign corporations. And yet, corporations could obviously operate in more than one state at a time, and could have large impacts on the economy and society of states other than their own. Disputes with a corporation would often arise in a state where that corporation did not legally "exist." Somehow, states needed a way to obtain jurisdiction in these types of situations. Various theories, such as implied consent, were tried, but the time was ripe for change when *International Shoe* came along.

■ CASE VOCABULARY

CAPIAS AD RESPONDENDUM: Method of commencing a court action in which the defendant is physically seized by the sheriff, and kept in custody until he is brought before the court.

DISTRAINT: Seizure of property.

McGee v. International Life Insurance Co.

(Beneficiary of Policy) v. (Holder of Policy)

355 U.S. 220, 78 S.Ct. 199 (1957)

U.S. SUPREME COURT RULES THAT SINGLE BUSINESS TRANSACTION IS ENOUGH TO SATISFY MINIMUM CONTACTS REQUIREMENT

■ **INSTANT FACTS** McGee (P), the beneficiary of a life insurance policy held by International Life (D), a Texas company, brought suit in California when International Life (D) refused to pay.

■ **BLACK LETTER RULE** A state may exercise jurisdiction over a defendant whose contacts with that state consist of only a single act, provided that that act is what gave rise to the claim for which jurisdiction is being sought, and was deliberately directed toward the state.

■ **PROCEDURAL BASIS**

Appeal from Texas court's refusal to enforce California judgment in action to recover proceeds of life insurance policy.

■ **FACTS**

Lowell Franklin, a resident of California, had a life insurance policy with the Empire Mutual Insurance Company, of Arizona. In 1948 International Life Insurance Company (D), of Texas, took over Empire Mutual's policies. International Life (D) sent statements to Franklin in California, and Franklin sent payments to International Life (D) in Texas. When Franklin died in 1950, International Life (D) refused to pay the proceeds of his policy to his designated beneficiary, McGee (P), claiming that Franklin had committed suicide. McGee (P) brought suit in California, under a state law that authorized service of process on out-of-state companies holding insurance contracts with in-state residents. McGee (P) won a judgment against International Life (D) in California, then tried to enforce it in Texas. The Texas courts, however, refused to enforce the judgment, claiming that California's exercise of jurisdiction was improper. McGee (P) appealed the Texas decision to the U.S. Supreme Court.

■ **ISSUE**

Can a state ever exercise jurisdiction over a defendant whose contacts with that state are limited to a single act or contract?

■ **DECISION AND RATIONALE**

Yes. A state can exercise jurisdiction over a defendant whose contacts with that state consist solely of a single act or contract, provided that that act is what gave rise to the claim, and was purposefully undertaken. Due to the fact that business has become increasingly nationalized in recent years, more and more contracts are between actors in different states. This trend has encouraged and necessitated an increasingly wide scope for the exercise of jurisdiction across state lines. California enacted this particular long-arm statute to protect the rights of its citizens against out-of-state insurance companies. Given the nature of the insurance business, it is much more likely that small policy holders would be denied justice if forced to file suit in a foreign jurisdiction, than that insurance companies would be more than slightly inconvenienced by having to defend a suit in California. True, in this particular case International Life (D)

---

claims to have had only the one policy holder in California, and not to have been in the habit of conducting business there. But it did knowingly hold that one policy, and communicated with the policy holder in California, so it shouldn't come as a complete surprise to be required to defend suit there after refusing to pay that policy holder's beneficiary. Also, the inconvenience involved in defending a suit in California cannot be much greater than defending the same suit in Texas, and having to transport all the witnesses and evidence found in California to Texas for the trial. Whatever inconvenience does arise from being subject to suit in California certainly does not amount to a denial of due process. International Life (D) had actual notice of the suit and plenty of time to prepare a defense. Therefore, justice is best served by allowing the California courts to exercise jurisdiction in this case. Reversed.

Analysis:

The *McGee* case represented a rather expansive application of the *International Shoe* guidelines. The Court explicitly approved the idea that minimum contacts could be very minimal indeed, so long as the case came out of those contacts. Although the Court did not use the term, this is now referred to as "specific jurisdiction"—that is to say, a defendant does not have extensive contacts with a state, but the nature of the contacts it does have is such as to justify the state's exercise of jurisdiction over cases arising from those contacts, but not over cases unrelated to those contacts. If a defendant's contacts are more extensive, they might give rise to "general jurisdiction," which would enable the state to exercise jurisdiction over any claim involving the defendant, whether or not it was related to the defendant's contacts with the state.

Hanson v. Denckla

(Not Stated) v. (Not Stated)

357 U.S. 235, 78 S.Ct. 1228 (1958)

SUPREME COURT RULES THAT NOT ALL CONTACTS ARE MINIMUM CONTACTS

■ **INSTANT FACTS** Various claimants to a Delaware trust filed suit against the trustee in Florida, claiming that the trust was invalid under Florida law.

■ **BLACK LETTER RULE** A state may not exercise jurisdiction over a defendant if the defendant's contacts with the state are negligible and non-deliberate, and the claim does not arise from those contacts.

■ **PROCEDURAL BASIS**

Appeal from conflicting judgments in two separate but related actions for final disposition of a trust.

■ **FACTS**

Dora Donner, a resident of Pennsylvania, established a trust with a Delaware bank as trustee. Donner was to collect the income from the trust during her lifetime; after her death the money would go to her beneficiary. She retained the power to change her beneficiary at any time. After establishing the trust, Donner moved to Florida, where she eventually drew up a will naming two of her daughters as her primary heirs. The same day, she named two of her grandchildren—the children of her third daughter, Elizabeth—as the beneficiaries of her trust. However, when Donner died several years later, the two daughters named in her will brought suit in Florida against the trust company (D), claiming that the appointment of beneficiaries had been invalid, and that the trust money should really go to the estate. [That is, to the two of them. How greedy can you get?! They were already getting more than half a million a piece. Are we talking, like, Cinderella here? Did they hate their sister *so much* that they would go to all this trouble to cheat her kids out of their grandmother's inheritance? To get another $200,000 each?] Anyway, while the Florida action was still pending, another action was filed in Delaware to determine the distribution of the trust money. The Florida court then decided that the trust was invalid, and that the money should go to the estate. The sisters tried to introduce this judgment in Delaware, as *res judicata.* The Delaware court held that the Florida court had not had jurisdiction over the trust company, however, and so refused to recognize the validity of that action. The Delaware court resolved that the trust had been valid, and that the grandchildren should get the money. Everybody appealed something, and the U.S. Supreme Court consolidated both actions for review.

■ **ISSUE**

May a state exercise jurisdiction over a non-resident defendant with only sporadic and inadvertent contacts with the state, when those contacts do not give rise to the claim for which jurisdiction is being sought?

■ **DECISION AND RATIONALE**

(Warren) No. A state may not exercise jurisdiction over a non-resident defendant with only sporadic and inadvertent contacts with the state, when those contacts do not give rise to the claim for which jurisdiction is being sought. Although the boundaries of a state's jurisdiction

---

over non-residents have been expanding ever since the decision in *International Shoe,* that does not mean that there are no longer any limits on a state's exercise of personal jurisdiction. There are restrictions on a state's power to exercise jurisdiction over non-residents not just to protect those non-residents from the burden of defending a suit in a distant, inconvenient court, but also to protect other states. In this case, the laws of Delaware allowed the trust to be created, maintained, and administered. Allowing Florida courts using Florida law to invalidate that trust is, in a way, like allowing Florida to overturn Delaware's laws and to legislate for the people of Delaware instead. Without minimum contacts between the trustee (D) and Florida, Florida cannot exercise jurisdiction over the trustee (D). The trustee (D) conducts no business in Florida, has no office there, solicits no business there. The fact that the trustee's (D) client, Mrs. Donner, moved to Florida after the trust had been created does not indicate any desire of the trustee (D) to take advantage of Florida's laws or to start doing business there. Without some action "by which the defendant purposefully avails itself of the privilege of conducting activities within the forum State, thus invoking the benefits and protections of its laws," it cannot be said to have the necessary contacts with that state. The fact that another, independent actor with a relationship to the defendant chose to interact with the forum state does not establish contact between the state and the defendant. Therefore, Mrs. Donner's contacts with Florida did not establish contacts between her trustee (D) and Florida, and Florida thus cannot exercise jurisdiction over the trustee (D). Since the trustee (D) was an essential party to the Florida action, that action is invalid, and the Delaware court was correct in not awarding that judgment res judicata value. The judgment of the Delaware courts is affirmed; that of the Florida courts is reversed.

■ DISSENT

(Black) Florida had a strong interest in overseeing this litigation, and would have been the most convenient forum. Donner lived in Florida, her heirs lived in Florida, her will was being administered in Florida. The trustee (D) chose to carry on business with a resident of Florida. The trust company (D) had sufficient contacts with Florida to justify Florida's exertion of jurisdiction over it, and there was nothing that unfair about subjecting it to suit there. Therefore, Florida's exercise of jurisdiction should have been upheld.

Analysis:

Hanson tried to reign in this enthusiasm. *Hanson* made clear that some exercises of jurisdiction would be struck down—if not to protect the due process interests of the defendants involved, then to protect the sovereignty of other states. *Hanson* also introduced the idea that a defendant must perform some purposeful, deliberate act in order to associate itself with the forum state. This was to prove a major sticking point between two separate factions of the Court, one of which endorsed the "purposeful availment" idea, and one of which, often led by Justice Brennan, preferred to focus on the relationship between the defendant, the litigation, and the interests of the forum state.

■ CASE VOCABULARY

LEGATEE: Heir designated to receive property in a will.

Shaffer v. Heitner

(Officer or Director) v. (Shareholder)

433 U.S. 186, 97 S.Ct. 2569 (1977)

THE SUPREME COURT EXTENDS THE MINIMUM CONTACTS TEST TO IN REM JURISDICTION

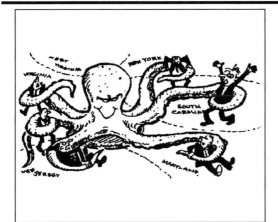

■ **INSTANT FACTS** Heitner (P) brought a shareholder's derivative suit against several officers and directors of Greyhound, a Delaware corporation, gaining in rem jurisdiction by attaching their stock in Greyhound.

■ **BLACK LETTER RULE** Minimum contacts must exist in order for in rem jurisdiction to attach.

■ **PROCEDURAL BASIS**

Writ of certiorari reviewing affirmance of rejection of arguments contesting jurisdiction for shareholder's derivative suit.

■ **FACTS**

Heitner (P), a nonresident of Delaware, owned one share of stock in Greyhound Corp., a business incorporated in Delaware. Heitner (P) filed a shareholder's derivative suit in Delaware state court, naming 28 officers or directors of Greyhound as defendants. Heitner (P) alleged that the officers and directors had breached their fiduciary duties. At the same time the complaint was filed, Heitner (P) filed a motion for sequestration of shares of approximately 82,000 shares of stock owned by 21 of the officers and directors, as allowed by Delaware law. Those 21 defendants entered a special appearance in Delaware, contending that the sequestration procedure violated due process and that the property was incapable of attachment in Delaware. In addition, the 21 defendants asserted that they did not have sufficient minimum contacts to justify Delaware jurisdiction. The Court of Chancery rejected these arguments, and the Delaware Supreme Court affirmed, holding that Delaware had a sufficient interest in the action to justify jurisdiction. The Supreme Court granted certiorari.

■ **ISSUE**

Is in rem jurisdiction subject to a minimum contacts analysis?

■ **DECISION AND RATIONALE**

(Marshall, J.) Yes. In rem jurisdiction is subject to a minimum contacts analysis. Traditionally, courts have ignored the lack of contacts between a defendant and a state in asserting quasi in rem jurisdiction. While the law governing in personam jurisdiction has expanded dramatically in recent years, no such change has occurred in the law governing in rem jurisdiction. In *Mullane v. Central Hanover Bank & Trust Co.* [Reasonable efforts must be made to give property owners actual notice of the action], we noted that, since an adverse judgment in rem directly affects the property owner by divesting him of his rights in property, certain Fourteenth Amendment rights must attach. Since jurisdiction over property involves jurisdiction over a person's interests in the property, the proper standard is the minimum contacts standard elucidated in *International Shoe Co. v. Washington* [Due process requires that minimum contacts exist for in personam jurisdiction]. We recognize that the presence of property in a State may impact this minimum contacts analysis, as a defendant having property in the state

---

would normally have purposefully availed himself of the jurisdiction of the state. However, in this case, we focus on a different type of quasi in rem action, in which the property serving as the basis for state-court jurisdiction is completely unrelated to Heitner's (P) cause of action. Since the assertion of jurisdiction over property is really just an assertion of jurisdiction over the owner of the property, we conclude that all assertions of state-court jurisdiction must be evaluated according to the standards set forth in *International Shoe* and its progeny. In the case at hand, the officers' and directors' holdings in Greyhound do not provide contacts with Delaware sufficient to support Delaware jurisdiction. Indeed, Delaware has a strong interest in supervising the management of a Delaware corporation, but the Delaware Legislature has failed to assert this interest. Moreover, Delaware is not a fair forum for this litigation. As far as the record indicates, the officers and directors had never set foot in Delaware, and they had not purposefully availed themselves of the benefits and protections of that State. It strains reason to suggest that anyone buying securities in a corporation formed in Delaware impliedly consents to Delaware jurisdiction on any cause of action. Reversed.

■ CONCURRENCE

(Powell, J.) While I reserve judgment on whether ownership of property in a State may provide the contacts necessary for jurisdiction, I favor the preservation of the common law concept of quasi in rem jurisdiction in the case of real property.

■ CONCURRENCE

(Stevens, J.) I would find the Delaware sequestration statute unconstitutional, creating an unacceptable risk of judgment without notice. Delaware denies a defendant the opportunity to defend the merits of a suit unless he subjects himself to the jurisdiction of the court. In effect, this creates a duty of inquiry upon every purchaser of securities to know the place of incorporation of the company and the unique requirements of Delaware law. However, I am uneasy with the reach of the opinion, and I concur with Justice Powell that the opinion should not be read so as to invalidate in rem jurisdiction over real property.

■ DISSENT

(Brennan, J.) While I agree that the minimum-contacts analysis represents a sensible approach to the exertion of state court jurisdiction, I dissent from the ultimate holding of the case. The majority has treated Delaware's statute as a long-arm statute requiring a minimum contacts analysis. However, the Delaware statute expressly denied such an approach. State court jurisdiction is proper only with notice and an applicable long-arm statute, and there was no such statute applicable in this case. Jurisdiction might indeed be in Delaware's best interest, and the problems with other states applying Delaware's laws argues against denying Delaware jurisdiction over this matter. Nothing noted in the majority opinion persuades me that it would be unfair to subject the officers and directors to suit in Delaware. They certainly associated themselves with the State of Delaware, thereby invoking the benefits and protections of its laws.

Analysis:

This is undoubtedly one of the most important of all of the cases pertaining to jurisdiction. In one broad opinion, Justice Marshall overturned the traditional approach to in rem jurisdiction, equating the in rem test with the minimum contacts test for personal jurisdiction. Thus, in rem jurisdiction is appropriate only where a defendant purposefully availed himself to the benefits and protections of the forum state, or where there is sufficient relatedness between the cause of action and the forum state. The opinion makes a number of logically sound conclusions on the way to its revolutionary holding. First, it is indeed true that in rem jurisdiction can affect a person just as much as in personam jurisdiction. Both affect a person's rights in money or property. Second, considerations of fairness dictate requiring some minimum contacts between the forum state and any person whose interests may be adversely affected by litigation. In the case at hand, the only contact between the property at issue and the state of Delaware was the fact that the stock happened to be in a Delaware corporation. If ever there was a case to deny jurisdiction, this seems to be a very strong one. Note that this decision is likely to have the most profound effect on in rem cases where there was no pre-existing legal interest between the plaintiff and the property, and where the suit is unrelated to the property. Otherwise, there may well be sufficient minimum contacts to justify in rem jurisdiction.

■ **CASE VOCABULARY**

SEQUESTRATION STATUTE: A law providing for the attachment of intangible personal property, such as stock, pending a litigation.

SHAREHOLDER'S DERIVATIVE SUIT: A suit by a shareholder raising a corporate cause of action, such as a suit against officers for a breach of fiduciary duty.

SPECIAL APPEARANCE: A submission to the jurisdiction of a court for limited purposes, including the contesting of jurisdiction.

World-Wide Volkswagen v. Woodson

(Regional Distributor of Defective Car) v. (Trial Court Judge)

444 U.S. 286, 100 S.Ct. 559 (1980)

U.S. SUPREME COURT RULES THAT A CORPORATION MUST HAVE PURPOSEFULLY AVAILED ITSELF OF A FORUM IN ORDER TO BE SUBJECT TO JURISDICTION THERE, REGARDLESS OF FAIRNESS OR CONVENIENCE

■ **INSTANT FACTS** A New York family passing through Oklahoma was in a car accident, and tried to bring suit there against the dealer who sold them the car in New York.

■ **BLACK LETTER RULE** In order to be subject to a state's jurisdiction, a defendant must have chosen to have some contact with that state; considerations of fairness, convenience, and the interests of the state in overseeing the litigation are otherwise irrelevant.

■ **PROCEDURAL BASIS**

Writ of Certiorari to the Supreme Court of Oklahoma, for its denial of the defendants' writ of prohibition to restrain the trial court judge from exercising personal jurisdiction over them.

■ **FACTS**

In 1976, the Robinson family—Harry, Kay, and their two kids—purchased a new Audi from Seaway Volkswagen, Inc. ("Seaway") (D), in Massena, New York. A year later, as the Robinsons were en route from their old home in New York to their new home in Arizona, disaster struck. While passing through Oklahoma, another car rear-ended the Robinsons' Audi, rupturing the gas tank and starting a fire that severely injured Kay and both children. Since the driver of the other car was unfortunately not wealthy, the Robinsons brought a product liability suit against the car's manufacturer, Audi NSU Auto Union Aktiengesellschaft ("Audi"), claiming that the gas tank and fuel system had been defective. They filed the action in Oklahoma state court, and named as additional defendants the car's importer, Volkswagen of America, Inc. ("Volkswagen"), its regional distributor, World-Wide Volkswagen Corporation ("World-Wide"), and Seaway, the retail dealer where they had purchased the car. World-Wide (D) and Seaway (D) challenged the Oklahoma court's exercise of jurisdiction, claiming that they did not have the necessary minimum contacts with Oklahoma. Seaway (D) claimed to do business in New York state only, and World-Wide (D) claimed to do business only within the tri-state area of New York, New Jersey, and Connecticut. Neither conducted any business in Oklahoma, employed anyone in Oklahoma, kept office space in Oklahoma, or directed advertising at the Oklahoma market. Both the trial court and the Supreme Court of Oklahoma rejected the claim that World-Wide (D) and Seaway (D) should not be subjected to jurisdiction there, based largely on the theory that they should have foreseen the possibility of litigation there, given the uniquely mobile nature of the product they sold. World-Wide (D) and Seaway (D) next appealed to the U.S. Supreme Court.

■ **ISSUE**

When a particular state would be the most convenient forum for a trial (i.e., all the witnesses are there, the plaintiffs are hospitalized there, the claim arose there, etc.), and the defendant

---

would not find it at all inconvenient to defend itself there, can that state exercise jurisdiction even if the defendant has not deliberately sought contacts with that state?

■ **DECISION AND RATIONALE**

(White) No. A state cannot exercise jurisdiction over a defendant who has not deliberately sought some contact with the state. Minimum contacts must be based on some act committed by the defendant. This is a result, in part, of the requirement, first stated in *International Shoe,* that jurisdiction should not be exercised when it is inconsistent with "traditional notions of fair play and substantial justice." It is fundamentally unfair to hold a defendant responsible for the actions of others, such as the action of the Robinsons in driving their car through Oklahoma. However, the minimum contacts requirement also stems from the idea that each state's jurisdiction is limited, not just to protect defendants, but to protect the interests of other states. It has been becoming less and less difficult for defendants to defend themselves in other states, as technology progresses, but the interests of other states in not having their own sovereignty infringed remains constant, as provided for in the Constitution. Unless a defendant had chosen to avail itself somehow of another state, that state's exercise of jurisdiction might very well conflict with the sovereignty of the state which the defendant did choose. It has been argued that the defendants in this case should have foreseen that their product might wind up in Oklahoma, especially given the mobile nature of automobiles. However, it is not the foreseeability that a given product might travel to a distant forum that is important, but rather the foreseeability that the defendant might be "haled into court there." It is reasonable to believe that neither Seaway (D) nor World-Wide (D) expected to be haled into court in Oklahoma. Since there is no evidence to support the view that either Seaway (D) or World-Wide (D) conducted business in Oklahoma, or intended their products to reach the Oklahoma market, there is basis for the Oklahoma court's exercise of jurisdiction over either defendant. Judgment reversed.

■ **DISSENT**

(Brennan) Yes. A state may exercise jurisdiction over a defendant who has not deliberately sought contacts with that state. Of course, the defendant must have *some* contacts with the state. For instance, in this case, if the Robinsons' car had blown up in Texas, the Oklahoma courts would obviously not have jurisdiction over the case. But the fact the defendants did sell the Robinsons the actual car which did reach Oklahoma and did blow up there, should be enough. Perhaps the Court is right to mock the idea of all chattels being treated in this way, but surely an exception should be made for a car, which by its very nature is meant to travel. It would be difficult to believe that the defendants truly believed that none of the cars they sold would ever leave the New York area. It is true that the contacts between Seaway (D) and World-Wide (D) and Oklahoma were not extensive, but given the other factors that must be considered—fairness and convenience—it is certainly reasonable to subject them to Oklahoma's jurisdiction for this case. There is no doubt that Oklahoma is the most efficient forum in which to try the case. The witnesses are there. The evidence is there. The plaintiffs were hospitalized there when they filed suit. And the defendants would only suffer minimal inconvenience, if any, in being required to defend themselves there. The two parent companies, Volkswagen and Audi, will be required to defend the case there one way or another. Expanding that defense to encompass World-Wide (D) and Seaway (D) would not be very difficult. Given these reasons, and Oklahoma's strong interest in the litigation, both Seaway (D) and World-Wide should be held subject to Oklahoma's jurisdiction.

Analysis:

WWVW is the first real indication of a serious split in the Court over what constitutes sufficient minimum contacts. The split stems from two different views on what the most important concern should be in exercising personal jurisdiction: the due process rights of the defendant, or the interests of the forum state in the litigation. Here, the winning side focused more on the former, and Justice Brennan, on the losing side, focused more on the latter. The great irony of this case, however, lies in the fact that neither side really cared whether or not Oklahoma had jurisdiction over Seaway (D) or World-Wide (D), or whether either of these defendants even stayed in the case—after all, Audi and Volkswagen were still in the case, and they were most likely capable of satisfying any judgment the Robinsons might be able to recover. What everybody involved really cared about was whether the case would be tried in Oklahoma state court or Oklahoma federal court. Apparently, the relevant federal and state courts must have drawn from significantly different jury pools, since the state court juries had a noticeable tendency to award more money, more often, to plaintiffs, than their federal court counterparts. The Robinsons therefore strategically filed their lawsuit in state court. The defendants, for the same reasons, wanted to be able to remove the action to federal court.

■ CASE VOCABULARY

CHATTEL: An item of personal property.

Burger King Corp. v. Rudzewicz

(Franchise Owner) v. (Franchisee)

471 U.S. 462, 105 S.Ct. 2174 (1985)

SUPREME COURT RULES THAT MINIMUM CONTACTS CAN BE A SINGLE CONTRACT

■ **INSTANT FACTS**   Rudzewicz (D) contracted with Burger King (D), a Florida corporation, to operate a Burger King restaurant in Michigan, then defaulted on payments, so Burger King (P) sued him in Florida.

■ **BLACK LETTER RULE**   Once it has been established that the defendant has minimum contacts with a state, it is up to the defendant to prove that being required to defend a suit there would be "fundamentally unfair."

■ **PROCEDURAL BASIS**

Appeal from reversal of judgment in action for damages and injunctive relief for breach of contract.

■ **FACTS**

John Rudzewicz (D) and Brian MacShara, both Michigan residents, entered into a franchise agreement with Burger King Corporation (P), a Florida company. The contract licensed Rudzewicz (D) and MacShara to use Burger King's (P) trademarks and service marks for a period of 20 years, in connection with their operation of a Burger King restaurant in Michigan. The contract provided that the agreement would be governed by Florida law, and called for payment of all franchise fees and royalties to Burger King's (P) Miami headquarters. In connection with establishing the restaurant, MacShara attended a training course at Burger King University in Miami. After operating the restaurant for a while, Rudzewicz (D) and MacShara fell behind in their monthly payments to Burger King (P). Burger King (P) then instituted an action in federal court in Florida, based on diversity jurisdiction. Rudzewicz (D) and MacShara claimed that they did not have sufficient contacts with Florida to be subjected to jurisdiction there. The District Court found that Florida could exercise jurisdiction in this case, based on a longarm statute which extends jurisdiction to anyone who breaches a contract within the state. The Court of Appeals reversed, however, finding that, although the defendants could be said to have the necessary contacts with Florida, such an exercise of jurisdiction would be fundamentally unfair, and an infringement of due process—and an especially dangerous precedent. Burger King (P) appealed to the U.S. Supreme Court.

■ **ISSUE**

In asserting jurisdiction against out-of-state defendants, does a state have to show both that the defendant has minimum contacts with the state, and that it would be fair and equitable to require the defendant to defend a suit there?

■ **DECISION AND RATIONALE**

(Brennan) No. The state does not have to show both that the defendant has minimum contacts with the state, and that it would be fair and equitable to require the defendant to defend a suit there. Once it has been established that the defendant has minimum contacts with a state, there is a presumption that it would be fair to require the defendant to defend a suit there. This presumption can of course be overcome, but it is the defendant who must show that it would be unfair to require him to defend there, and not the state which must show that it would be fair. In deciding the question of fairness, the court may look to and balance the forum state's interest in the litigation, the plaintiff's interest in efficient and convenient relief, the demands and best interests of the federal system as a whole, and the defendant's interest in not having to defend a suit in an extremely remote or disadvantageous forum. In the case at hand, Rudzewicz (D) deliberately and voluntarily entered into a 20-year-long contract with a Florida corporation, governed by Florida law. That contract required that someone associated with the new restaurant attend training in Florida at Burger King University. While Rudzewicz (D) himself did not go, and in fact has never been to Florida at all, it can hardly have come as a complete shock to him to learn that Burger King (P) might sue him there should he breach the agreement. Florida is certainly the most convenient forum for this case, and while this is not the determining factor, it is something to consider. Rudzewicz (D) has not shown that his case would be unfairly prejudiced or harmed by a trial in Florida. Of course he will be somewhat inconvenienced, but doesn't the mere fact of being sued cause some inconvenience in and of itself? We shouldn't therefore prohibit all lawsuits. And undoubtedly Burger King (P) was inconvenienced by not receiving the monthly payments. In short, Rudzewicz's (D) purposeful involvement with a Florida company provides the necessary minimum contacts for Florida to exercise jurisdiction, and he has failed to show that it would be fundamentally unfair to allow Florida to do so. Reversed and remanded.

■ DISSENT

(Stevens) Rudzewicz (D) did no business in Florida. He sold no products there, did not anticipate that any of his products would ever wind up there, maintained no offices there, and had in fact never been there. His principal contact with Burger King (P) was through its Michigan branch office, not its Florida headquarters. There is no reason to believe that Rudzewicz (D) ever anticipated any involvement with the Florida office, and every reason to think that he would have expected to resolve any problems that arose with the Michigan office—including any potential litigation. Also, the typical franchise is at best a very local operation, with far less capital or bargaining power than a huge national corporation like Burger King (P). Therefore, it would be fundamentally unfair to require local franchise operators like Rudzewicz (D) to defend themselves in a forum as distant and unfamiliar as Florida. The judgment of the Court of Appeals dismissing the Florida action should be upheld.

Analysis:

The swing votes must have come over to Justice Brennan's side this time because here, unlike in cases such as *World-Wide Volkswagen,* the defendant had taken some purposeful action to associate himself with the forum state. One interesting question to ponder, however, is why Rudzewicz (D) took this case all the way up to the Supreme Court. It's not as if, had Burger King (P) been denied the right to sue him in Florida, the case would have ended. Burger King (P) would probably have just turned around and sued him in Michigan. Do you think that having the "home-court" advantage is worth that much effort? The action was in federal court, and one of the main reasons for establishing a federal court system in the first place was to provide a neutral forum where non-residents could see justice without the interference of local prejudice against out-of-staters.

(Web Site Creator) v. (State Court)

29 Cal.4th 262, 58 P.3d 2 (2002)

POSTING INFORMATION ON A WEB SITE DOES NOT ESTABLISH PERSONAL JURISDICTION IN ALL STATES

■ **INSTANT FACTS** A Texas resident who posted information infringing upon the licensing rights of a California business on a Web site created in Indiana was sued in California state court for misappropriation of trade secrets.

■ **BLACK LETTER RULE** A court may exercise personal jurisdiction over a nonresident defendant only if the defendant has purposefully availed himself of the benefits of the forum state, the action relates to the defendant's contacts with the forum state, and jurisdiction would not offend notions of fair play and substantial justice.

■ **PROCEDURAL BASIS**

On appeal to consider the trial court's decision denying the plaintiff's motion to quash service of process.

■ **FACTS**

Pavlovich (D) was a Texas resident and the president of Media Driver, LLC. Before moving to Texas, Pavlovich (D) studied at Purdue University in Indiana and was employed in Indiana. He never lived in California, owned property in California, maintained a place of business in California, or otherwise had any business contact with California. While in Indiana, Pavlovich (D) created a Web site containing text and links to other Web sites. The Web site was informational only and neither solicited nor transacted any business. The Web site was designed to provide information to those interested in improving "video and DVD support for Linux" by defeating technology used to encrypt DVDs and prevent the unauthorized duplication of copyrighted material. The Web site provided its end users with a code that could be used to circumvent encrypted data on copyrighted DVDs. DVD Copy Control Association, Inc. (DVD CCA) (P), a Delaware corporation with its principal place of business in California, owned the licensing rights to the encryption technology. Although Pavlovich (D) was aware that circumventing the encryption technology was probably illegal and suspected that a license was required to access the encryption technology, he was unaware that DVD CCA (P) owned the licensing rights. DVD CCA (P) sued Pavlovich (D) in California state court for misappropriating trade secrets through his Web site. Pavlovich (D) filed a motion to quash service of process, contending that the California court lacked personal jurisdiction. After the motion was denied, the California Supreme Court heard the appeal.

■ **ISSUE**

Does the court have personal jurisdiction over a nonresident defendant who posts information on a Web site that injures a California resident?

■ **DECISION AND RATIONALE**

(Brown, J.) No. A court may exercise personal jurisdiction over a nonresident defendant only if the defendant has purposefully availed himself of the benefits of the forum state, the action relates to the defendant's contacts with the forum state, and jurisdiction would not offend notions of "fair play and substantial justice." Generally, the United States Supreme Court has established that a party purposefully avails itself of a forum state if the foreseeable effects of the out-of-state action would be to injure a person within the forum state. Here, Pavlovich's (D) only contact with California is through the publication of material on the Internet that can be accessed by any Internet user in any state, including California. Although other courts have found that reaching out to a foreign state through the Internet may be a proper basis for personal jurisdiction, jurisdiction is generally based on the business advantage obtained by the Web site or the interactive exchange between the defendant and residents of the foreign state. The mere creation of an informational Web site, however, is insufficient to establish personal jurisdiction. Here, there is no evidence that Pavlovich (D) specifically targeted California residents nor that any California residents ever accessed the Web site. To find personal jurisdiction on such facts would support minimum contacts in every state for all Internet-related claims. Such a notion would violate longstanding and well-established principles of personal jurisdiction. Although Pavlovich (D) was aware that his Web site may injure some entity that owned the licensing rights to the encryption technology, he did not know the identity of that entity nor that the entity maintained its principal place of business in California. The general knowledge that his actions may injure the motion picture industry in California is insufficient to establish that Pavlovich (D) purposefully availed himself to that jurisdiction. To hold that Pavlovich (D) purposefully availed himself to California because he should have known that his actions may harm certain California interests, though not the plaintiff's, would destroy the concept of purposeful availment. While a defendant's knowledge that his actions may affect California interests may help support personal jurisdiction, it is insufficient, by itself, to establish jurisdiction. The plaintiff may still pursue an action against the defendant, but must do so in either Indiana or Texas. Reversed and remanded.

■ **DISSENT**

(Baxter, J.) By posting information to be used to defeat the encryption technology used to protect DVDs from unauthorized misappropriation of copyrighted material, the defendant's intent was to damage not DVD CSS (P), but the entire motion picture and computer industries. He specifically knew that these industries were either established in or maintained a substantial presence in California. It matters not whether he specifically knew the exact identity of the party to be injured or its exact location. By specifically targeting the motion picture and computer industries in California, the defendant established minimum contacts with that state and reasonably should expect to be sued in California for injuries arising out of his conduct.

Analysis:

Most critics of the court's holding believe the California Supreme Court set the bar too high by requiring proof of the specific intended target of Internet conduct, rather than mere knowledge of the situs of the harm to be caused. This exacting knowledge requirement, it is argued, fosters intentional ignorance of a true copyright or trademark owner in order to avoid exposing oneself to jurisdiction. The opposing view, however, points out the court's insistence that such ignorance does not insulate a person from liability, but merely the necessary ties required to establish jurisdiction.

■ **CASE VOCABULARY**

MINIMUM CONTACTS: A nonresident defendant's forum-state connections, such as business activity or actions foreseeably leading to business activity, that are substantial enough to bring the defendant within the forum-state court's personal jurisdiction without offending traditional notions of fair play and substantial justice.

MOTION TO QUASH: A party's request that the court nullify process or an act instituted by the other party, as in seeking to nullify a subpoena.

SPECIFIC JURISDICTION: Jurisdiction that stems from the defendant's having certain minimum contacts with the forum state so that the court may hear a case whose issues arise from those minimum contacts.

J. McIntyre Machinery, Ltd. v. Nicastro

(Manufacturer) v. (Injured Worker)

131 S. Ct. 2780 (2011)

AN ENGLISH CORPORATION'S SINGLE SALE IN NEW JERSEY DID NOT SUBJECT IT TO THE JURISDICTION OF NEW JERSEY COURTS

I predict your products will reach New Jersey, but nevertheless it will not have jurisdiction over you.

stus.com

■ **INSTANT FACTS** Nicastro (P) sued J. McIntyre Machinery (D) in New Jersey for injuries caused by a machine manufactured by McIntyre (D), but McIntyre (D) had no contacts with New Jersey.

■ **BLACK LETTER RULE** Personal jurisdiction over an out-of-state defendant requires some showing that the defendant purposefully availed itself of the privilege of conducting activities within the state.

■ **PROCEDURAL BASIS**

Appeal from an order of the New Jersey Supreme Court finding personal jurisdiction over McIntyre (D).

■ **FACTS**

Nicastro (P) seriously injured his hand while using a machine manufactured by J. McIntyre, Ltd. (D) in England. Nicastro (P) brought a products liability suit against McIntyre (D) in New Jersey state court. McIntyre (D) was incorporated in England and operated in England. It never marketed goods in New Jersey or shipped them there. Nicastro's (P) counsel noted that an independent company sold McIntyre's (D) machines to buyers in the United States. McIntyre (D) officials attended conventions in the United States to market their products, but none of these conventions was in New Jersey. No more than four (and perhaps no more than one) machines manufactured by McIntyre (D) ended up in New Jersey. In addition, the New Jersey court noted that the U.S. distributor structured advertising and sales efforts in accordance with McIntyre's (D) direction and guidance, when possible, and that at least some of the machines manufactured by McIntyre (D) were sold on consignment to the distributor. Even so, the New Jersey Supreme Court held that New Jersey courts could exercise jurisdiction over McIntyre (D).

■ **ISSUE**

Did the New Jersey courts properly exercise jurisdiction over McIntyre (D)?

■ **DECISION AND RATIONALE**

(Kennedy, J.) No. Personal jurisdiction over an out-of-state defendant requires some showing that the defendant purposefully availed itself of the privilege of conducting activities within the state. In a products liability case such as this one, it is a defendant's purposeful availment that makes the exercise of jurisdiction consistent with traditional notions of fair play and substantial justice. A person may submit to the authority of a state in a number of ways, such as by consent, physical presence within the state, or citizenship or domicile. There is also a limited form of submission to authority that is found when a defendant conducts activities within the state. Submission to jurisdiction through contact with and an activity directed at the sovereign may justify specific jurisdiction in a suit arising out of or related to the defendant's contact with the forum.

Personal jurisdiction calls for a forum-by-forum, or sovereign-by-sovereign, analysis. The question is whether a defendant followed a course of conduct directed at the society or economy within a jurisdiction, so that a sovereign may lawfully render judicial judgment over the defendant. A defendant who is a domestic domiciliary has the courts of its home state available, and those courts can exercise general jurisdiction. If another state were to exercise jurisdiction in an inappropriate case, the federal balance, which posits that each state has a sovereignty that is not subject to unlawful intrusion by the others, would be upset. Foreign corporations often will target or concentrate on specific states, which would make them subject to specific jurisdiction in those forums. In addition, because the United States is a distinct sovereign, a defendant could be subject to the courts of the United States, but not the courts of any particular state. Such a situation would be an exceptional case.

The New Jersey Supreme Court relied on the case of *Asahi Metal Industry Co. v. Superior Court of Cal., Solano Cty.,* 480 U.S. 102 (1987), for its finding that jurisdiction was proper in New Jersey. In *Asahi,* Justice Brennan, writing for four Justices, outlined an approach to jurisdiction that discarded sovereign authority in favor of considerations of fairness and foreseeability. Justice Brennan's concurrence contended that jurisdiction premised on placing a product into the stream of commerce without more is consistent with due process. As long as a participant in this process is aware that the final product is being marketed in the forum state, the possibility of a lawsuit there cannot come as a surprise. According to Justice Brennan, the ability to anticipate suit rendered the assertion of jurisdiction fair. Justice O'Connor, also writing for four Justices, rejected Justice Brennan's opinion and stated that the minimum contacts necessary for personal jurisdiction must come about by an action of the defendant purposefully directed toward the forum state. Justice Brennan's concurrence is inconsistent with the premises of lawful judicial power. Precedent makes it clear that it is a defendant's actions, not his expectations, that empower a state's courts to subject him to judgment. If foreseeability were the controlling criterion, a person who sold products to a large distributor could be subject to suit in any state without ever leaving town. In addition, the issue of foreseeability itself might be contested so that significant expenses would be incurred just to litigate the preliminary issue of jurisdiction. Jurisdictional rules should avoid those costs whenever possible.

The conclusion that the authority to subject a defendant to judgment depends on purposeful availment does not resolve all of the questions of jurisdiction that will arise in the future. The defendant's conduct and economic realities will differ across cases, and judicial exposition will clarify the contours of that principle. In the case at bar, McIntyre (D) directed marketing and sales efforts at the United States. Congress may be able to authorize jurisdiction in appropriate cases, but it is not necessary to decide that issue. Nicastro (P) did not show that McIntyre (D) engaged in conduct purposefully directed at New Jersey, and the trial court found that the only contact shown was that the machine that injured Nicastro (P) ended up in New Jersey. McIntyre (D) may have intended to serve the U.S. market, but that does not show an intent to avail itself of the New Jersey market. Reversed.

■ CONCURRENCE

(Breyer, J.) It is unwise to announce a broad rule based on changes in commerce and communication. The outcome of this case is determined by precedent. No prior case has found that a single isolated sale, even if accompanied by the kind of sales effort engaged in by McIntyre (D), is sufficient for a finding of personal jurisdiction. The incident at issue in this case does not implicate modern concerns. What do the standards stated by the plurality mean when a company targets the world by selling products from a website? Does it matter if products are shipped through an intermediary? What if the company markets through popup advertisements that will be viewed in a forum? Those issues have serious consequences, but are totally absent in this case.

■ DISSENT

(Ginsburg, J.) McIntyre (D) has avoided the jurisdiction of state courts, except perhaps in those states where it sells a sizeable quantity of its machines. The Court has previously made clear that legal fictions such as "presence" and "implied consent" should be discarded. The relationship among the defendant, the forum, and the litigation determines whether due process permits the exercise of personal jurisdiction. The plurality also puts United States plaintiffs at a disadvantage in comparison to similarly situated plaintiffs elsewhere in the world. In the European Union, the jurisdiction New Jersey would have exercised would not have been exceptional.

Analysis:

The plurality draws a distinction between marketing efforts directed at residents of the United States and efforts directed at the residents of a particular state. This distinction may be splitting hairs, since a resident of the United States is necessarily a resident of a state. The plurality also seems to assume that all sales are alike. There is, however, a great difference between a single sale of a consumer product and a single sale of a large industrial machine. One machine could represent a significant part of a manufacturer's sales.

■ CASE VOCABULARY

GENERAL JURISDICTION: The authority of a court to hear all claims against a defendant at the place of the defendant's domicile or the place of service, without any specific connection between the claims and the forum state.

SPECIFIC JURISDICTION: Jurisdiction stemming from the defendant's minimum contacts with the forum state, such that the court may hear a case arising from those minimum contacts.

Goodyear Dunlop Tire Operations, S.A. v. Brown

(Tire Manufacturer) v. (Parent of Decedent)

131 S. Ct. 2846 (2011)

GENERAL JURISDICTION IS RARELY EXERCISED OVER OUT-OF-STATE CORPORATIONS

General Jurisdiction*

*If you're asking, the answer is probably "no"

stus.com

■ **INSTANT FACTS** The sons of Brown (P) and Helms (P) were killed in a bus accident, allegedly because of tires manufactured by a foreign subsidiary of Goodyear (D), and the subsidiaries (D) claimed that the state court did not have jurisdiction.

■ **BLACK LETTER RULE** Sale of an out-of-state manufacturer's products in a forum state will justify the exercise of specific jurisdiction only with regard to the product that was sold in the state.

■ **PROCEDURAL BASIS**

Appeal from an order affirming a denial of a motion to dismiss.

■ **FACTS**

The sons of Brown (P) and Helms (P) were killed in a bus accident in France. The cause of the accident allegedly was a failure of the tires on the bus. The tires were manufactured by subsidiaries (D) of Goodyear (D) at a plant in Turkey. Brown (P) and Helms (P) brought wrongful death suits against Goodyear (D) and its subsidiaries (D) in North Carolina state court.

The subsidiaries (D) were three corporations. One was incorporated in France, one in Luxembourg, and one in Turkey. They had no physical presence in North Carolina, and did not market tires in North Carolina. A small number of specialty tires manufactured by the subsidiaries (D) were sold in North Carolina, but the type of tire involved in the bus accident was not sold in the United States. The subsidiaries moved to dismiss for lack of jurisdiction. The trial court denied the motion, and the North Carolina Court of Appeals affirmed the denial.

■ **ISSUE**

Did the North Carolina court have jurisdiction over the Goodyear subsidiaries (D)?

■ **DECISION AND RATIONALE**

(Ginsburg, J.) No. Sale of an out-of-state manufacturer's products in a forum state will justify the exercise of specific jurisdiction only with regard to the product that was sold in the state. The canonical opinion regarding a state court's jurisdiction over out-of-state defendants is *International Shoe Co. v. Washington,* 326 U.S. 310 (1945). That case authorized the exercise of jurisdiction if the defendant had certain minimum contacts with the state, such that the maintenance of the suit does not offend traditional notions of fair play and substantial justice. The Court in *International Shoe* classified two types of cases involving out-of-state corporate defendants. The first is when the defendant's in-state activity was continuous and systematic and that activity gave rise to the lawsuit. This category of cases is referred to as "specific jurisdiction." Specific jurisdiction is distinguished from general jurisdiction. General jurisdiction will arise when continuous corporate operations in a state are so substantial and of such a nature as to justify suits on causes of action arising from dealings entirely distinct from those activities. An individual's domicile, or the equivalent for a corporation, is the paradigm forum for the exercise of general jurisdiction.

Since *International Shoe,* the Supreme Court has addressed the issue of whether a corporate defendant's contacts with a forum state were sufficient for general jurisdiction only twice. In *Perkins v. Benguet Consol. Mining Co., 342 U.S. 437 (1952),* the Court held that the Ohio courts had general jurisdiction over a corporate defendant organized and doing business only in the Philippines. The corporation had ceased doing business during the Second World War, and the records of the corporation were kept and maintained in Ohio. The claim involved in the suit did not arise in Ohio, but the Supreme Court held that the exercise of jurisdiction by the Ohio courts would not violate due process. In *Helicopteros Nacionales de Colombia v. Hall,* 466 U.S. 408 (1984), the suit involved a helicopter crash in Peru. The plaintiff brought a wrongful death suit in Texas state court against the owner and operator of the helicopter, a Colombian corporation. The defendant's contacts with Texas were limited to sending an officer to Houston to negotiate a contract, accepting checks drawn on a bank in Houston, and purchasing helicopters and training services from businesses located in Texas. The defendant was not licensed to do business in Texas and had no place of business in the state. These links were insufficient to confer jurisdiction over a claim that neither arose out of nor related to the Texas activities. Mere purchases, even those occurring at regular intervals, are not sufficient contacts to confer general jurisdiction over a non-resident defendant in a cause of action not related to those purchases. There is no reason to differentiate the insufficient ties to Texas in *Helicopteros* from the sporadic sales in North Carolina of tires manufactured by the Goodyear subsidiaries (D).

Brown (P) and Helms (P) also assert a "single enterprise" theory, which would consolidate the subsidiaries' (D) ties to North Carolina with those of Goodyear (D). In effect, Brown (P) and Helms (P) are asking the Court to pierce Goodyear's (D) corporate veils, at least for jurisdictional purposes. This argument was not raised below, so Brown (P) and Helms (P) have forfeited it. Reversed.

Analysis:

The Court in this case seems to suggest that there is rarely general jurisdiction over an out-of-state corporation. *Perkins v. Benguet Consol. Mining* represented an unusual case in which the out-of-state defendant existed, if at all, in the forum state. In other situations, it would appear that the question of the level of contacts an out-of-state defendant has with the forum state is moot, unless the suit arose out of those contacts.

■ **CASE VOCABULARY**

PIERCING THE CORPORATE VEIL: The judicial imposition of personal liability on otherwise immune corporate officers, directors, and shareholders for the corporation's wrongful acts, when, for instance, the corporation has failed to comply with corporate formalities, or is merely a sham.

Burnham v. Superior Court

(Prospective Divorcee) v. (Court)

495 U.S. 604, 110 S.Ct. 2105 (1990)

TRANSIENT JURISDICTION REMAINS AVAILABLE WITHOUT CONDUCTING A MINIMUM CONTACTS ANALYSIS

■ **INSTANT FACTS** While visiting California for business and vacation, Dennis Burnham (D) was served with process for a divorce proceeding, and Burnham (D) contends that California jurisdiction violates due process.

■ **BLACK LETTER RULE** Jurisdiction based on physical presence comports with due process, regardless of the defendant's contacts with the forum State.

■ **PROCEDURAL BASIS**

Writ of certiorari reviewing denial of mandamus relief following denial of motion to quash service of process in divorce action.

■ **FACTS**

Francie Burnham (P), a resident of California, brought suit for divorce against her husband, Dennis Burnham (Burnham) (D), in California state court. Mr. Burnham (D) was served with the summons and complaint while voluntarily visiting California for three days. Burnham's (D) presence in California did not relate to the divorce action, as he was initially on business and later traveled to San Francisco to visit his daughters [That's what he gets for trying to do something nice]. Subsequently, Burnham (D) made a special appearance in California Superior Court, moving to quash the service of process. Burnham (D) argued that the court lacked personal jurisdiction because his only contacts with the state were a few short trips on business and to visit his daughters. The Superior Court denied the motion. Thereafter, the California Court of Appeal denied mandamus relief, holding that physical presence and personal service in the forum state constituted valid grounds for jurisdiction. The Supreme Court granted certiorari.

■ **ISSUE**

Does transient jurisdiction, obtained by a defendant's physical presence in the forum state, violate due process?

■ **DECISION AND RATIONALE**

(Scalia, J.) No. Transient jurisdiction, obtained by a defendant's physical presence in the forum state, does not violate due process. In order to decide whether the assertion of personal jurisdiction comports with due process, we have relied on well-established traditional principles of jurisdiction. Jurisdiction based on physical presence is one of these traditional forms of in personam jurisdiction. On occasion, we have held that deviations from the traditional 19th century rules are permissible, but only with respect to suits arising out of the absent defendant's contacts with the forum state. Thus, in *International Shoe Co. v. Washington* [Minimum contacts are required in order to satisfy the traditional notions of fair play and substantial justice], we established a minimum contacts test for such situations. In the instant action, Burnham (D) contends that the *International Shoe* minimum contacts test should also be applied to a situation where a nonresident defendant is physically present in the forum

---

state. However, we find nothing in *International Shoe* or its progeny requiring an extension to situations of transient jurisdiction. We therefore hold that jurisdiction based on physical presence alone satisfies due process because it is one of the continuing traditions of our legal system and, therefore, is consistent with "traditional notions of fair play and substantial justice." Burnham's (D) argument, that our decision in *Shaffer v. Heitner* [Quasi in rem jurisdiction is subject to the same minimum contacts analysis as is in personam jurisdiction] requires reversal, is likewise unavailing. Burnham (D) misinterprets our statement in *Shaffer* that "all assertions of state-court jurisdiction must be evaluated according to the standards set forth in *International Shoe* and its progeny." The context of this statement reveals that only quasi in rem jurisdiction must be subjected to the minimum contacts analysis. *Shaffer* does not, therefore, compel the conclusion that physically present defendants must be treated identically to absent ones. Where a jurisdictional principal is firmly approved by tradition and still favored, such as the doctrine of jurisdiction by physical presence, due process is not violated by obtaining such jurisdiction. Thus, the California courts could exercise jurisdiction over Burnham (D) based on in-state service of process. Affirmed.

■ **CONCURRENCE**

(White, J.) I concur in the affirmance and in Justice Scalia's conclusion that jurisdiction by personal service is so widely accepted that it should not be struck down as violative of the Fourteenth Amendment Due Process Clause.

■ **CONCURRENCE**

(Brennan, J.) While I concur in the judgment, I do not agree with the unshakable reliance on tradition as supporting all forms of jurisdiction. Unlike Justice Scalia, I would undertake an independent inquiry into the fairness of the prevailing in-state service rule. Justice Scalia's historical approach is foreclosed by our decisions in *International Shoe* and *Shaffer v. Heitner*. Pursuant to *Shaffer*, I believe that all rules of jurisdiction, even ancient ones, must satisfy the contemporary notions of due process elucidated in *International Shoe's* minimum contacts analysis. However, as transient jurisdiction is consistent with the reasonable expectations of a nonresident defendant, it is entitled to a strong presumption that it comports with due process. By visiting the forum State, a nonresident defendant purposefully avails himself of the benefits and protections of the forum State. Moreover, the potential burdens on a transient defendant are slight. Thus, I believe that, as a rule the exercise of personal jurisdiction over a defendant based on his voluntary presence in the forum state will satisfy the requirements of due process.

■ **CONCURRENCE**

(Stevens, J.) I am concerned with the broad reach of Justice Scalia's majority opinion. However, the historical evidence identified by Justice Scalia, the considerations of fairness identified by Justice Brennan, and the common sense displayed by Justice White convince me that this is a very easy case. I agree that the judgment should be affirmed.

Analysis:

This is an extremely important case in ascertaining the correct application of *Shaffer v. Heitner* and *International Shoe*. Although *Shaffer* apparently stated that all jurisdictional issues must now be evaluated by the *International Shoe* minimum contacts test, Justice Scalia's opinion makes it clear that this is not the case. Rather, the traditional notion of jurisdiction based on physical presence can survive even absent sufficient minimum contacts between the defendant and the forum State. Justice Scalia's rule has the advantages of certainty and judicial efficiency. But Justice Brennan's concurrence argues that *all* forms of jurisdiction, including jurisdiction based on physical presence, must satisfy the minimum contacts test in order to comport with due process. In reality, it appears that Justices Scalia and Brennan reached essentially the same result, however, although they took different approaches to get there. Indeed, it may be inferred that the only difference between Scalia's rule and Brennan's involves cases of involuntary physical presence. Nevertheless, these situations of involuntary presence in a forum state are likely so rare that Scalia and Brennan have, in effect, adopted the same rule: jurisdiction based on in-state service of process over a defendant physically present in the forum state comports with due process.

■ CASE VOCABULARY

MANDAMUS: A proceeding in some superior court, seeking an order for an inferior court to perform some duty, such as quashing a service of process.

TRANSIENT JURISDICTION: Jurisdiction over a nonresident defendant based on service of process on the defendant while present in the forum State.

Carnival Cruise Lines v. Shute

(Cruise Line) v. *(Passenger)*

499 U.S. 585, 111 S.Ct. 1522 (1991)

REASONABLE FORUM SELECTION CLAUSES VALIDLY ESTABLISH JURISDICTION BY CONSENT

■ **INSTANT FACTS** In response to a suit for injuries occurring on one of its cruise ships, Carnival Cruise Lines (D) argued that the forum selection clause contained on the ticket should establish jurisdiction.

■ **BLACK LETTER RULE** Reasonable forum selection clauses are effective in imposing jurisdiction.

■ **PROCEDURAL BASIS**

Writ of certiorari reviewing reversal of dismissal of action for damages for negligence due to lack of jurisdiction.

■ **FACTS**

Eulala and Russel Shute (P) purchased tickets for a cruise on Carnival Cruise Lines (D). The tickets were purchased from a travel agent in Washington, who forwarded the payment to Carnival's (D) headquarters in Florida. A provision on the tickets stated that all disputes were required to be litigated in Florida. While sailing from Los Angeles to Mexico, Mrs. Shute (P) slipped on a deck mat and was injured. The Shutes (P) filed suit in a Washington district court, alleging damages for negligence on the part of Carnival (D) and its employees. However, the District Court ruled that Carnival's (D) contacts with Washington were insufficient to support jurisdiction. The Court of Appeals reversed, and the Supreme Court granted certiorari.

■ **ISSUE**

Is a reasonable forum selection clause enforceable to establish consent to jurisdiction?

■ **DECISION AND RATIONALE**

(Justice Not Stated) Yes. A reasonable forum selection clause is enforceable in order to establish consent to jurisdiction. The minimum contacts analysis is inapplicable in the instant action, as the forum selection clause contained on the ticket was reasonable for several reasons. First, a cruise line has a special interest in limiting the potentially vast number of forums in which it could be sued. Second, a forum selection clause has the beneficial effect of sparing litigants and courts the time and expense of pretrial motions to determine the correct forum [although it does not spare parties the cost of litigating in a distant jurisdiction!]. Third, passengers who purchase tickets containing a forum selection clause presumably benefit in the form of reduced fares, reflecting the savings that cruise lines enjoy by limiting the forums in which they may be sued.

Analysis:

This decision essentially reiterates the reasonableness requirement for forum selection clauses, established in *Bremen v. Zapata*. However, the Court's reasoning can be questioned on a number of fronts. First, while a cruise line certainly has an interest in limiting the number

---

of forums in which it can be sued, the court fails to consider the interests and burdens suffered by passengers who must litigate in a distant state. Arguably, it would be less burdensome for a large corporate cruise line to defend suits in distant states than it would be for passengers to litigate in far-away locales. The Court's holding could have the effect of dissuading passengers from bringing valid claims due to the expense involved. Second, in reality it is unlikely that passengers such as the Shuttes (P) benefitted very much in the form of reduced fares by the insertion of the forum selection clause. Perhaps the Court should have conducted a modified minimum-contacts test, weighing the benefits and burdens of each of the parties and determining whether passengers or the cruise line purposefully availed themselves of jurisdiction in a distant state.

■ CASE VOCABULARY

EX ANTE: Beforehand; ahead of time.

FORA: The plural form of "forum."

Mullane v. Central Hanover Bank & Trust Co.

(Special Guardian) v. *(Common Trustee)*

339 U.S. 306, 70 S.Ct. 652 (1950)

NOTICE BY PUBLICATION IS RARELY "REASONABLY CALCULATED" TO PROVIDE NOTICE WHEN ADDRESSES OF THE PARTIES ARE KNOWN

■ **INSTANT FACTS** Central Hanover Bank and Trust Company (P) petitioned for a judicial settlement of a trust and provided notice by publication to all of the beneficiaries.

■ **BLACK LETTER RULE** Notice by publication fails to comply with due process where the names and addresses of the parties are known.

■ **PROCEDURAL BASIS**

Writ of certiorari reviewing affirmance of order overruling due-process objection to service of process in petition for settlement of trust.

■ **FACTS**

Central Hanover Bank and Trust Company (P) established a common trust fund, in which 113 small trusts were pooled into one fund for investment administration. Central Hanover (P) petitioned the Surrogate's Court of New York for judicial settlement of this account as common trustee. If granted, the decree would settle all questions respecting the management of the common fund, terminating all rights of beneficiaries against the trustee for improper management. Pursuant to New York statute, all beneficiaries of this common trust were notified by publication in a local newspaper for four successive weeks. [After all, everyone reads the "legal notices" section of the newspaper, don't they?] Mullane (D), who was appointed special guardian for all beneficiaries not otherwise appearing in the action, entered a special appearance in New York in order to object to the notice. According to Mullane (D), the Trust Company (P) should have provided notice by mail, as the company had actual knowledge of the names and addresses of the beneficiaries. Therefore, Mullane (D) argued that the statutorily-endorsed notice was inadequate to afford due process under the Fourteenth Amendment, and therefore that the court was without jurisdiction to enter a final decree. The Surrogate overruled Mullane's (D) objections, and a final decree accepting the accounts was entered. The Appellate Division of the New York Supreme Court and the Court of Appeals of New York affirmed. The Supreme Court granted certiorari.

■ **ISSUE**

Where the names and addresses of parties are known, does notice by publication comply with due process?

■ **DECISION AND RATIONALE**

(Jackson, J.) No. Where the names and addresses of parties are known, notice by publication does not comply with due process. Due process requires that notice be provided prior to the deprivation of life, liberty or property by adjudication. In the situation at hand, the proceeding had the possibility of depriving the beneficiaries of property, as a decree would cut off their rights to hold the common trustee liable for negligence. Further, we hold that due process requires that this notice be reasonably calculated, under the circumstances, to apprise

---

interested parties of the pendency of the action and afford them and an opportunity to be heard. Personal service of written notice always complies with due process. However, parties residing outside of the forum state do not necessarily have to be provided with written notice, as this would place impossible obstacles in the instant action where the number of interested beneficiaries is numerous. Indeed, in many circumstances, notice by mail complies with due process, even though there is a risk that notice may not actually reach all interested parties. Where a large number of parties share a common interest, it can be assumed that those beneficiaries present will defend the rights of the absent parties. However, in the instant action, Central Hanover (P) only provided notice by publication. Such notice was not reasonably calculated to provide notice to those parties whose names and addresses were known. Notice by publication is certainly not a reliable method of apprising interested parties of the pending adjudication of their rights. The record indicates that, upon the foundation of the common trust, Central Hanover (P) had mailed information to a number of the beneficiaries. Likewise, Central Hanover (P) should have mailed notice of the legal proceeding to all of these beneficiaries, as this would not seriously burden the trust. Thus, the New York statute providing for service by publication in such circumstances is unconstitutional, as it fails to comply with the Fourteenth Amendment. However, with regard to those beneficiaries whose addresses were not known, or whose interests in the trust were uncertain, we hold that notice by publication did comply with due process. Reversed in part.

Analysis:

Whenever legal proceedings affect the life, liberty or property interests of parties, these parties must be provided with notice reasonably calculated under the circumstances to apprise them of the proceedings and give them an opportunity to be heard. The focus of the case is on the phrase "reasonably calculated under the circumstances." There is a wide spectrum of potential notice devices, ranging from personal service (the best form of notice) to notice by publication (the least reliable method). Whenever possible, personal service should be provided, although this may be impossible when the parties are numerous or reside in distant states. In such circumstances, it is easy to see that mailed notice is sufficient, even though some of the parties might not receive the notice. However, courts generally disfavor notice by publication unless parties' addresses are unknown or not easily ascertainable. Indeed, notice by publication is really just a legal fiction, since no reasonable person would regularly read the legal notices of a newspaper (published in a distant state!).

■ CASE VOCABULARY

INTER VIVOS TRUST: A trust created by distribution of property to a trustee during the lifetime of the settlor (the entity creating the trust), in which the property is held for the benefit of the beneficiaries.

SURROGATE COURT: A court with jurisdiction over probate matters, including wills and trusts.

TESTAMENTARY TRUST: A trust created by will upon the death of the settlor.

Gibbons v. Brown

(Direction Giving Passenger) v. (Passenger)

716 So.2d 868 (Fla.App.1998)

STATE LONG-ARM STATUTES MAY RESTRICT PERSONAL JURISDICTION EVEN IF THE CONSTITUTION WOULD PERMIT IT

■ **INSTANT FACTS** Passenger versus passenger lawsuit where personal jurisdiction was asserted based upon non-resident Brown (D) having filed a lawsuit in the state two years prior against a non-party driver.

■ **BLACK LETTER RULE** Jurisdiction over a non-resident defendant is not proper where the only contact with the state was filing a lawsuit two years earlier against a defendant not a party to the current suit.

■ **PROCEDURAL BASIS**

Appeal from order denying motion to quash service of process and, alternatively, motion to dismiss complaint for damages for personal injuries.

■ **FACTS**

Gibbons (D), a passenger in the car driven by Mr. Brown, was sued by Mrs. Brown (P), also a passenger, for injuries sustained in an automobile accident that occurred in Canada. Gibbons (D) had given wrong directions to Mr. Brown, the driver of the car, which caused him to turn onto a one-way street, resulting in a head-on collision. Gibbons (D) resided in Texas and Brown (P) resided in Florida. Brown (P) brought the action in Florida [asserting a theory of bad direction giving]. However, a prior lawsuit had been brought in Florida by Gibbons as a plaintiff against Mr. Brown, the driver, two years earlier. [Gibbons felt that Mr. Brown caused the accident notwithstanding her bad directions.] In the current lawsuit, Brown (P) contended that non-resident Gibbons (D) subjected herself to the personal jurisdiction of Florida because she had brought the prior lawsuit against Mr. Brown in Florida. However, she did not name Mrs. Brown as a defendant in that suit. Florida's long-arm statute provides that "a defendant who is engaged in substantial and not isolated activity within this state, whether such activity is wholly intrastate, interstate, or otherwise, is subject to the jurisdiction of the courts of this state, whether or not the claim arises from that activity." Gibbons (D) challenges Florida's jurisdiction over her because her prior lawsuit, although involving the same accident, did not include Brown (P) as a defendant, and there were two years between that lawsuit and this action.

■ **ISSUE**

Is jurisdiction over a non-resident defendant proper where the only contact with the state was filing a lawsuit two years earlier against a defendant not a party to the current suit?

■ **DECISION AND RATIONALE**

(Per Curiam) No. To come within Florida's jurisdiction under its long-arm statute, a defendant must be "engaged in substantial and not isolated activity" within the state. Even if we were to assume [by stretching it to the extreme] that bringing an action in Florida can constitute "substantial and not isolated activity", there is nevertheless no showing by Brown (P) that Gibbons (D) "is engaged" in any activity in the state other than defending this lawsuit. Because of the length of time between the two lawsuits and the fact that the prior suit did not

---

name Brown (P) as a defendant, we conclude that Brown (P) has not alleged a satisfactory ground for personal jurisdiction pursuant to Florida's long-arm statute. The trial court is directed to dismiss Brown's (P) complaint.

Analysis:

This case is an example of a state's long-arm statute limiting jurisdiction even where the Constitution would permit such jurisdiction absent the statutory restrictions. In this Florida Court of Appeal case, the decision states that Florida's long-arm statute requires more activities or contacts than are currently required by the decisions of the United States Supreme Court. The statute at issue limits jurisdiction to specified occurrences, whereas other states, such as California, permit jurisdiction on any basis not inconsistent with the Constitution. For example, in *Adam v. Saenger,* the Supreme Court upheld California's jurisdiction over a non-resident whose only contact with the state was commencing a lawsuit that resulted in the defendant filing a counterclaim against him. In *Gibbons,* the court was unwilling to hold that a person's bringing of a prior lawsuit in the state should indefinitely prevent challenging jurisdiction in a separate suit, even one arising from the same subject matter. The court relied upon the length of time between the two actions and the fact that a non-party to the instant action was named as a defendant in the prior action.

■ **CASE VOCABULARY**

MOTION TO DISMISS COMPLAINT: Challenging the right of the court to entertain the lawsuit based on various legal theories.

MOTION TO QUASH SERVICE OF PROCESS: To void the act of legally serving documents, such as the summons and complaint.

PER CURIAM: An opinion by the whole court, rather than one judge.

Dee-K Enterprises, Inc. v. Heveafil Sdn. Bhd.

(Rubber Thread Purchaser) v. (Distributors)

982 F.Supp. 1138 (E.D.Va.1997)

VENUE DETERMINATIONS ARE MADE SOLELY FROM STATUTORY RATHER THAN CONSTITUTIONAL SOURCES

■ **INSTANT FACTS** Manufacturers of rubber thread outside of the United States challenge jurisdiction and venue to sue them in federal district court.

■ **BLACK LETTER RULE** General federal venue statute subjecting alien corporations to suit in any judicial district overrides other federal statutes that may contain specific venue provisions.

■ **PROCEDURAL BASIS**

Decision by federal district court judge ordering plaintiff to amend antitrust complaint to allege, with specificity, venue in the district in which complaint was filed.

■ **FACTS**

Dee-K Enterprises, Inc. (Dee-K) (P) and other American purchasers of rubber thread used in the making of bungee cords brought suit against various foreign governments and distributors of the thread alleging an international conspiracy to restrain trade in, and fix prices of, the thread in the United States. [The defendants must have foreseen big business in bungee jumping and wanted to make lots of money from their rubber threads.] Heveafil Sdn. Bhd. (Heveafil) (D) and other defendants moved to dismiss on the grounds of 1) lack of personal jurisdiction over a manufacturer from a foreign country where it consummates sales of the thread in the foreign country, and 2) improper venue in the Eastern District of Virginia.

■ **ISSUE**

Does the general federal venue statute subjecting alien corporations to suit in any judicial district override other federal statutes that may contain specific venue provisions?

■ **DECISION AND RATIONALE**

(Ellis) Yes. The federal venue statute, 28 U.S.C. §1391(d), provides that aliens may be sued in any district. This statute overrides any special venue provision contained in other federal statutes. We first address the issue of jurisdiction. Jurisdiction is based upon a federal antitrust statute and a federal rule of civil procedure which provide for worldwide service of process when the antitrust defendant is a corporation. We initially must determine whether under the federal statute or rule, due process is complied with pursuant to the "fair play and substantial justice" test of *International Shoe* [personal jurisdiction over a non-resident defendant corporation exists where the defendant has certain minimum contacts with the state and maintenance of the suit does not offend traditional notions of fair play and substantial justice]. We find that due process was satisfied [hands down] by Heveafil's (D) appointment of exclusive U.S. sales agents and the customizing of its products for the U.S. markets. We next must consider venue. The antitrust statute provides that venue is proper in any district where the defendant is "found" or where it "transacts business." Although Heveafil (D) and the other foreign defendants conduct their business abroad, [no need to worry,] this is not fatal. The Supreme Court has held that the general federal venue statute, 28 U.S.C. §1391(d), which

---

provides that aliens may be sued in any district, overrides any special venue provision contained in other federal statutes such as the one pertaining to antitrust actions. With respect to the American defendants, subsection (b) of 28 U.S.C. §1391 provides that venue is proper, among other things, in a "judicial district in which any defendant may be found, if there is no district in which the action may otherwise be brought." Although (Dee-K) (P) has alleged that some defendants have contact with Virginia, additional allegations are necessary to show that the contacts or businesses are located in the Eastern District so that venue here is proper.

Analysis:

The court shows here how the issue of venue is one determined by statute rather than upon a constitutional review. This case is somewhat complicated in that there are multiple defendants. The court found proper venue with respect to the foreign corporations, but required Dee-K (P) to amend its complaint with respect to allegations of venue for the American defendants. Note that venue further defines the location where the trial will occur. Whereas jurisdiction may place the matter in a particular state, venue determines which district within the state is proper. Also, the case demonstrates statutory interpretation and illustrates the overriding of the antitrust statute by the general federal venue statute. Finally, notice that there is a very broad venue statute applicable to alien corporations.

■ CASE VOCABULARY

ALIENS: Foreign persons or companies that are citizens or subjects of a foreign nation.

ANTITRUST ACTION: Lawsuit alleging unlawful monopolies or restraints on trade and commerce.

Piper Aircraft Co. v. Reyno

(Plane Manufacturer) v. (Estate Representative)

454 U.S. 235, 102 S.Ct. 252, 70 L.Ed.2d 419 (1981)

SUPREME COURT ANNOUNCES THAT DISMISSAL FOR FORUM NON CONVENIENS IS NOT AN ABUSE OF JUDICIAL DISCRETION MERELY BECAUSE THE LAW OF THE ALTERNATIVE FORUM IS LESS FAVORABLE TO PLAINTIFFS

■ **INSTANT FACTS** The Scottish heirs of plane crash victims in Scotland try to sue for wrongful death in an American court because American courts recognize wrongful death as a cause of action and are known generally to be more favorable to plaintiffs than the courts in Scotland.

■ **BLACK LETTER RULE** The fact of a substantive law being less favorable to plaintiffs in an alternative forum should not be given conclusive or even substantial weight in applying the doctrine of forum non conveniens.

■ **PROCEDURAL BASIS**

Appeal from order of the Court of Appeals granting jurisdiction in Pennsylvania District Court.

■ **FACTS**

A commercial aircraft manufactured in Pennsylvania by Piper (D) crashed in the Scottish highlands. Reports suggested either that the airplane suffered mechanical failure or pilot error. (Legend says only the Lochness monster witnessed it.) At the time of the crash, the plane was registered in Great Britain, operated by a Scottish air taxi service, subject to Scottish air traffic patrol, and full of Scottish residents. Naturally, then, Gaynell Reyno (P), the estate administratrix and legal secretary to the attorney who filed the wrongful death suit on behalf of the Scottish families, brought the action in California state court. Claiming negligence and strict liability, Reyno (P) admits that the choice of forum was determined by the fact that the laws regarding liability, capacity to sue, and damages are more favorable in America than in Scotland. Oddly enough, Piper (D) didn't see this as a boon and moved to transfer the case to a Pennsylvania District Court and subsequently motioned to dismiss it under the doctrine of forum non conveniens. The District Court granted the motion but the Circuit Court overruled it and remanded for trial in Pennsylvania because the plaintiffs would be disadvantaged more by the law in Scotland than the law in Pennsylvania.

■ **ISSUE**

Should a motion to dismiss for forum non conveniens be denied merely because the substantive law of an alternative forum is less favorable to plaintiffs?

■ **DECISION AND RATIONALE**

(Marshall, J.) No. In analyzing a motion to dismiss for forum non conveniens, courts should not give dispositive or even substantial weight to the fact that the alternative forum is less favorable to plaintiffs than the one in which the action was initially brought. At present, the doctrine of forum non conveniens is designed to avoid conducting complex exercises in comparative law. Giving substantial weight to such a consideration, however, would render the doctrine effectively moot. On the one hand, if courts give much weight to change in substantive law, they will be forced to interpret the law of foreign jurisdictions to make the determination of which is the more favorable forum. On the other hand, it is clear that plaintiffs initially select the most favorable forum to them so courts won't even have to consider a motion to dismiss for forum non conveniens because any alternative forum will be less favorable to plaintiffs than the one they selected for themselves. Of course, substantial weight may be given to the disadvantaging law of an alternative forum if the remedy would be so clearly inadequate that dismissal would not be "in the interests of justice." This is not the case for the Scottish plaintiffs, though. Other considerations are more important in this case. First, the strong presumption in *Gulf Oil Corp. v. Gilbert* [creating a balancing test of public and private interests between plaintiffs and defendants to determine the appropriateness of a forum non conveniens dismissal] in favor of the plaintiff's choice of forum applies with less force when, as in this case, the plaintiffs are foreign. It is unreasonable to assume that a foreign plaintiff's choice of an American forum is for the sake of convenience. Great deference to a foreign plaintiff would also encourage an onslaught of litigation to be brought in the United States which could and should have been brought in a foreign forum. Second, private policy interests dictate that the result of the District Court should have been upheld. Because witnesses and much relevant evidence are more easily located in Great Britain, there would be fewer evidentiary problems in Scotland. Furthermore, because it is far more convenient to resolve all claims in one trial and because Piper (D) would have a hard time impleading potential third party defendants in the United States, the trial should be held in Scotland. Third, public policy interests recommend toward trial in Scotland because Piper (D) and Hartzell, the other defendant, would have two different sets of law applied to them. Piper (D) would be subject to Pennsylvania law whereas Hartzell would still be subject to Scottish law, with which the Pennsylvania court is understandably unfamiliar. In addition, Scotland has a greater interest in this litigation than does the United States because, apart from Piper (D) and Hartzell, all potential plaintiffs and defendants are either Scottish or English. Finally, the important base consideration is that reversal of a dismissal for forum non conveniens should only be granted if the District Court abused its discretion. In the instant case, it is apparent that the District Court did no such thing, but the Circuit Court simply disagreed with their analysis. Reversed.

Analysis:

Piper represents the current approach to the forum non conveniens doctrine. An underlying tenet of *Piper* is that the doctrine applies only when venue is proper in the initial forum and there is an alternative forum available. In *Piper,* for example, the choice was clearly between the United States and Scotland; both the litigants and the courts were aware of this. The crucial progressive step that *Piper* takes is to establish a balancing test, without allowing any one factor to be dispositive. The result of such a balancing test is rarely removal to another country. Most courts would not grant such a drastic forum non conveniens motion until all other jurisdictional possibilities had been exhausted. Once the case is out of the dismissing court's hands, the burden falls on the plaintiffs to re-submit the case in the alternate forum. There is a notable distinction between the application of forum non conveniens dismissal in federal and state courts. Federal courts rarely utilize the dismissal option because if another federal court is available as a proper forum, they need only resort to transfer. Only when the more convenient forum is foreign, which is a rare occurrence, will the federal courts have to dismiss. State courts, on the other hand, end up exercising their right to dismiss for forum non conveniens because the more convenient forum is often another state and state courts can't transfer a case to a court in another state.

■ CASE VOCABULARY

ADMINISTRATRIX: One (female) appointed to handle the affairs of one who has died intestate, or who has left no executor.

CHOICE-OF-LAW RULES: Rule applied in a court to determine whether federal or state law is applicable and/or whether the law of the forum or some other state applies.

FORUM NON CONVENIENS: Discretionary doctrine whereby a court which has jurisdiction over a case may decline to exercise it, as there is no substantive reason for the case to be brought there, or if in presenting the case in that court it would create a hardship on the defendants or witnesses.

IMPLEAD: To bring a third party, who is allegedly liable, into a lawsuit for purposes of indemnity or contribution.

INDEMNITY: The obligation of one person to make good on a loss of another; an assurance to compensate for the damage caused by another.

CHAPTER 3

Subject Matter Jurisdiction of Federal Courts

Louisville & Nashville Railroad v. Mottley

Instant Facts: Injured railroad customers sought to enforce the use of their free passes in the wrong court.

Black Letter Rule: The plaintiff's federal question must appear in the allegations of the complaint, and anticipated defense, involving federal law are inadequate for federal question jurisdiction.

Redner v. Sanders

Instant Facts: Redner (P), a United States citizen living in France, sued three New York citizens in federal court.

Black Letter Rule: Residency is not synonymous with citizenship.

Hertz v. Friend

Instant Facts: Friend (P) and other California employees (P) of Hertz (D) brought a class action suit for wage and hour law violations, and Hertz (D) sought to remove the suit to federal court based on diversity jurisdiction.

Black Letter Rule: For purposes of diversity jurisdiction, a corporation's principal place of business is the location of the corporation's headquarters.

In re Ameriquest Mortgage Co. Mortgage Lending Practices Litigation

Instant Facts: A borrower sued a lender in federal court for violations of the Truth in Lending Act and fraud, and the lender moved to dismiss the fraud claims, arguing that, because they were based on state law, the federal court did not have jurisdiction to hear them.

Black Letter Rule: Under 28 U.S.C. § 1367, in any action in which the federal court has jurisdiction over a federal claim, it has supplemental jurisdiction over state claims that are so related to claims in the action within such original jurisdiction that they form part of the same case or controversy under Article III of the Constitution.

Szendry-Ramos v. First Bancorp

Instant Facts: A bank's in-house counsel sued the bank when it fired her after she disclosed the bank's allegedly unethical practices.

Black Letter Rule: When the plaintiff's state law claims substantially predominate over the federal claims or raise complex or novel issues of state law, the federal court may decline to exercise supplemental jurisdiction over the state law claims.

Caterpillar, Inc. v. Lewis

Instant Facts: Lewis's (P) state case was improperly removed to federal court because there was not completed diversity of the parties. The jurisdictional defect was cured before judgment.

Black Letter Rule: A district court's error in failing to remand a case improperly removed is not fatal to the ensuing judgment if federal jurisdictional requirements are met at the time judgment is entered.

Louisville & Nashville Railroad v. Mottley

(Railroad) v. *(Victim)*

211 U.S. 149, 29 S.Ct. 42 (1908)

TO INVOKE FEDERAL JURISDICTION, THE FEDERAL QUESTION MUST APPEAR IN THE COMPLAINT; ANTICIPATED DEFENSES INVOLVING FEDERAL QUESTIONS ARE INADEQUATE

■ **INSTANT FACTS** Injured railroad customers sought to enforce the use of their free passes in the wrong court.

■ **BLACK LETTER RULE** The plaintiff's federal question must appear in the allegations of the complaint, and anticipated defense, involving federal law are inadequate for federal question jurisdiction.

■ **PROCEDURAL BASIS**

objection b/c P's facts, while true, are insufficient.

Appeal by the Railroad (D) when a demurrer in their favor was overruled.

■ **FACTS**

The Mottleys (P) were injured in a railway accident on Louisville & Nashville Railroad (D) and given lifetime passes on the railroad to settle their claims. Many years later, Congress made free passes unlawful, believing that railroads were using free passes to bribe public officials. When the railroad (D) refused to honor the Mottleys' (P) passes, they sued in federal court asking for specific performance. The Mottleys (P) alleged that the Railroad (D) would raise the federal law as a defense, and that applying this law to them would be unconstitutional.

■ **ISSUE**

Is a plaintiff's allegation that a defense to his complaint will raise an issue of federal or constitutional law adequate to give a federal court jurisdiction over the suit?

■ **DECISION AND RATIONALE**

(Moody, J.) No, the plaintiff's federal question must appear in the complaint. Louisville & Nashville Railroad (D) filed a demurrer to the bill and raised two questions of law which are presented here on appeal. The first is whether the act of Congress at issue prohibits the giving of passes under the circumstances of this case, and secondly, if the act does apply to this case, whether the statute is in violation of the Fifth Amendment of the Constitution of the United States. We are not going to consider these issues because the court below was without jurisdiction. Neither party questioned that jurisdiction, but we may on our own see to it that the jurisdiction of the Circuit Court is not exceeded. There is no diversity of citizenship here so the only possible ground for jurisdiction is that the case was a suit "arising under the Constitution and laws of the United States" as the jurisdiction statute provides. The settled meaning of this statute is that a suit arises under the Constitution and laws of the United States when the plaintiff's statement of his own cause of action shows that it is based upon those laws or the Constitution. It is not enough that the plaintiff alleges that some anticipated defense to his suit will be unconstitutional. While some question under the Constitution will likely arise at some point in the litigation, this does not mean that the original suit arises under the Constitution. The plaintiff should be confined to his own statement in the complaint. The defendant should

---

be left to set up the defense. We find that the application of this rule to the present case shows that the Circuit Court had no subject matter jurisdiction. Reversed and remanded with instructions to dismiss for lack of jurisdiction.

Analysis:

This case presents the well-pleaded complaint rule under which the plaintiff's federal question must appear in the allegations of the complaint. This rule allows for an early determination of whether the federal court has jurisdiction. It is difficult, if not impossible, to predict what defenses a defendant may raise in the answer or at a later point in the litigation. Therefore, it is reasonable to disallow the consideration of possible defenses in determining whether a federal question exists. Note how the court raised the issue of jurisdiction on its own, or sua sponte. Unlike personal jurisdiction, subject matter jurisdiction cannot be waived by the parties. A defect in subject matter jurisdiction can be raised at any time by the court.

■ **CASE VOCABULARY**

BILL: The first pleading by the plaintiff. It is now called a complaint.

DEMURRER: A motion arguing that even if the facts as alleged are true, they are legally insufficient to make a claim. It is now called a motion to dismiss.

SUA SPONTE: This means to take action on its own will without the suggestion of another.

Redner v. Sanders

(French Resident) v. (New York Citizen)

2000 WL 1161080 (S.D.N.Y. 2000)

DIVERSE *RESIDENCES* DO NOT SUPPORT DIVERSITY JURISDICTION

■ **INSTANT FACTS** Redner (P), a United States citizen living in France, sued three New York citizens in federal court.

■ **BLACK LETTER RULE** Residency is not synonymous with citizenship.

■ **PROCEDURAL BASIS**

On consideration of the defendant's motion to dismiss for lack of subject matter jurisdiction.

■ **FACTS**

Redner (P) sued two individual defendants and one corporate defendant, all citizens of New York, in New York federal court. In the complaint, Redner (P) alleged that he was a United States citizen residing in France, without establishing his state of citizenship. The defendants filed a motion to dismiss under Federal Rule of Civil Procedure 12(b)(1) for lack of subject matter jurisdiction.

■ **ISSUE**

Did Redner (P) sufficiently establish diversity of citizenship by virtue of his residency in a foreign country?

■ **DECISION AND RATIONALE**

(Griesa, J.) No. Under 28 U.S.C. § 1332, a federal district court has jurisdiction over actions involving citizens of different states as well as citizens of a state and a foreign country. Redner (P), in his complaint, apparently seeks diversity jurisdiction by virtue of his current residency in France. Residency, however, is not synonymous with citizenship. Based on Redner's (P) allegations in the complaint that he is a United States citizen residing in France, the case does not involve an action between a citizen of a state and a citizen of a foreign country. Neither does the complaint sufficiently establish that the action involves citizens of different states. At the hearing, the plaintiff asserted that he maintains United States citizenship in California, as demonstrated by his license to practice law in that state, his driver's license from that state, and his modest attempts at gaining employment in that state. The plaintiff fails, however, to explain his residency in France, including his purpose for living there and his intentions to return to California. Absent such a factual showing, the plaintiff has failed to establish his domicile. Motion granted.

Analysis:

Redner's (P) problem may have been avoided through more careful pleading. The problem Redner (P) faced may not be so much that he lacked the citizenship to create diversity, but that he failed to properly assert his citizenship. But as a United States citizen residing in France, Redner's (P) California citizenship would have been retained if he did not intend to

---

remain in France; a temporary change in residence does not change a person's domicile for jurisdictional purposes if the person intends to return at some point in the future.

■ **CASE VOCABULARY**

CITIZEN: A person who, by either birth or naturalization, is a member of a political community, owing allegiance to the community and being entitled to enjoy all its civil rights and protections; a member of the civil state, entitled to all its privileges.

DIVERSITY JURISDICTION: A federal court's exercise of authority over a case involving parties from different states and an amount in controversy greater than a statutory minimum.

DIVERSITY OF CITIZENSHIP: A basis for federal-court jurisdiction that exists when (1) a case is between citizens of different states, or between a citizen of a state and an alien, and (2) the matter in controversy exceeds a specific value.

DOMICILE: The place at which a person is physically present and that the person regards as home; a person's true, fixed, principal, and permanent home, to which that person intends to return and remain even though currently residing elsewhere.

RESIDENT: A person who lives in a particular place; a person who has a home in a particular place.

Hertz v. Friend

(Employer) v. (Employee)

130 S. Ct. 1181 (2011)

A CORPORATION'S "NERVE CENTER" IS ITS PRINCIPAL PLACE OF BUSINESS FOR PURPOSES OF DIVERSITY JURISDICTION

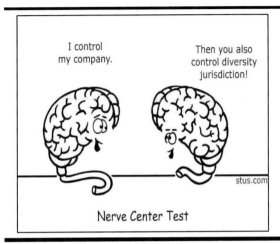

I control my company.

Then you also control diversity jurisdiction!

stus.com

Nerve Center Test

■ **INSTANT FACTS** Friend (P) and other California employees (P) of Hertz (D) brought a class action suit for wage and hour law violations, and Hertz (D) sought to remove the suit to federal court based on diversity jurisdiction.

■ **BLACK LETTER RULE** For purposes of diversity jurisdiction, a corporation's principal place of business is the location of the corporation's headquarters.

■ **PROCEDURAL BASIS**

Appeal from an order affirming a remand of the case to state court.

■ **FACTS**

Friend (P) and other California employees (P) of Hertz (D) brought a class action suit against Hertz (D) in California state court. The suit alleged violations of California wage and hours laws. Hertz (D) moved to remove the case to federal court based on diversity of citizenship. The diversity jurisdiction statute, 28 U.S.C. § 1332 (c)(1), states that a corporation is deemed a citizen of the state of its incorporation and of the state where it has its principal place of business. Friend (P) resisted removal, claiming that there was no diversity because California was a principal place of business for Hertz (D). Friend (P) argued that Hertz (D) derived more revenue from California than from any other state, and that the plurality of Hertz's (D) business occurred there.

■ **ISSUE**

Was there diversity of citizenship?

■ **DECISION AND RATIONALE**

(Breyer, J.) Yes. For purposes of diversity jurisdiction, a corporation's principal place of business is the location of the corporation's headquarters. The term "principal place of business" is best understood as referring to the place where a corporation's officers direct, control, and coordinate the activities of the corporation. In practice, this will normally be the place where the corporation maintains its headquarters, assuming that the headquarters is the actual center of direction, control, and coordination (the "nerve center"), and not simply an office where board meetings are held. There are three considerations that make this rule the best approach. The first is that the diversity statute refers to a principal "place" of business. The language is singular, not plural. The second is that administrative simplicity is a major virtue in a jurisdictional statute. Complex jurisdictional tests complicate a case and consume time and money by forcing the parties to litigate jurisdiction, rather than the merits of their claims. Courts also have an independent obligation to determine whether subject-matter jurisdiction exists, even if the parties don't challenge it. Courts benefit from straightforward rules under which they can readily assure themselves of jurisdiction. Third, the legislative history of the diversity statute supports this reading. The initial version of the proposed statutes suggested a numerical test, in which a corporation would be deemed a citizen of the state that accounted for more than half its gross income. This approach was criticized as too complex and impractical to apply. The legislative history suggests that "principal place of business" should be interpreted to be no more complex than the initial "half the gross income" test. A "nerve center" test offers such a possibility, but a "general business activities" test does not.

There may be no perfect test for citizenship that satisfies every criterion. There will be hard cases under the "nerve center" test. For example, some corporations may divide functions among officers who work at several different locations, perhaps communicating over the internet. Nonetheless, under the "nerve center" test, courts will not have to try to weigh corporate functions, assets, or revenues. Our approach provides a sensible test that is relatively easier to apply, not one that will, in all instances, automatically generate a result. A "nerve center" test may produce results that seem to cut against the basic rationale for diversity jurisdiction. For example, if the bulk of a company's business activities visible to the public take place in New Jersey, while its top officers direct those in New York, the "principal place of business" is New York. One could argue that members of the public in New Jersey would be less likely to be prejudiced against the corporation than persons in New York, but the corporation will still be entitled to remove a New Jersey state case to federal court. Such seeming anomalies will arise. However, in view of the necessity of a clearer rule, we must accept them. Reversed and remanded.

Analysis:

The examples of jurisdictional anomalies and hard cases mentioned by Justice Breyer raise a larger question for policy-makers: Is diversity jurisdiction necessary anymore? The "nerve center" of a corporation could be an elusive place, as many companies have decentralized operations. In addition, state boundaries can be blurred, especially in metropolitan areas that cross three or four state lines. A new test may evolve over time, if more cases like this come before the Court.

■ CASE VOCABULARY

REMOVAL: Transferring an action from state to federal court upon a litigant's timely filing of removal papers showing a valid basis for federal-court jurisdiction.

In re Ameriquest Mortgage Co. Mortgage Lending Practices Litigation

(Borrower) v. (Lender)

2007 WL 2815952 (N.D. Ill. 2007)

FEDERAL COURTS MAY HEAR STATE LAW CLAIMS CLOSELY RELATED TO THE FEDERAL CLAIMS BEFORE THEM

Back in 2004, this place appraised for $163,000.

stus.com

■ **INSTANT FACTS** A borrower sued a lender in federal court for violations of the Truth in Lending Act and fraud, and the lender moved to dismiss the fraud claims, arguing that, because they were based on state law, the federal court did not have jurisdiction to hear them.

■ **BLACK LETTER RULE** Under 28 U.S.C. § 1367, in any action in which the federal court has jurisdiction over a federal claim, it has supplemental jurisdiction over state claims that are so related to claims in the action within such original jurisdiction that they form part of the same case or controversy under Article III of the Constitution.

■ **PROCEDURAL BASIS**

Federal district court consideration of the defendant's motion to dismiss two state law counts of the plaintiff's amended complaint.

■ **FACTS**

The plaintiff alleged in her complaint that she entered into a mortgage transaction with Ameriquest (D) in April 2004. An appraisal conducted at Ameriquests's (D) request shortly before closing valued the mortgaged property at $163,000. Skanes, the mortgagee, argued that the appraised value was falsely inflated in order to increase the amount that could be lent and thus Ameriquest's (D) potential profits, in violation of the federal Truth in Lending Act (TILA). Skanes sued, alleging various claims under TILA and state law fraud claims. The defendant moved to dismiss the state law fraud claims, arguing that the federal court lacked jurisdiction over them.

■ **ISSUE**

Was there a sufficient nexus between the plaintiff's state law claims and her TILA claims to support the federal court's exercise of supplemental jurisdiction?

■ **DECISION AND RATIONALE**

(Aspen, J.) Yes. Under 28 U.S.C. § 1367, in any action in which the federal court has jurisdiction over a federal claim, it has supplemental jurisdiction over state claims that are so related to claims in the action within such original jurisdiction that they form part of the same case or controversy under Article III of the Constitution. A loose factual connection is sufficient, as long as those facts are both common and operative. In determining the requisite connection, courts routinely compare the facts required to prove the elements of the federal claim with those necessary to the success of the state claim. The court may also ask whether the state claims can be resolved or dismissed without affecting the federal claims.

Here, the facts underlying the state and federal claims combine to tell one story. Skanes did not fully know about her right to cancel her mortgage at its outset, which may be a TILA violation as well as fraud. Moreover, we cannot say that dismissal of the state claims would not have an effect on the resolution of the federal claims, so we cannot deny our supplemental jurisdiction here. Although we may decline to exercise supplemental jurisdiction under the circumstances presented in 28 U.S.C. § 1367(c), none of those circumstances exists here. The claims do not raise a novel or complex issue of state law, they do not substantially predominate over the federal claims, the court has not dismissed the federal claims, and there are no other compelling reasons for declining jurisdiction. Accordingly, we choose to exercise our discretion in favor of retaining jurisdiction over the state law counts in the complaint.

Analysis:

The concept of supplemental jurisdiction embodies two earlier jurisdictional concepts that were distinctly applied until about 1990: ancillary jurisdiction and pendent jurisdiction. Ancillary jurisdiction related to a court's jurisdiction to adjudicate claims and proceedings related to another claim that was properly before the court. If a plaintiff brought a lawsuit in federal court based on a federal question (such as a claim under Title VII), for instance, the defendant could assert a counterclaim over which the court would not otherwise have jurisdiction (such as a state law claim for stealing company property). Pendent jurisdiction applied to a court's authority to determine claims over which they would not otherwise have jurisdiction, because the claims arose from the same transaction or occurrence as another claim that was properly before the court. If a plaintiff brought suit in federal court claiming, for example, that the defendant violated both a federal and a state law, the federal court had jurisdiction over the federal claim under federal question jurisdiction and over the state claim that was pendent to the federal claim. Pendent jurisdiction, as well as ancillary jurisdiction, have now been codified under 28 U.S.C. § 1367 as supplemental jurisdiction.

■ CASE VOCABULARY

SUPPLEMENTAL JURISDICTION: Jurisdiction over a claim that is part of the same case or controversy as another claim over which the court has original jurisdiction.

Szendry-Ramos v. First Bancorp

(Bank's Counsel) v. (Bank)

512 F.Supp.2d 81 (D.P.R. 2007)

VIOLATIONS OF STATE ETHICAL CANONS MAY REQUIRE CONSIDERATION IN STATE, RATHER THAN FEDERAL, COURT

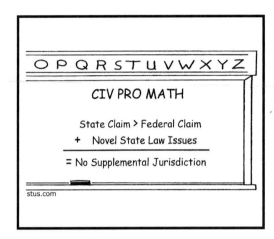

O P Q R S T U V W X Y Z

CIV PRO MATH

State Claim > Federal Claim

  +   Novel State Law Issues

= No Supplemental Jurisdiction

stus.com

■ **INSTANT FACTS** A bank's in-house counsel sued the bank when it fired her after she disclosed the bank's allegedly unethical practices.

■ **BLACK LETTER RULE** When the plaintiff's state law claims substantially predominate over the federal claims or raise complex or novel issues of state law, the federal court may decline to exercise supplemental jurisdiction over the state law claims.

■ **PROCEDURAL BASIS**

Federal district court consideration of the defendant's motion to dismiss.

■ **FACTS**

Szendry-Ramos (P) worked for First Bancorp (D) as its general counsel. In March 2005, she received information from outside counsel indicating that the bank may have been involved in some unethical conduct relating to the bulk purchase of mortgage loans from other financial institutions. Szendry-Ramos (P) conducted an investigation that led to the conclusion that ethical violations had occurred, so she reported this conclusion to outside counsel for the bank, bank officials, and the board of directors. Szendry-Ramos (P) was blamed for some of the very conduct she had investigated and was fired, and she sued under Title VII and Puerto Rico law, claiming wrongful discharge, violations of the P.R. Constitution, defamation, and tortious interference with contracts.

■ **ISSUE**

Could the federal district court in a Title VII case decline to exercise supplemental jurisdiction over the plaintiff's claims based on Puerto Rico law?

■ **DECISION AND RATIONALE**

(Casellas, J.) Yes. When the plaintiff's state law claims substantially predominate over the federal claims or raise complex or novel issues of state law, the federal court may decline to exercise supplemental jurisdiction over the state law claims. Here, the plaintiff's complaint includes two lonesome claims under Title VII, for discrimination and retaliation. The remaining claims all arise under Puerto Rico law. The P.R. claims not only outnumber the federal claims, their scope also far exceeds that of the federal claims. Moreover, the P.R. claims require proof that is not necessary to establish the federal claims. Thus, on that basis alone, we could decline to exercise supplemental jurisdiction in this case.

In addition, however, the plaintiff's P.R. claims have the potential to run afoul of Canon 21 of the Puerto Rico Code of Professional Ethics, which arguably forbids an attorney to disclose client confidences even in litigation between lawyer and client. Canon 21 is clearly within the province of the Puerto Rico courts, and is decidedly different from the American Bar Association's Model Rules. But Puerto Rico courts have not yet applied the Canon in a case

---

like this. Thus, because the plaintiff's claims also posit novel and complex issues of state law, we decline to exercise supplemental jurisdiction on that basis as well.

Analysis:

Although the federal district court declined to exercise supplemental jurisdiction and dismissed the plaintiff's Puerto Rico law claims, the plaintiff was not left without recourse. She had the opportunity to bring a separate case in Puerto Rico court. The federal court retained jurisdiction, however, to hear the Title VII causes of action, thus forcing the plaintiff to litigate in two separate forums. Note that the plaintiff could have originally brought all of her claims in Puerto Rico court, and in this case she may have been better off doing so.

■ **CASE VOCABULARY**

DEFAMATION: The act of harming the reputation of another by making a false statement to a third person; a false written or oral statement that damages another's reputation. If the alleged defamation involves a matter of public concern, the plaintiff is constitutionally required to prove both the statement's falsity and the defendant's fault.

TITLE VII: Title VII of the Civil Rights Act of 1964. A federal law that prohibits employment discrimination and harassment on the basis of race, sex, pregnancy, religion, and national origin, as well as prohibiting retaliation against an employee who opposes illegal harassment or discrimination in the workplace. This term is often referred to simply as Title VII.

TORTIOUS INTERFERENCE WITH CONTRACT: A third party's intentional inducement of a contracting party to break a contract, causing damage to the relationship between the contracting parties.

WRONGFUL DISCHARGE: A discharge for reasons that are illegal or that violate public policy.

Caterpillar, Inc. v. Lewis

(Manufacturer) v. (Injured Operator)

519 U.S. 61, 117 S.Ct. 467 (1996)

A FEDERAL TRIAL COURT'S ERROR IN FAILING TO REMAND A CASE IMPROPERLY REMOVED IS NOT FATAL TO THE FINAL JUDGMENT IF THE JURISDICTIONAL REQUIREMENTS ARE MET AT THE TIME THE JUDGMENT IS ENTERED

■ **INSTANT FACTS** Lewis's (P) state case was improperly removed to federal court because there was not completed diversity of the parties. The jurisdictional defect was cured before judgment.

■ **BLACK LETTER RULE** A district court's error in failing to remand a case improperly removed is not fatal to the ensuing judgment if federal jurisdictional requirements are met at the time judgment is entered.

■ **PROCEDURAL BASIS**

Appeal from vacation of district court judgment for lack of jurisdiction.

■ **FACTS**

James David Lewis (P), a resident of Kentucky, was injured while operating a bulldozer. He brought state law claims in Kentucky state court for breach of warranty, defective manufacture, negligent maintenance, and failure to warn against Caterpillar (D), a Delaware corporation with its principal place of business in Illinois. Lewis (P) also made claims against Whayne Supply Company, a Kentucky corporation with its principal place of business in Kentucky, who serviced the bulldozer. Later, the insurance carrier for Lewis' (P) employer, Liberty Mutual, intervened in the lawsuit as a plaintiff seeking subrogation against both Caterpillar (D) and Whayne Supply Company for workers' compensation benefits Liberty Mutual had paid to Lewis (P). Lewis (P) subsequently settled with Whayne Supply. Caterpillar (D) then asked for removal to the District Court for the Eastern District of Kentucky on the basis of diversity of citizenship. Caterpillar (D) satisfied with only one day to spare the statutory requirement that diversity removal take place within one year of the lawsuit's commencement as required by 28 U.S.C. §1446(b). The case was not removable at the lawsuit's commencement because complete diversity was absent as Lewis (P) and Whayne Supply were both citizens of Kentucky. Caterpillar (D) assumed that the settlement agreement between Lewis (P) and Whayne Supply would result in Wayne Supply being dismissed from the lawsuit. However, Lewis (P) argued the case should be remanded to state court because Liberty Mutual had not yet settled its subrogation claim against Whayne Supply, and Whayne Supply's presence in the lawsuit defeated diversity jurisdiction. The district court rejected Lewis' (P) argument. Three years later, before a verdict was rendered in favor of Caterpillar (D), Liberty Mutual and Whayne Supply settled.

■ **ISSUE**

Is the absence of complete diversity at the time of removal fatal to federal court jurisdiction where the jurisdictional requirements are ultimately met at the time the judgment is entered?

■ DECISION AND RATIONALE

(Ginsburg, J.) No. The District Court erred in failing to remand the case to state court because it was improperly removed. It incorrectly treated Whayne Supply, the nondiverse defendant, as effectively dropped from the suit. Whayne Supply, however, remained in the suit as a defendant of Liberty Mutual. However, this error is not fatal to federal jurisdiction because the jurisdictional requirements were ultimately met before judgment when Liberty Mutual and Whayne Supply settled. Lewis (P) did all that was required to preserve his objection to removal by filing a motion to remand to state court. Lewis (P) argues that the ultimate satisfaction of the complete diversity requirements should not swallow up previous statutory jurisdictional violations. Lewis (P) also emphasizes that Caterpillar (D) was only able to get into federal court by removing prematurely. If Caterpillar (D) had waited until Whayne Supply had been dismissed from the case, the 1-year limitation of §1446(b) would have barred removal, and the case would have remained in state court. These arguments are not without merit. However, they run up against the overriding considerations of finality, efficiency, and economy. If a federal court judge denies a motion to remand, and the jurisdictional defect remains uncured, the judgment must be vacated. In the present case, however, no jurisdictional defect lingered through judgment. To wipe out the judgment at this point and return to state court a case now satisfying all federal jurisdictional requirements would impose a huge cost on our court system that is incompatible with the fair administration of justice. Lewis (P) argues that if we allow the judgment against him to stand, defendants will have an incentive to attempt wrongful removals. We do not believe these dire consequences are likely. Federal trial court judges will still enforce the removal requirements and remand improper cases. Defendants are not likely to gamble that a jurisdictional defect will escape detection and then disappear prior to judgment. The judgment of the court of appeals is reversed.

Analysis:

When federal and state court jurisdiction overlap, the plaintiff has the initial choice of forum. However, removal gives the defendant the power to challenge this choice and move the case to federal court. Caterpillar (D) eventually won the suit in federal court, and the judgment was upheld. It could be said that Caterpillar (D) benefitted from the district court erroneously refusing to remand the case. Generally, complete diversity must exist at the time the case is filed for a federal court to have proper diversity jurisdiction. Can this rule be reconciled with the Court's ruling in *Caterpillar* that a jurisdictional defect can be corrected sometime before judgment?

■ CASE VOCABULARY

REMAND: When an appellate court sends a case back to the trial court. In the case of removal, the federal district court sends the case back to the state court.

REMOVAL OF CAUSES: The transfer of a case from one court to another.

SUBROGATION: The right of one who has paid an obligation on behalf of another to be compensated for these payments. Insurance companies often have the right to take the place of their insured and sue any party their insured could have sued to recover insurance payouts.

CHAPTER 4

The *Erie* Problem

Erie Railroad v. Tompkins

Instant Facts: Lower federal court refused to apply state decisional law concerning duty of due care owed by railroad to injured person in federal diversity case.

Black Letter Rule: In federal diversity cases, the substantive laws of the state must be applied.

Guaranty Trust Co. v. York

Instant Facts: State statute of limitations applied to bar federal diversity case, rather than more lenient equitable federal rules concerning delay in bringing suit.

Black Letter Rule: State statute of limitations applies in federal diversity case where, disregarding it, would significantly affect the result of the litigation, as compared with the outcome had it been tried in state court.

Byrd v. Blue Ridge Rural Electric Cooperative

Instant Facts: Injured worker sued employer for personal injuries in federal court and state law required the judge, not jury, to decide issue of application of workman's compensation law.

Black Letter Rule: State decisional law did not apply in federal diversity case where it allowed a judge, and not jury, to determine a factual issue.

Hanna v. Plumer

Instant Facts: Executor of estate of automobile driver was sued, and summons and complaint were served on spouse in accordance with federal rule, but contrary to state rule requiring in-hand service.

Black Letter Rule: Federal Rules of Civil Procedure governing service of process apply to federal diversity cases, notwithstanding conflicting state rule.

Semtek Int'l Inc. v. Lockheed Martin Corp.

Instant Facts: After a California federal court dismissed the plaintiff's action on the basis of the state statute of limitations, a Maryland state court dismissed a subsequent suit brought by the plaintiff on the same grounds.

Black Letter Rule: The claim-preclusive effect of a judgment on the merits in a federal diversity action is governed by the law of the state in which the federal court sits.

Erie Railroad v. Tompkins

(Railroad) v. (Injured person)

304 U.S. 64, 58 S.Ct. 817, 82 L.Ed. 1188 (1938)

NO MORE FEDERAL GENERAL COMMON LAW; STATE LAW APPLIES INSTEAD

■ **INSTANT FACTS** Lower federal court refused to apply state decisional law concerning duty of due care owed by railroad to injured person in federal diversity case.

■ **BLACK LETTER RULE** In federal diversity cases, the substantive laws of the state must be applied.

■ **PROCEDURAL BASIS**

Writ of certiorari granted by Supreme Court to interpret meaning of federal statute and constitutionality of its application in negligence action following judgment.

■ **FACTS**

Tompkins (P) was injured by an Erie Railroad (D) train. Suit was brought in federal court based upon diversity of citizenship. Erie Railroad (D) contended that its liability for injuries sustained by Tompkins (P) should be determined in accordance with Pennsylvania case law, as decided by Pennsylvania's highest court. Pennsylvania law provided that the duty of due care of a railroad to someone on its land is no greater than that owed to a trespasser, e.g., to refrain from willful or wanton injury. [In other words, it's okay to negligently hit a trespasser with a train.] Erie Railroad (D) contended that the federal Rules of Decision Act [which says that laws of the states shall be regarded as rules of decision in federal civil cases, unless otherwise provided by the Constitution or federal statute] required the application of the state case law to the federal case. The lower court did not apply Pennsylvania common law, and instead held that the issue of liability should be based upon federal general common law. The lower court held that Pennsylvania's case law was not within the meaning of the "laws of the states" as used in the Rules of Decision Act. The state's substantive law concerning the duty of due care was thus not applied by the federal court.

■ **ISSUE**

In federal diversity cases, must the substantive laws of the state be applied?

■ **DECISION AND RATIONALE**

(Brandeis) Yes. We hold that in federal diversity cases the law to be applied is the law of the State, except in matters governed by the Federal Constitution or by Acts of Congress. In so doing, we disapprove of *Swift v. Tyson* [federal courts hearing diversity of citizenship cases are not required to apply the unwritten state laws, i.e., the decisions by the state courts, but may exercise an independent judgment as to what is the common law of the state]. Criticism of the *Swift v. Tyson* doctrine has become widespread following a [really terrible] decision where a company was permitted to reincorporate under the laws of another state and sue under its laws for the purpose of avoiding the laws of the first state of incorporation. [This is known as forum-shopping at its worst!] Application of the *Swift v. Tyson* doctrine has revealed defects, and no benefits derived therefrom. There is no uniformity of common law and no certainty regarding what is general law and local law. The purpose of diversity of citizenship is

---

to prevent discrimination in State courts against non-citizens. However, discrimination by non-citizens against citizens has resulted. The rights under the unwritten law vary depending upon whether they are being enforced in state or federal court, and the choice of court is with the non-citizen. Therefore, the doctrine of *Swift v. Tyson* must be disapproved. We hold that the law to be applied is the law of the State, except in matters governed by the Federal Constitution or by Acts of Congress. It does not matter if the State law is pursuant to statute or case law. There is no federal general common law. Congress has no power to declare substantive rules of common law applicable in a State whether they be local in their nature or general, be they commercial law or a part of the law of torts. No clause in the Constitution purports to confer such a power upon the federal courts. The doctrine of *Swift v. Tyson* is an unconstitutional assumption of powers by the courts of the United States. By applying this doctrine, the lower courts have invaded rights reserved by the Constitution to the states. The issue of liability must therefore be decided based upon state law. Judgment is reversed and case remanded.

■ CONCURRENCE

(Reed) I concur with the majority decision disapproving of *Swift v. Tyson.* However, it is unnecessary to declare that the "course pursued" therein was "unconstitutional," instead of merely erroneous. The unconstitutional course is apparently the ruling in *Swift v. Tyson* that the supposed omission of Congress to legislate as to the effect of decisions leaves federal courts free to interpret general law for themselves. I am not sure whether federal courts would be compelled to follow state decisions.

Analysis:

The *Erie* case is a landmark decision in that it held that the state's substantive law must be applied in federal diversity cases, except in matters governed by the federal Constitution or by acts of congress. In so holding, the Supreme Court interpreted the meaning of the phrase "laws of the several states" in the Rules of Decision Act to include state common law. Thus, this case reflects the rejection of a federal common law in favor of individual states' substantive common law. In the cases following *Erie*, the issues turned toward whether or not the law was substantive or procedural. Finally, although the court declared in the decision that there is no federal general common law, this is not entirely accurate. There are certain federal statutes that allow the federal courts to create common law for cases pertaining to such statutes. Thus, *Erie* prohibits a general federal common law from displacing the states' common laws in areas where the states have lawmaking powers under the Constitution.

■ CASE VOCABULARY

COMMON LAW: Law which originated in England and developed over the years from case law decisions, as opposed to statutory laws.

DIVERSITY OF CITIZENSHIP: It creates federal jurisdiction when party on one side of a lawsuit is a citizen of one state and the party on the other side is a citizen of another state.

EQUITY: A claim or remedy based upon the underlying principles of fairness and justice, and not part of legal or common law claims and remedies.

GENERAL LAW: A law that affects all, and is not local or unique to one group.

Guaranty Trust Co. v. York

(Bond Trustee) v. (Victim of Misrepresentations)

326 U.S. 99, 65 S.Ct. 1464, 89 L.Ed. 2079 (1945)

SUPREME COURT DEVELOPS "OUTCOME-DETERMINATIVE TEST" FOR WHETHER STATE LAW IS SUBSTANTIVE

■ **INSTANT FACTS** State statute of limitations applied to bar federal diversity case, rather than more lenient equitable federal rules concerning delay in bringing suit.

■ **BLACK LETTER RULE** State statute of limitations applies in federal diversity case where, disregarding it, would significantly affect the result of the litigation, as compared with the outcome had it been tried in state court.

■ **PROCEDURAL BASIS**

Appeal to Supreme Court following judgment on equitable causes of action for misrepresentation and breach of trust.

■ **FACTS**

York (P) sued Guaranty Trust Co. (D) in a federal diversity action alleging misrepresentation and breach of trust. One of the defenses invoked by Guaranty Trust (D) was the New York statute of limitations. York (P) contended that the statute of limitations did not bar the suit because the suit was one based on equity and, although federal courts in equity consider the delay in bringing suit, they are not strictly bound by the statute of limitations. The lower court [to the joy of York(P)] held that York's (P) suit was not barred. [Unfortunately for York (P)] the Supreme Court disagreed and reversed.

■ **ISSUE**

In a federal diversity case, must the federal court apply the state statute of limitations?

■ **DECISION AND RATIONALE**

(Frankfurter) Yes. New York's statute of limitations governs the matter. In determining whether or not to apply the state statute of limitations, characterization of the statute as "substance" or "procedure" is not altogether determinative because these same key words are used throughout law for very different issues. Each implies different variables depending on the particular problem for which it is used. The intent of the *Erie Railroad v. Tompkins* decision [state substantive laws apply to federal diversity cases] was to insure that in federal diversity cases, the outcome of the litigation in federal court should be substantially the same as it would be if tried in a state court. [Remember forum-shopping is a *no no* under Erie.] Thus, the proper method of determining if the state statute of limitations will be applied in federal diversity cases is to ask if the federal court were to disregard it, would so doing significantly affect the result of the litigation. If this matter had been tried in state court, no recovery could be had because the action was barred by the statute of limitations. However, by using the federal method of merely considering the delay in bringing suit and disregarding the state statute of limitations, if desired, the claims could proceed. Thus, the outcome of the litigation would have different results, although upon the same claim by the same parties, if litigated in federal instead of state court. If permitted, this would be contrary to the intent of Erie. Judgment reversed and case remanded.

Analysis:

This case addresses the issue of whether or not a state statute of limitations is, in effect, substantive, and therefore controlling in federal litigation. However, the Court attacked the use of the terms "substantive" and "procedural" because of their differing meanings depending on the particular circumstances in which they are used. The court developed an "outcome-determinative test": a state rule that was outcome-determinative should be followed no matter whether it is labeled procedural or substantive. In its holding, the Court referenced other diversity cases where it held that federal courts must follow the law of the state including burden of proof, conflict of laws, and contributory negligence. The Court commented that state law must not be disregarded in federal diversity cases, and that a policy so important to federalism, "must be kept free from entanglements with analytical or terminological niceties." The "outcome-determinative" test has become just one factor, among several, for determining whether to apply state or federal rules. The case that follows, *Byrd v. Blue Ridge Rural Electric Cooperative*, created an "interest balancing" approach, in which the *York* outcome-determinative test is just one of three main factors to consider in choosing between state and federal rules.

■ **CASE VOCABULARY**

STATUTE OF LIMITATIONS: A statute used as a defense to bar untimely filed claims.

Byrd v. Blue Ridge Rural Electric Cooperative

(Injured Worker) v. (Employer)

356 U.S. 525, 78 S.Ct. 893, 2 L.Ed.2d 953 (1958)

SUPREME COURT DEVELOPS "INTEREST BALANCING" APPROACH FOR WHETHER STATE LAW IS SUBSTANTIVE

■ **INSTANT FACTS** Injured worker sued employer for personal injuries in federal court and state law required the judge, not jury, to decide issue of application of workman's compensation law.

■ **BLACK LETTER RULE** State decisional law did not apply in federal diversity case where it allowed a judge, and not jury, to determine a factual issue.

■ **PROCEDURAL BASIS**

Appeal to Supreme Court from judgment in personal injury case seeking damages.

■ **FACTS**

Byrd (P), an independent contractor, was employed by Blue Ridge Rural Electric Cooperative (Blue Ridge) (D) as a construction worker. He was injured on the job and sued Blue Ridge (D) in federal court under diversity jurisdiction for the personal injuries he sustained. As a defense, Blue Ridge (D) contended that Byrd (P) was a "statutory" employee whose exclusive remedy was under the state's Workmen's [or, better stated, "workers"] Compensation Act. If this were true, the tort action would be barred. Blue Ridge (D) argued that a state Supreme Court decision should be controlling on remand in the federal court. The decision provided that the judge, rather than the jury, is to decide the issue of whether the workman's personal injury claim is within the workman's compensation jurisdiction. If so, Blue Ridge (D) would be immune to the tort action.

■ **ISSUE**

In a federal diversity case, must the federal court apply state decisional law that allows a judge, and not a jury, to determine a factual issue?

■ **DECISION AND RATIONALE**

(Brennan) No. We hold that the decision of the State Supreme Court that a judge, and not a jury, shall determine factual issues, shall not be applied in this federal case. There are several factors that bear on our decision. The state court decision must be examined to determine whether its holding must be applied in the federal case. Using the [very limited] outcome-determinative test, consideration must be given to whether disregarding the state rule would significantly affect the result of the litigation, as compared with the outcome had the matter been tried in state court. The state court decision which provides that the judge, rather than the jury, shall decide the issue of immunity appears to be merely a form and mode of enforcing the immunity against tort actions. It does not appear to be a rule bound up with the definition of the rights and obligations of the parties. In other words, it is not an integral part of a state substantive right. However, the outcome of Byrd's (P) case may be substantially affected by whether the issue of immunity is decided by a judge or jury. Therefore, if the [very limited] outcome-determinative test were the only consideration, a strong case might be had for requiring the federal court to follow state practice. Other countervailing considerations should be reviewed [so that we can expand on the very limited outcome-determinative test and create our own balancing test]. There is a strong federal policy against allowing state rules to interfere with the federal court's distribution of functions between the judge and the jury. The function assigned to the jury by the federal courts should not yield to the state rule in order to further the objective of the same outcome in federal and state courts. Finally, it cannot be assumed that the outcome may, with certainty, be different if decided by a judge or a jury. There are factors here which reduce the possibility of differing results. Federal judges have powers denied to many state judges to comment on the weight of evidence and credibility of witnesses, and to exercise discretion in granting new trials. The likelihood of a different result is not so strong as to require the federal practice of allowing a jury to determine the issues to yield to the state rule. Reversed and remanded.

Analysis:

This case expands on *Guaranty Trust Co. v. York*'s outcome-determinative test and develops an "interest balancing" approach to *Erie* problems. The Court held that there are several factors that must be balanced in deciding whether to apply federal or state rules to federal diversity cases. Consideration must be given to the relationship between the state rule and the underlying state right. The strength of the federal policy must be examined before holding that it must yield to a counter state policy. In this case, there was obviously a strong federal policy, based on the Constitution, to allow juries to decide factual issues. Finally, the *York* outcome-determinative test must still be considered. The Court concluded that it was far from certain that a different result would occur if decided by a judge or a jury. In later years, the interest balancing approach was virtually ignored by the Supreme Court in favor of the principles articulated in the following case, *Hanna v. Plumer*.

■ **CASE VOCABULARY**

INDEPENDENT CONTRACTOR: Employment relationship where one works pursuant to his own rules and control.

REMAND: Sending the case back to the same court from which it came, such as after reversal on appeal and further proceedings ordered.

Hanna v. Plumer

(Injured Person) v. *(Executor of Estate)*

380 U.S. 460, 85 S.Ct. 1136, 14 L.Ed.2d 8 (1965)

SUPREME COURT HOLDS THAT *ERIE* IS NOT THE APPROPRIATE TEST TO DETERMINE THE VALIDITY AND APPLICATION OF FEDERAL RULES OF CIVIL PROCEDURE

■ **INSTANT FACTS** Executor of estate of automobile driver was sued, and summons and complaint were served on spouse in accordance with federal rule, but contrary to state rule requiring in-hand service.

■ **BLACK LETTER RULE** Federal Rules of Civil Procedure governing service of process apply to federal diversity cases, notwithstanding conflicting state rule.

■ **PROCEDURAL BASIS**

Writ of certiorari granted by Supreme Court following the affirming of summary judgment in action for negligence seeking damages.

■ **FACTS**

Hanna (P) filed a federal court lawsuit for personal injuries against Plumer (D), the executor of the estate of an alleged negligent automobile driver. Service of the summons and complaint was made pursuant to the Federal Rules of Civil Procedure by leaving copies with Plumer's (D) wife at his residence. Plumer (D) contended that the lawsuit could not proceed because the service of the summons and complaint was not in compliance with the statutory *state* law requiring actual in-hand service on the person being sued. The federal district court granted Plumer's (D) motion for summary judgment [and promptly threw the matter out of court]. On appeal, Hanna (P) contended that the Federal Rules of Civil Procedure governed the method of service of process in diversity actions [and begged to have the lawsuit reinstated]. The Court of Appeals affirmed, finding that the state law involved a substantive rather than a procedural matter and thus should have been applied.

■ **ISSUE**

In a federal diversity case, must the federal court apply state rules concerning service of process?

■ **DECISION AND RATIONALE**

(Warren) No. The Federal Rules of Civil Procedure govern the method of service of process in diversity actions, and the federal rule shall apply notwithstanding a conflicting state rule. The federal statute, known as the Rules Enabling Act, provides that the Supreme Court shall have the power, among other things, to prescribe, by general rules, the forms of process, and the practice and procedure of the federal courts in civil actions. It further provides that such rules shall not abridge, enlarge or modify any substantive right and shall preserve the right of trial by jury. It is clear from existing case law that the federal rule regarding service of process at issue herein clearly complies with the Rules Enabling Act. Thus, without a conflicting state law, the federal rule would certainly control. Plumer (D) contends that federal courts must apply state law whenever the application of federal law, in place of the state law, would alter the outcome of the case. In this case, if the state law concerning service of process was applied, Plumer (D) would win. If federal law was applied, litigation would continue and he could lose. Thus,

Plumer (D) [seeing an easy way out of the lawsuit] asserts that state law must apply. However, this argument cannot stand for several reasons. First, even if there was no federal rule allowing for service on a spouse at home, it is doubtful that the federal court would have been required to follow the state law. The outcome-determinative test cannot be read without reference to the "twin aims" of the *Erie* rule: discouragement of forum-shopping and avoidance of inequitable administration of the laws. If the test were taken to its extreme, every procedural variation would be outcome-determinative. Although the choice between federal and state rules in this matter will affect the outcome of the case, the difference between the two rules would be of scant relevance to the choice of a forum. In other words, when Hanna (P) decided where to file the complaint, she was not presented with a situation where applicability of the state rule would wholly bar recovery; rather, the state rule merely would alter the way in which process was served. In addition, it cannot be said that serving the spouse in lieu of personal in-hand service substantially alters the mode of enforcement of state rights so as to result in inequitable administration of the laws. *Erie* [substantive state laws must be applied] is not the proper test for determining the validity and applicability of a Federal Rule of Civil Procedure. Instead, we consider the scope of the Enabling Act and the constitutionality of the specific federal rules. Congress has the power to prescribe housekeeping rules for federal courts even though they may differ [in a big way] from comparable state rules. The federal rule considered herein is valid. Judgment reversed.

■ CONCURRENCE

(Harlan) The proper approach in determining whether to apply a state or federal rule, whether substantive or procedural, is to ask if the choice of rule would substantially affect those primary decisions respecting human conduct which our constitutional system leaves to state regulation. If so, the state rule should prevail, even when there is a conflicting federal rule. The majority's opinion can be understood to mean that so long as a reasonable man could characterize a federal rule as procedural, it would have to apply even if the rule frustrated a state's substantive rule. The majority's test goes too far. However, the facts of the present case cause me to concur in the opinion.

Analysis:

This case has two important holdings. First, it modified the outcome-determinative test so it applies only in those situations where the rule would encourage forum shopping or cause inequitable administration of the laws. Second, it held that where federal rules of procedure conflict with state rules, the federal procedural rule will prevail unless it violates the Constitution or the terms of the Rules Enabling Act. Thus, as long as the rules are procedural in nature and do not abridge, enlarge, or modify any substantive right, they will be upheld. The Court indicated a very strong presumption in favor of the validity of the Federal Rules. The *Hanna* case demonstrates that the source of the federal practice must be considered. If it is a federal rule of civil procedure, there is a very strong chance that it will prevail.

■ CASE VOCABULARY

INTER ALIA: Latin for among other things.

MOTION FOR SUMMARY JUDGMENT: A legal motion requesting the judge to enter judgment, before trial, on the ground that the action has no merit or there is no defense to the action.

SERVICE OF PROCESS: Transmitting to another legal documents such as summons and complaints in a manner provided by rules which thereby constitutes serving the documents.

SYLLOGISM: An argument which has two premises resulting in a conclusion.

Semtek Int'l Inc. v. Lockheed Martin Corp.

(Plaintiff) v. (Defendant)

531 U.S. 497, 121 S.Ct. 1021 (2001)

CALIFORNIA LAW GOVERNS WHETHER A CLAIM DISMISSED BY A CALIFORNIA
FEDERAL COURT MAY BE RELITIGATED ELSEWHERE

■ **INSTANT FACTS** After a California federal court dismissed the plaintiff's action on the basis of the state statute of limitations, a Maryland state court dismissed a subsequent suit brought by the plaintiff on the same grounds.

■ **BLACK LETTER RULE** The claim-preclusive effect of a judgment on the merits in a federal diversity action is governed by the law of the state in which the federal court sits.

■ **PROCEDURAL BASIS**

Certiorari to review a decision of the Maryland Court of Special Appeals affirming a trial court dismissal of the plaintiff's action.

■ **FACTS**

Semtek International, Inc. (P) sued Lockheed Martin Corp. (D) in California state court for breach of contract and various torts. Lockheed Martin (D) removed the case to California federal court on the basis of diversity of citizenship and successfully moved for dismissal of the action with prejudice on the merits as barred by the state statute of limitations. Thereafter, Semtek (P) refiled its case against Lockheed Martin (D) in Maryland state court within the Maryland statute of limitations. On the defendant's motion, the Maryland court dismissed the complaint on the basis of res judicata, reasoning that the decision of the California federal court was on the merits and precluded the subsequent suit. After a Maryland court of appeals affirmed, Semtek (P) sought a writ of certiorari.

■ **ISSUE**

Is the claim-preclusive effect of a federal judgment dismissing a diversity action on statute-of-limitations grounds determined by the law of the state in which the federal court sits?

■ **DECISION AND RATIONALE**

(Scalia, J.) Yes. Under Federal Rule of Civil Procedure 41(b), a court order dismissing a plaintiff's complaint "operates as an adjudication on the merits" unless otherwise specified. "On the merits" is generally understood as a determination of the substance of the claim. While traditionally judgments on the merits have invoked the doctrines of res judicata and claim preclusion, no longer do all adjudications on the merits have a claim-preclusive effect under Rule 41(b). In this instance, Rule 41(b) governs the internal procedures of the California federal court, declaring its decision on the merits by default. To hold this procedural declaration binding upon the plaintiff's substantive state-law rights to pursue its claims in another jurisdiction, though not in California, would violate the principles of the Rules Enabling Act, which specifically preserves a party's substantive rights. Further, any claim-preclusive effect of the federal court judgment on the plaintiff's state-law rights would raise the risk conflicting decisions based on the forum in which the decision is rendered. For instance, under California state law, a party may not recover after the expiration of the state statute of limitations. Yet, the claims remain viable for consideration in an appropriate foreign jurisdiction.

Accordingly, the reasonable understanding of the default language of Rule 41(b) is that "adjudication on the merits" is the opposite of "dismissal without prejudice" as discussed in Rule 41(a). Although a dismissal with prejudice may, under certain circumstances, bar a party from relitigating his claims in other courts, the default provisions of Rule 41(b) should be construed only to preclude relitigation of the claims in the same court in which the adjudication on the merits was decided. Rule 41(b) does not determine the claim-preclusive effect of the California federal court judgment in the Maryland state court.

Since Rule 41(b) does not control the preclusive effect of the federal court judgment, the court must fashion a rule to be applied. In *Dupasseur v. Rochereau*, the Court applied a since-repealed statute to determine that the claim-preclusive effect of a federal diversity judgment is properly determined by the law of the state in which the federal court sits. Although *Dupasseur* does not apply to this matter given its reliance on a repealed statute, its reasoning continues to be appropriate in diversity actions. Because the substantive rights involved in a federal diversity action are governed by state law, the claim-preclusive effect of a federal court judgment applying state law should similarly be governed by state law. A uniform federal rule would promote forum shopping of claims and promote removal, where available, for a tactical advantage. Only where federal interests directly conflict with the state-law interests will the federal interests prevail. Here, because the California federal court granted dismissal on the merits only because state law so required, California state law governs the issue of claim preclusion. Because California does not prohibit the plaintiff from bringing its claims in another jurisdiction, the Maryland court erred in dismissing the plaintiff's claims. Reversed and remanded.

Analysis:

Semtek is controversial, in part, because it endeavors to apply state procedural law in a federal diversity case. Under *Erie v. Tompkins* and its progeny, a federal court sitting in diversity generally applies the substantive law of the state in which the action arose and the procedural rules of the federal court, most notably the Federal Rules of Civil Procedure. The problem encountered in *Semtek*, however, is that the Federal Rules of Civil Procedure fail to discuss the claim-preclusive effect of federal diversity judgments. With no procedural rule to enforce, the court created federal common law to resolve the issue.

■ **CASE VOCABULARY**

MERITS: The elements or grounds of a claim or defense; the substantive considerations to be taken into account in deciding a case, as opposed to extraneous or technical points, especially of procedure.

RES JUDICATA: An issue that has been definitively settled by judicial decision; an affirmative defense barring the same parties from litigating a second lawsuit on the same claim, or any other claim arising from the same transaction or series of transactions and that could have been—but was not—raised in the first suit.

CHAPTER 5

Incentives to Litigate

State Farm Mut. Automobile Ins. Co. v. Campbell

Instant Facts: After State Farm (D) failed to settle claims against Campbell (P) for its policy limits and altered information to lessen his culpability, a jury awarded Campbell $1 million in compensatory damages and $145 million in punitive damages.

Black Letter Rule: In evaluating the appropriateness of a punitive damages award, a court must weigh the reprehensibility of the defendant's conduct, the disparity between the actual harm caused and the amount of the punitive damages awarded, and the difference between the punitive damages awarded and the civil penalties imposed under state law.

Sigma Chemical Co. v. Harris

Instant Facts: A company sought to enforce a restrictive covenant by enjoining one of its former employees from continuing to work for one of the company's major competition.

Black Letter Rule: The determination whether to issue an injunction involves a balancing of the interests of the parties who might be affected by the court's decision.

Evans v. Jeff D.

Instant Facts: While negotiating a settlement for his clients, a class of handicapped children, a Legal Aid attorney was forced to waive his claim for legal fees provided by statute in order to obtain all of the injunctive relief his clients sought from the state.

Black Letter Rule: The civil rights fee shifting provision does not prohibit settlements conditioned on the waiver of fees.

Buckhannon Board and Care Home, Inc. v. West Virginia Department of Health and Human Resources

Instant Facts: Buckhannon Board and Care Home's (P) suit was dismissed as moot after the defendant changed its conduct during litigation.

Black Letter Rule: Under federal fee-shifting statutes, a party must obtain a judgment on the merits or court-ordered consent decree to qualify as the "prevailing party."

Winter v. Natural Resources Defense Council, Inc.

Instant Facts: The Natural Resources Defense Council (P) obtained a preliminary injunction against a training exercise conducted by the Navy (D), and the Ninth Circuit Court of Appeals affirmed.

Black Letter Rule: When ruling on a request for a preliminary injunction, a court must consider the consequences to the public of granting the request.

Fuentes v. Shevin

Instant Facts: Margarita Fuentes (P) and other debtors challenge the constitutionality of Florida and Pennsylvania statutes allowing seizure of goods covered by an installment sales contract without providing an opportunity for the debtor to be heard prior to seizure.

Black Letter Rule: In order to comply with procedural due process, notice and an opportunity to be heard must be provided prior to seizure of any protected property interest.

State Farm Mut. Automobile Ins. Co. v. Campbell

(Insurance Company) v. (Insured)

538 U.S. 408, 123 S.Ct. 1513 (2003)

PUNITIVE DAMAGES AWARDS MUST BE VIEWED WITH REFERENCE TO THE COMPENSATORY DAMAGES

■ **INSTANT FACTS** After State Farm (D) failed to settle claims against Campbell (P) for its policy limits and altered information to lessen his culpability, a jury awarded Campbell $1 million in compensatory damages and $145 million in punitive damages.

■ **BLACK LETTER RULE** In evaluating the appropriateness of a punitive damages award, a court must weigh the reprehensibility of the defendant's conduct, the disparity between the actual harm caused and the amount of the punitive damages awarded, and the difference between the punitive damages awarded and the civil penalties imposed under state law.

■ **PROCEDURAL BASIS**

Certiorari to review the excessiveness of a punitive damages verdict.

■ **FACTS**

Campbell (P) held an automobile policy with State Farm Mutual Automobile Insurance Co. (D). While traveling in Utah, Campbell, (P) decided to pass six vans traveling slowly in front of him. As Campbell (P) was driving in the wrong direction, Ospital was forced onto the shoulder to avoid a head-on collision. In the process, Ospital lost control of his vehicle, collided with a vehicle driven by Slusher, and died. Slusher became permanently disabled. An investigation of the incident determined that Campbell's unsafe pass had caused Ospital's death and Slusher's injuries. Nonetheless, State Farm (D) decided to contest liability and declined offers from Ospital's estate and Slusher to settle both claims for its total policy limit of $50,000. At trial, a jury found Campbell (P) liable for the accident and returned a verdict for $185,849. State Farm (D) refused to pay the verdict in excess of its $50,000 policy limits and refused to post a supersedeas bond required for Campbell's (P) appeal. Campbell (P) subsequently obtained independent counsel and appealed the verdict. During the appeal, Campbell (P) agreed to pursue a bad faith action against State Farm (D) in exchange for an agreement by Ospital's estate and Slusher not to seek satisfaction of the judgment against Campbell (P). Ospital's estate and Slusher agreed to accept ninety percent of any proceeds received from State Farm (D) in the bad faith suit. The Utah Supreme Court denied Campbell's (P) appeal from the wrongful death judgment, and State Farm (D) subsequently agreed to pay the full amount of the judgment against him. Campbell (P) then commenced his bad faith suit, alleging State Farm's (D) refusal to accept the settlement offer was a product of a national scheme to control the amount of claims paid. Campbell (D) offered at trial evidence of State Farm's (D) business practices throughout the country over a twenty-year period, although little pertained to payment of third-party automobile claims similar to that asserted by Campbell (D). A jury awarded Campbell $2.6 million in compensatory damages and $145 million in punitive damages. After the compensatory damages award was reduced to $1 million, State Farm (D) appealed.

■ ISSUE

Where compensatory damages are $1 million, is an award of $145 million in punitive damages against a defendant excessive in violation of the Due Process Clause of the Fourteenth Amendment?

■ DECISION AND RATIONALE

(Kennedy, J.) Yes. Unlike compensatory damages, which serve to compensate an injured person for the wrongful conduct of another, punitive damages are aimed at deterrence and retribution against the wrongdoer. Because punitive damages serve a purpose similar to criminal sanctions, but without the procedural protections accompanying criminal punishment, a court must weigh the reprehensibility of the defendant's conduct, the disparity between the actual harm caused and the amount of the punitive damages awarded, and the difference between the punitive damages awarded and the civil penalties imposed under state law. Weighing these factors, the jury's $145 million punitive damages award was excessive.

First, State Farm's (D) conduct cannot be considered so reprehensible as to justify the award. In gauging a defendant's conduct, a court should consider whether the harm caused was physical rather than economic, whether the defendant acted with reckless disregard for the health and safety of others, whether the plaintiff was financially vulnerable, whether the conduct involved a repetitive pattern or an isolated incident, and whether the conduct was intentional. Here, while State Farm's (D) handling of Campbell's (P) insurance claims is not laudable, its conduct does not justify such an excessive punitive damages award. Rather than focusing on the particular conduct of the case, the award focuses on State Farm's (D) nationwide handling of claims. A state court, however, has no authority to punish a defendant for conduct that occurred outside its territorial limits and involving parties who were directly affected by the out-of-state conduct. A defendant's dissimilar conduct, bearing no relation to the harm involved in a particular lawsuit, may not be taken into account when determining punitive damages. Due process does not permit a court to award a party punitive damages merely because the defendant may have caused some harm to others who were not proper parties to the litigation.

Second, although there is no bright-line ratio between the amount of punitive damages and the harm caused to a plaintiff, an award 145 times the actual harm suffered is excessive. Generally, anything over a single-digit ratio calls for close judicial scrutiny. Likewise, as the compensatory damages award increases, the appropriate proportion to the punitive damages award decreases since a larger ratio is unnecessary to serve the purposes of deterrence and retribution. Here, the 145:1 ratio between the punitive award and the compensatory award is unreasonable given the $1 million compensatory damages award for emotional distress.

Finally, the $145 million punitive damages award is grossly in excess of the maximum civil penalty of $10,000 imposed under Utah law. Under this factor, the punitive damages award is excessive. Because a punitive award more closely approximating the compensatory award would be an adequate and rational punishment for the defendant's conduct, the award is excessive. Reversed and remanded.

■ DISSENT

(Ginsburg, J.) The three-factor analysis applied by the Court in reversing the state court's punitive damages award inappropriately threatens to create a bright-line test for determining the appropriateness of a punitive damages award.

Analysis:

The Court's focus on with the appropriate ratio between compensatory and punitive damages is interesting. If punitive damages serve a separate and distinct purpose from compensatory damages, why should the amount of compensatory damages affect the amount of punitive damages? If a defendant commits intentional conduct worthy of punishment, should it matter whether the compensatory damages were substantial or not?

■ CASE VOCABULARY

BAD FAITH: Dishonesty of belief or purpose.

COMPENSATORY DAMAGES: Damages sufficient in amount to indemnify the injured person for the loss suffered.

PUNITIVE DAMAGES: Damages awarded in addition to actual damages when the defendant acted with recklessness, malice, or deceit.

SUPERSEDEAS BOND: A bond that suspends a judgment creditor's power to levy execution, usually pending appeal.

Sigma Chemical Co. v. Harris

(Employer) v. (Former Employee)

605 F.Supp. 1253 (E.D. Mo. 1985)

A DECISION TO ISSUE AN INJUNCTION INVOLVES A BALANCING OF INTERESTS—THE BENEFIT TO THE MOVING PARTY AGAINST THE HARM TO THE OPPOSING PARTY

■ **INSTANT FACTS** A company sought to enforce a restrictive covenant by enjoining one of its former employees from continuing to work for one of the company's major competition.

■ **BLACK LETTER RULE** The determination whether to issue an injunction involves a balancing of the interests of the parties who might be affected by the court's decision.

■ **PROCEDURAL BASIS**

Decision of the Federal District Court enjoining a salesman from competing with his former employer.

■ **FACTS**

Sigma Chemical Co. (Sigma) (P) is a company that sells chemicals used in research, production, and analysis. Sigma's (P) knowledge of which supplier sells a particular chemical of a certain quality that satisfied a particular purpose at the right price is a trade secret. Foster Harris (D) went to work for Sigma (P) in 1979, after signing an agreement that he would not work for a competitor for two years after leaving Sigma (P) and that he would never disclose confidential information acquired from Sigma (P). In 1983, Harris (D) went to work for ICN, one of Sigma's (P) five major competitors. Sigma (P) sought to enjoin Harris (D) from working for ICN.

■ **ISSUE**

Does a company's interest in keeping a trade secret sufficiently outweigh a former employee's interest in seeking other employment, so that the latter may be enjoined from competing against the former?

■ **DECISION AND RATIONALE**

(Nangle, C.J.) Yes. The restrictive covenant at issue here is valid because it is necessary to protect Sigma's (P) legitimate interest in keeping a trade secret and because it is reasonable in both temporal and geographic scope. The determination whether to issue an injunction involves a balancing of the interests of the parties who might be affected by the Court's decision. The main prerequisite to obtaining injunctive relief is a finding that the plaintiff is being threatened by some injury for which he has no adequate legal remedy. First, it is clear that Harris (D) is violating the terms of the covenant. Harris (D) is contributing knowledge to the sale of a product that is in competition with that of Sigma (P). Harris (D) is also in a position that makes it likely he will use or disclose trade secret information that Harris (D) learned from Sigma's (P) product files. Under these circumstances there is a serious threat of irreparable harm to Sigma (P), for the company stands to lose its competitive edge. Harris (D) also faces substantial harm. He will be prevented from working for ICN for two years and likely will forever be prevented from using his knowledge of Sigma's (P) trade secrets. But the threat to Harris (D) is diminished by the fact that other former Sigma (P) employees have obtained

---

employment with companies not in competition with Sigma (P). The balance of the equities do not favor Harris (D) because he was aware of the restrictions when he took employment with Sigma (P). On balance, the threat to Sigma (P) outweighs the detriment to Harris (D). It is ordered that Harris (D) be enjoined from: [1] rendering services to ICN as a purchasing agent involved in the purchase of products also sold by Sigma (P) for a period of two years; and [2] using or disclosing any trade secret that is the property of Sigma (P) and which Harris (D) acquired by reason of his employment with Sigma (P).

Analysis:

Before issuing an injunction, the court must balance the interests of the parties involved. Using a two-step approach. First, the court determines the relative harm to each party. The second step is the balancing of the equities—a sort of fairness determination. The court holds that an injunction should issue here because (a) the benefit to Sigma (P) outweighs the harm to Harris (D), and (b) fairness demands that Harris (D) be held to the terms of a contract he freely entered. One other point is notable. The court states that before Sigma (P) can obtain an injunction it must show that there is no available remedy at law.

Evans v. Jeff D.

(State Governor) v. *(Group of Handicapped Children)*

475 U.S. 717, 106 S.Ct. 1531 (1986)

FEE SHIFTING STATUTES MAY CREATE A CONFLICT BETWEEN THE LAWYER'S DUTY TO HIS CLIENT AND HIS INTEREST IN BEING COMPENSATED

■ **INSTANT FACTS** While negotiating a settlement for his clients, a class of handicapped children, a Legal Aid attorney was forced to waive his claim for legal fees provided by statute in order to obtain all of the injunctive relief his clients sought from the state.

■ **BLACK LETTER RULE** The civil rights fee shifting provision does not prohibit settlements conditioned on the waiver of fees.

■ **FACTS**

A class of mentally and emotionally handicapped children (plaintiff class) (P) sued the State of Idaho (D) seeking injunctive relief for improved treatment under the federal civil rights statute, 42 U.S.C. §1983. The attorney for the plaintiff class was employed by the Legal Aid Society; and his representation agreement contained no provision for legal fees. Before trial, the State of Idaho (D) offered a settlement proposal which granted the plaintiff class (P) virtually all of the relief it was seeking. The settlement, however, was conditioned on the waiver of any claim of legal fees provided by 42 U.S.C. §1988(b), the Civil Rights Attorney's Fees Award Act (Fees Act). This provision permits a District Court to allow a prevailing party in a civil rights action to recover reasonable attorney's fees. Although the waiver was unacceptable to the Legal Aid Society, the attorney felt compelled by his ethical obligations to his clients and accepted the settlement. The District Court rejected the attorney's ethical argument and approved of the settlement conditioned upon the waiver of fees.

■ **ISSUE**

Does the federal civil rights fee shifting provision prohibit a court from accepting a settlement conditioned upon the waiver of fees?

■ **DECISION AND RATIONALE**

(Stevens, J.) No. The Fees Act does not embody a general rule prohibiting settlements conditioned on the waiver of fees in order to be faithful to the purposes of that Act. Although we believe that the Legal Aid attorney was faced with a conflict of interest between pursuing relief for his clients and obtaining a fee for the Legal Aid Society, we do not view this as an "ethical dilemma." The attorney had no ethical duty to recover a fee [it is perfectly okay for the attorney's family to starve]; his only ethical duty was to obtain relief for the plaintiff class. Since the settlement offer was more favorable than any probable outcome at trial, the attorney's decision to settle was consistent with the highest standards of our profession. Any defect in the negotiated fee waiver must stem from a prohibition in the Fees Act, and not the rules of ethics. We, however, can deduce no such prohibition from the fees Act. The statute and its legislative history do not suggest that Congress intended to prohibit all waivers of attorney's fees. In fact, we believe that such a prohibition may impede the vindication of civil rights by reducing the attractiveness of settlement. We must then decide whether the District Court abused its discretion in this case when it approved the settlement and fee waiver. We believe the District Court acted within its discretion. It is argued that a court's authority to

---

approve of class-action settlements must be exercised in accordance with the Fees Act to ensure the availability of attorneys in civil rights cases. We disagree. The question a court must ask is whether the settlement is fair; and in doing so, the court may consider the waiver. We do not decide whether the availability of fee waivers will actually diminish the availability of attorneys in civil rights cases. That question is best left to Congress. Thus far, the Legislature has failed to prohibit such waivers.

Analysis:

The Court notes the attorney in this case was pressured into waiving his fee in order to secure a favorable result for his client, but in the Court's opinion, this conflict was not an "ethical" one since the rules of the profession do not require an attorney to seek a fee, they only require an attorney to protect the interests of the client. Second, the Court goes on to hold that neither the statute authorizing a court to award attorney's fees in civil rights cases, nor its legislative history, indicate an intent on the part of Congress to prohibit a ban on settlements conditioned on a fee waiver. The Court noted that such a rule may actually interfere with the purposes of the statute by making settlement less attractive. But the purpose of the fee shifting statute is not to make settlement more attractive; rather, it is to make attorneys available in civil rights cases. Ethical rules will always require an attorney in this situation to take the settlement and waive his fee.

Buckhannon Board and Care Home, Inc. v. West Virginia Department of Health and Human Resources

(Nursing Home Operator) v. (State Agency)

532 U.S. 598, 121 S.Ct. 1835 (2001)

A POST-COMPLAINT CHANGE IN LAW MAKING A CLAIM MOOT DOES NOT RENDER THE PLAINTIFF A "PREVAILING PARTY"

■ **INSTANT FACTS** Buckhannon Board and Care Home's (P) suit was dismissed as moot after the defendant changed its conduct during litigation.

■ **BLACK LETTER RULE** Under federal fee-shifting statutes, a party must obtain a judgment on the merits or court-ordered consent decree to qualify as the "prevailing party."

■ **PROCEDURAL BASIS**

Certiorari to review a decision of the Fourth Circuit Court of Appeals.

■ **FACTS**

Buckhannon Board and Care Home (P) had been issued cease and desist orders from the West Virginia Department of Health and Human Resources (D), calling for the plaintiff to close its nursing home facilities for failure to comply with a state law requiring all nursing home patients to be capable of exiting a burning building. The plaintiff filed suit against the defendant for declaratory and injunctive relief, alleging the regulation violated the federal Fair Housing Amendments Act and the Americans with Disabilities Act. After discovery began, the West Virginia legislature enacted legislation eliminating the law at issue. The district court dismissed the plaintiff's complaint as moot since compliance was no longer required. Thereafter, the plaintiff requested attorney's fees as the "prevailing party" under the Fair Housing Amendments Act.

■ **ISSUE**

Does the term "prevailing party" include a party that has failed to secure a judgment on the merits or a court-ordered consent decree, but has nonetheless achieved the desired result because the lawsuit brought about a voluntary change in the defendant's conduct?

■ **DECISION AND RATIONALE**

(Rehnquist, C.J.) No. Under the American rule, each party generally is responsible to pay his or her own attorney's fees. However, many fee-shifting statutes, such as the Fair Housing Amendments Act, authorize an award of attorney's fees to the "prevailing party." Past court precedent confirms the dictionary definition of prevailing party as one "in whose favor a judgment is rendered, regardless of the amount of damages awarded." Here, no such judgment has been entered. Nonetheless, the plaintiff argues it is entitled to an award of attorney's fees under the catalyst theory recognized by many federal courts of appeal. Under the catalyst theory, a party is the prevailing party if its desired result is achieved as a result of the litigation, regardless whether the litigation resulted in a judgment or court-ordered decree.

There exists insufficient legislative history to demonstrate an explicit congressional intent to depart from the traditional understanding of the term "prevailing party." The only means of determining the prevailing party, therefore, is through a judgment on the merits or court-

---

ordered consent decree. No evidence has been presented to demonstrate that without the catalyst theory, plaintiffs will be deterred from bringing meritorious claims. In contrast, the American rule encourages voluntary settlement and remedial action by defendants, who realize that a judgment on the merits could result in a large attorney's fee award. Moreover, the catalyst theory would apply only to the small percentage of cases seeking equitable relief, since an action for damages will remain regardless of any change in a defendant's conduct. The catalyst theory threatens to prolong and complicate litigation by creating a second dispute over the reasons for the defendant's change in conduct and the impact the litigation had on such a change. Thus, without a judgment or court-ordered decree, a plaintiff simply is not the prevailing party. Affirmed.

■ DISSENT

(Ginsburg, J.) The Court's decision that a court-ordered resolution to the case is required to grant an award of attorney's fees ignores the well-established practice in the courts of appeal and jeopardizes Americans' access to the courts to redress violations of their civil rights. Congress established federal fee-shifting statutes to enable parties who have been wronged to litigate meritorious claims without absorbing litigation costs to vindicate their individual rights. The catalyst theory is an important element of these federal statutes and must be preserved.

Analysis:

Although most fee-shifting statutes allow an award of attorneys' fees for "the prevailing party," different standards apply depending on whether the plaintiff or the defendant prevails. When the plaintiff is the prevailing party, he naturally has succeeded in vindicating his rights and established some wrongdoing on the defendant's part. When the defendant is the prevailing party, however, attorneys' fees are usually not awarded unless the action was frivolous or brought in bad faith. To do otherwise would create a chilling effect on a plaintiff's ability to prosecute civil rights claims for fear of paying the defendant's legal fees.

■ CASE VOCABULARY

AMERICAN RULE: The general policy that all litigants must bear their own attorney's fees, including the prevailing party.

A LIKELIHOOD OF INJURY, NOT JUST A POSSIBILITY, MUST BE SHOWN IN ORDER TO OBTAIN A PRELIMINARY INJUNCTION

Hey, men!
The Supreme Court confirmed it is in the "public interest" to not lose wars.

stus.com

■ **INSTANT FACTS** The Natural Resources Defense Council (P) obtained a preliminary injunction against a training exercise conducted by the Navy (D), and the Ninth Circuit Court of Appeals affirmed.

■ **BLACK LETTER RULE** When ruling on a request for a preliminary injunction, a court must consider the consequences to the public of granting the request.

■ **PROCEDURAL BASIS**

Appeal from an order affirming the granting of a temporary injunction.

■ **FACTS**

The Marine Mammal Protection Act (MMPA) prohibits the harming of marine mammals, but the Secretary of Defense is authorized to grant an exemption for activities that are necessary for national defense. The Navy (D) was granted a two-year exemption from the MMPA on the condition that it adopt mitigation procedures. After the exemption was granted, the Navy (D) issued an environmental assessment that concluded that its training exercises would not have a significant impact on the environment. The Natural Resources Defense Council (P) brought suit against the Navy (D) to stop the exercises, claiming that the Navy's use of sonar would endanger marine mammals. The District Court granted the Council's (P) motion for a preliminary injunction barring the Navy (D) from using sonar in its training exercises, holding that the Council (P) had "demonstrated a probability of success" on their claims. The court also determined that a preliminary injunction was appropriate because the Council (P) had established at least a "possibility" of irreparable harm to the environment. Based on the evidence in the record, the court concluded that there was a "near certainty" of irreparable injury to the environment, and that this injury outweighed any possible harm to the Navy (D). The preliminary injunction stated that, during the exercises, the Navy (D) would be required to shut down its sonar in a certain area and to power-down its sonar under certain conditions.

The Ninth Circuit Court of Appeals affirmed the granting of the preliminary injunction. The appellate court held that the Council (P) had carried their burden of establishing a "possibility" of irreparable injury. It concluded that the training exercises would cause physical injuries to and would disturb the behavior of marine mammals. The court also held that the balance of hardships and consideration of the public interest weighed in favor of the Council (P). The impact on the Navy (D) was speculative, since it had never conducted exercises under the circumstances ordered by the district court, and the district court's restrictions were not unreasonable.

■ **ISSUE**

Was the Council (P) entitled to a preliminary injunction?

■ DECISION AND RATIONALE

(Roberts, C.J.) No. When ruling on a request for a preliminary injunction, a court must consider the consequences to the public of granting the request. A preliminary injunction is an extraordinary remedy, and it is not granted as a matter of right. Here, the public interest, and the Navy's (D) interest, in training sailors requires denial of the injunctive relief.

The District Court used an incorrect standard when it granted the Council's (P) request for a preliminary injunction. The Council (P) should have been required to demonstrate a likelihood of irreparable injury, and not just a possibility. The Navy (D) argued that the Council's (P) claimed injuries were too speculative, in that there has been no documented case of a sonar-related injury to a marine mammal in the forty years that the Navy (D) has conducted training exercises. The Council (P) argued that, even under the more restrictive standard, it was entitled to relief because the District Court found a "near certainty" of irreparable harm. Even if the Council (P) has shown irreparable injury from the Navy's (D) exercises, any such injury is outweighed by the public interest in training sailors.

This case involves professional military judgments. The Court gives great deference to the professional judgment of military authorities regarding the relative importance of a particular military interest. The record in the instant case contains declarations from some of the Navy's (D) most senior officers, all of whom underscored the need for sonar training to counter the threat posed by enemy submarines. These interests must be balanced against the harm to ecological, scientific, and recreational interests that are before the Court. The balance of equities and consideration of the overall public interest tip strongly in favor of the Navy (D). The most serious harm alleged by the Council (P) is possible harm to an unknown number of marine mammals. In contrast, deploying inadequately trained forces jeopardizes the safety of the Navy (D) fleet. The public interest in allowing the sonar training exercises plainly outweighs the interests advanced by the Council (P). Military interests will not always trump other considerations, but in this case the determination of the public interest is not even a close question. Reversed.

■ DISSENT

(Ginsburg, J.) Flexibility is a hallmark of equity jurisdiction. Courts have evaluated claims for equitable relief on a "sliding scale," and have not required that litigants uniformly show a particular, predetermined quantum of probable success or injury before awarding equitable relief.

Analysis:

The Court states that military considerations do not always trump other considerations for equitable relief. At the same time, the Court notes the great deference that is to be afforded decisions of military authorities. Given that deference, it is hard to imagine a court deciding that other interests outweigh a claim that a proposed military action is of the "utmost importance." In this case, the possibility of some unknown quantum of harm did not convince the Court that an injunction should issue.

■ CASE VOCABULARY

PRELIMINARY INJUNCTION: A temporary injunction issued before or during trial to prevent an irreparable injury from occurring before the court has a chance to finally decide the case on its merits.

Fuentes v. Shevin

(Debtor) v. (Not Stated)

407 U.S. 67, 92 S.Ct. 1983 (1972)

SEIZURE OF A PROTECTED PROPERTY INTEREST MUST BE PRECEDED BY NOTICE AND AN OPPORTUNITY TO BE HEARD

■ **INSTANT FACTS** Margarita Fuentes (P) and other debtors challenge the constitutionality of Florida and Pennsylvania statutes allowing seizure of goods covered by an installment sales contract without providing an opportunity for the debtor to be heard prior to seizure.

■ **BLACK LETTER RULE** In order to comply with procedural due process, notice and an opportunity to be heard must be provided prior to seizure of any protected property interest.

■ **PROCEDURAL BASIS**

Writ of certiorari reviewing affirmance of rejection of constitutional claims concerning replevin of chattels.

■ **FACTS**

In this case, the Supreme Court reviews two separate appellate rulings regarding the constitutionality of state replevin statutes. One ruling involved Margarita Fuentes (P), who had purchased a stove and stereo system under a conditional sales contract. The supplier, Firestone Tire and Rubber Company, was to retain title to the merchandise until Mrs. Fuentes (P) made all of her payments, although Mrs. Fuentes (P) was allowed to possess the items in the interim. After more than a year of progress payments, a dispute developed regarding servicing of the stove. Firestone instituted an action in small claims court for repossession of the items, claiming that Mrs. Fuentes (P) had refused to make her payments. Firestone simultaneously obtained a writ of replevin, pursuant to Florida statute, ordering a sheriff to seize the goods without providing Mrs. Fuentes (P) with a preseizure hearing. Thereafter, Mrs. Fuentes (P) instituted the present action in federal district court, challenging the constitutionality of Florida's replevin statute. A similar action was brought in Pennsylvania by four other consumers who had entered into similar conditional sales contracts. In each suit, the district courts rejected the constitutional claims, and three-judge district courts considered the appeal and upheld the constitutionality of the statutes. The Supreme Court granted certiorari to review both appellate rulings.

■ **ISSUE**

Absent extraordinary circumstances, must notice and an opportunity to be heard be provided prior to depriving a party of a protected property interest?

■ **DECISION AND RATIONALE**

(Stewart, J.) Yes. Absent extraordinary circumstances, notice and an opportunity to be heard must be provided *prior* to depriving a party of a protected property interest. Consistent with procedural due process, we have repeatedly held that, prior to depriving a party of a property interest, an opportunity to be heard must be granted at a meaningful time. We now hold that, if notice and a hearing is to serve its full purpose, then the hearing must be granted at a time when the deprivation still can be prevented. Indeed, the Florida statute requires a post-seizure hearing in which the aggrieved party can argue her right to the goods. And in Pennsylvania,

---

the aggrieved party can institute a lawsuit for the return of wrongfully-seized goods. Furthermore, pursuant to both statutes, the creditor seeking replevin must post a bond and may be forced to pay damages for wrongful repossession. However, no later hearing and no damage award can undo the fact that the arbitrary taking that was subject to procedural due process has already occurred. We have never embraced the position that a wrong may be done if it can be undone. Thus, we now hold that, in order to comply with due process, notice and an opportunity to be heard must be provided *prior* to any deprivation of a property interest protected by the Fourteenth Amendment. In the present cases, the Florida and Pennsylvania statutes are unconstitutional, as they provide for the replevin of chattels without the benefit of a hearing. Although Mrs. Fuentes (P) and the Pennsylvania appellants lacked full title to the replevied goods, the Fourteenth Amendment's property protection covers both possession and ownership. There are, however, extraordinary situations that justify postponing notice and opportunity for a hearing. In each such case, the seizure must be directly necessary to secure an important governmental or general public interest, there must be a special need for prompt action, and the statute must be narrowly drawn. For example, the Court has allowed summary seizure of property to collect the internal revenue of the United States, to meet the needs of a national war effort, to protect against the economic disaster of a bank failure, and to protect the public from mislabeled drugs and contaminated food. Since the Florida and Pennsylvania statutes serve no such important interests, and since the facts of the cases at hand are not these unusual situations, we hold that the statutes are unconstitutional. Vacated and remanded.

■ DISSENT

(White, J.) I believe that the Florida and Pennsylvania statutes represent fair, constitutionally valid methods of reconciling the conflicting interests of the debtor and creditor in an installment sales contract. Both statutes immobilize the property during the pendency of the action, allowing the aggrieved debtor to reclaim the goods and recover damages if the seizure was invalid. The majority wrongfully ignores the creditor's interest in preventing further use and deterioration of a property in which he has a substantial interest. Finally, the majority's result will have little impact on seizure in the installment sales context. A creditor could withstand attack under the majority's opinion by simply making clear in the original credit documents that they may retake possession without a hearing. Alternatively, they need only give a few days' notice of a hearing, and they need only establish probable cause for the default at the hearing. It is doubtful that such a hearing would result in protections for the debtor substantially different from those the present laws provide.

Analysis:

In this case, the majority presents compelling arguments for providing notice and an opportunity to be heard prior to seizure of goods via a writ of replevin. As already shown in *Mullane v. Central Hanover Bank & Trust Co.*, due process requires that notice be provided prior to the deprivation of life, liberty, or property by adjudication. The case at hand substantially broadens a party's due process rights, providing an almost universal *opportunity to be heard* prior to the deprivation of property. However, it should be noted that the unconstitutional "seizure" in this case was really only an *attachment,* as the debtor retained an ability to contest the "seizure" after it occurred. Thus, the case stands for the proposition that a preattachment opportunity to be heard is consistent with procedural due process.

■ CASE VOCABULARY

CHATTEL: An item of personal property.

DETINUE: Common law action allowing creditor to recover goods wrongfully detained.

REPLEVIN: Modern action allowing the title holder to repossess goods or chattels from a person who has wrongfully obtained or retained them.

CHAPTER 6

Pleading

Haddle v. Garrison (I)

Instant Facts: Whistleblower (P), who is an at-will employee, alleges an injury from being fired as part of a conspiracy to deter him from testifying in federal court.

Black Letter Rule: As a matter of law, an at-will employee who was fired is not "injured," and therefore a claim for injury cannot be sustained.

Haddle v. Garrison (II)

Instant Facts: An at-will employee was fired for cooperating (including willingness to testify in front of a federal grand jury) with the federal criminal investigation of his employer for welfare fraud.

Black Letter Rule: Firing an at-will employee causes injury because it is an interference with employment relationship, which is a tort under state law.

Ashcroft v. Iqbal

Instant Facts: Iqbal (P) brought a *Bivens* action complaining about his treatment while detained after the 9/11 attacks, and Ashcroft's (D) motion to dismiss the complaint was denied.

Black Letter Rule: A complaint will not be dismissed if it contains sufficient factual matter, taken as true, to state a claim for relief that is plausible on its face.

Stradford v. Zurich Insurance Co.

Instant Facts: After Stradford's (P) insurance policy lapsed and was reinstated, Stradford (P) filed a large claim under the policy, prompting the defendant to file a counterclaim for fraud.

Black Letter Rule: Claims of fraud or mistake must be asserted with particularity to provide the party against whom such claims are made fair notice of the claim and the grounds on which it is based.

Jones v. Bock

Instant Facts: A prisoner brought suit for violation of his rights under 42 U.S.C. § 1983, and the Supreme Court consolidated his case with those of other prisoners to determine the pleading requirements applicable to their complaints.

Black Letter Rule: Failure to exhaust administrative remedies is an affirmative defense in prisoner lawsuits, and inmates are therefore not required to specially plead or demonstrate exhaustion in their complaints.

Walker v. Norwest Corp.

Instant Facts: The plaintiffs' complaint was dismissed and sanctions were imposed because the plaintiffs failed to assert the citizenship of all defendants necessary to establish diversity jurisdiction.

Black Letter Rule: Sanctions are appropriate when an attorney, through court submissions, raises allegations or factual contentions that are not supported by evidence or likely to be supported upon reasonable discovery.

Christian v. Mattell, Inc.

Instant Facts: Christian (P) sued Mattell, Inc. (D) for copyright infringement in federal court over the creation and distribution of a doll.

Black Letter Rule: Rule 11 sanctions are appropriate only when an attorney, through court submissions, raises allegations or factual contentions that are not supported by evidence or likely to be supported with an opportunity to conduct reasonable discovery.

Zielinski v. Philadelphia Piers, Inc.

Instant Facts: A man who was hit by a forklift claims that it was owned by large company which denies owning it at the time of the accident.

Black Letter Rule: A general denial will not be valid if any of the allegations being denied have been admitted by both parties as true.

Beeck v. Aquaslide N' Dive Corp.

Instant Facts: Defendant admits manufacturing the defective water slide at issue in the case but a year later moves the court to amend the answer to deny manufacture.

Black Letter Rule: A court does not abuse its discretion by allowing an amendment to an answer, which initially admitted responsibility for the manufacture of the product at issue but now seeks to deny manufacturing it.

Moore v. Baker

Instant Facts: A patient who was disabled after an operation sued the doctor for violation of the informed consent law, and later tried to amend the complaint to include allegations of negligence.

Black Letter Rule: In order to relate back to the time of the original complaint, a proposed amendment must have its basis in the same facts that are alleged in the original complaint.

Bonerb v. Richard J. Caron Foundation

Instant Facts: Patient originally sued the Rehab Center for negligent maintenance of its basketball court, and later tried to amend the complaint to include a claim for counseling malpractice.

Black Letter Rule: A claim will relate back if the operational facts set out in the original complaint are sufficient to put the defendant on notice that the amended claim could be brought.

Haddle v. Garrison (I)

(Whistleblower Employee) v. (Employer)

Unpublished Opinion. Docket No. 96-00029-CV-1 (1996)

A RULE 12(B)(6) MOTION WILL BE GRANTED IF NO SET OF FACTS IN SUPPORT OF PLAINTIFF'S CLAIM WILL ENTITLE PLAINTIFF TO RELIEF

■ **INSTANT FACTS** Whistleblower (P), who is an at-will employee, alleges an injury from being fired as part of a conspiracy to deter him from testifying in federal court.

■ **BLACK LETTER RULE** As a matter of law, an at-will employee who was fired is not "injured," and therefore a claim for injury cannot be sustained.

■ **PROCEDURAL BASIS**

District court sustains a motion to dismiss a complaint for failure to state a claim upon which relief may be granted.

■ **FACTS**

Haddle (P) is a former employee of Healthmaster Home Health Care, Inc. (Healthmaster). Haddle (P) alleges that he was fired because he was planning to be a witness against Garrison (D) and others in a Federal criminal trial, that the firing was in retaliation for his planned testimony, and that the firing has caused Haddle (P) an actual injury. Haddle (P) concedes that he was an at-will employee at all relevant times. Haddle is suing his former employers for a violation of his civil rights under 42 U.S.C. §1985(2) [making it a crime to conspire to cause an injury to any witness in order to deter the witness from testifying in federal court.]

■ **ISSUE**

Does an at-will employee state a cause of action by alleging that his termination from employment is an "injury?"

■ **DECISION AND RATIONALE**

(Alaimo) No. Rule 12(b)(6) permits a defendant to move to dismiss a complaint on the ground that the complaint fails to state a claim upon which relief can be granted. In other words, a defendant is saying to a plaintiff, "Even if everything you allege is true, the law affords you no relief." In deciding a 12(b)(6) motion, a court must assume that all of the factual allegations in the complaint are true. In the present case, Haddle (P) claims that his allegations will sustain a cause of action under §1985(2) despite his status as an at-will employee. However, Haddle's (P) claim is contrary to binding 11th Circuit precedent in *Morast v. Lance* [a plaintiff must have been actually injured in order to sustain a claim under §1985(2), and the discharge of an at-will employee is not an actual injury.] Under *Morast*, Haddle (P) has not been "injured." Therefore he has not stated a claim upon which relief can be granted. Dismissed.

Analysis:

The court reasoned that at-will employees have no guarantee of work the next day. Therefore, an at-will employee who is fired has not been injured, because he was not entitled to be

---

working in the first place. Since Haddle (P) was an at-will employee, he was not injured, and thus could not make out a claim under the law invoked in the complaint. Even if every fact that Haddle (P) alleged was true, and he really did get fired in retaliation for cooperating with the authorities, since there was no injury, the law allows for no recovery. Notice also that the district court here did not make an independent determination of whether there had been an injury. Rather, it applied a case from the Eleventh Circuit, which said that there is no injury in this situation. Since the Georgia district court is in the Eleventh Circuit, the court was bound by its determination of the question.

■ **CASE VOCABULARY**

AT-WILL EMPLOYMENT: Absent a contract or statutory protection, an employer may fire an employee for any reason or for no reason at all.

(Whistleblower Employee) v. (Employer)

525 U.S. 121, 119 S.Ct. 489 (1998)

A RULE 12(B)(6) MOTION TO DISMISS SHOULD BE DENIED IF ANY SET OF FACTS ALLEGED IN THE COMPLAINT WILL ENTITLE PLAINTIFF TO RELIEF

■ **INSTANT FACTS** An at-will employee was fired for cooperating (including willingness to testify in front of a federal grand jury) with the federal criminal investigation of his employer for welfare fraud.

■ **BLACK LETTER RULE** Firing an at-will employee causes injury because it is an interference with employment relationship, which is a tort under state law.

■ **PROCEDURAL BASIS**

Appeal from dismissal of claim.

■ **FACTS**

Haddle (P) is an at-will employee at Healthmaster, Inc. Haddle (P) was cooperating with a federal investigation of Healthmaster and its officers (including Garrison (D)) for allegations of Medicare fraud. Garrison (D) personally could not participate in the affairs of Healthmaster while he was under investigation, but he conspired with another officer of the corporation to have Haddle (P) fired. Haddle (P) alleged that he was fired in retaliation for his cooperation in the federal investigation, and that the termination was to discourage him from cooperating further with the authorities. Haddle (P) included in his complaint claims for relief under 42 U.S.C. §1985(2) [making it a crime to conspire to cause an injury to any witness in order to deter the witness from testifying in federal court.] The district court dismissed the action for failure to state a claim upon which relief may be granted. *Rule 12(b)(6)*. It reasoned that because Haddle (P) was an at-will employee, he could not have suffered an "injury" by being fired. Injury is an essential element under the statute. The Eleventh Circuit Court of Appeals affirmed, relying on its precedent in *Morast* [holding that firing an at-will employee does not cause an "injury"].

■ **ISSUE**

Can an at-will employee suffer a legal "injury" if his employer fires him?

■ **DECISION AND RATIONALE**

(Rehnquist) Yes. Since the Eleventh Circuit's rule in *Morast* conflicts with rulings of the First and Ninth Circuits, we granted certiorari to resolve the question of whether an at-will employee is "injured in his person or property" under §1985(2) if his employer fires him. Since this case was dismissed under Rule 12(b)(6), we must take all of the facts as alleged in Haddle's (P) complaint as true. We disagree with the Eleventh Circuit and hold that the firing of an at-will employee in this context does constitute a harm under §1985(2). The harm alleged by Haddle (P) is a third-party interference with an at-will employment relationship. This is analogous to the long-standing tort of interference with contract. Wrongful interference with employment relations is a tort under the state law of Georgia, which is where the action here took place.

Therefore, we find ample support for our holding that the harm occasioned by the conspiracy to fire Haddle (P) may give rise to a claim for damages under §1985(2). Reversed and Remanded.

Analysis:

Here the Supreme Court reversed the Eleventh Circuit's holding that discharge from at-will employment does not cause injury. Remember, this is still a case about whether the law will allow recovery under the facts as alleged by Haddle (P). This case is still at the pre-discovery stage, so the Court assumes that all of the allegations in the complaint are true for purposes of deciding whether or not it should allow the dismissal to stand. The ultimate disposition is that the case is remanded for further action consistent with the Supreme Court's decision, which means that the case will be allowed to go forward, but it does not mean that Haddle (P) is guaranteed to win. Haddle (P) must still gather enough evidence to survive summary judgment, and to convince a jury that he had proven all of the elements of his claims.

■ **CASE VOCABULARY**

CERTIORARI: When the Supreme Court agrees to hear a case.

INTERFERENCE WITH CONTRACT: A common law tort where one party causes another party damage by creating a situation where the second party, due to some action of the first party, cannot receive the benefits of a contract that it has made.

Ashcroft v. Iqbal

(Attorney General) v. (Former Prisoner)

556 U.S. 662 (2009)

CONCLUSORY AND LEGAL, AS OPPOSED TO FACTUAL, ALLEGATIONS ARE INSUFFICIENT TO STATE A VIABLE CLAIM

■ **INSTANT FACTS** Iqbal (P) brought a *Bivens* action complaining about his treatment while detained after the 9/11 attacks, and Ashcroft's (D) motion to dismiss the complaint was denied.

■ **BLACK LETTER RULE** A complaint will not be dismissed if it contains sufficient factual matter, taken as true, to state a claim for relief that is plausible on its face.

■ **PROCEDURAL BASIS**

Decision on a writ of certiorari to the Second Circuit Court of Appeals, to review an order affirming denial of a motion to dismiss Iqbal's (P) complaint.

■ **FACTS**

After the September 11, 2001 terrorist attacks, federal law enforcement agencies began an investigation to identify the attackers and prevent them from attacking again. Some of the people questioned were deemed to be of high interest to the investigation and were detained. The high-interest detainees were held under restrictive conditions, to prevent them from communicating with other prisoners or with the outside world. Iqbal (P), a citizen of Pakistan and a Muslim, was one of those high-interest detainees. He was arrested on fraud charges relating to immigration documents, and on charges of conspiracy to defraud the United States. Pending trial, Iqbal (P) was housed in a detention facility. After he was designated a person of high interest, he was transferred to a secure housing unit at the detention center. Iqbal (P) and the other inmates in the secure unit were kept in lockdown for twenty-three hours each day. When they were outside their cells, inmates were in handcuffs and leg irons, and were accompanied by a four-officer escort.

Iqbal (P) pleaded guilty to the charges against him. After a term of imprisonment, he was removed to Pakistan. Iqbal (P) then filed a *Bivens* action against thirty-four current and former federal officials (D) and nineteen "John Doe" federal corrections officers (D). The defendants included the correctional officers (D) who had day-to-day contact with Iqbal (P), the wardens of the facility (D), and all the way up to Ashcroft (D) and Mueller (D), officials who were at the highest level of federal law enforcement. The allegations against Ashcroft (D) and Mueller (D), the only allegations considered in this case, stated that Iqbal (P) was designated a person of high interest because of his race, religion, or national origin, contrary to the First and Fifth Amendments. The complaint alleged that the FBI, under the direction of Mueller (D), arrested and detained "thousands of Arab Muslim men." The complaint further alleged that the policy of holding post-September 11 detainees in secure units was approved by Ashcroft (D) and Mueller (D). Finally, the complaint alleged that Ashcroft (D) and Mueller (D) each "knew of, condoned, and willfully and maliciously agreed to subject" Iqbal (P) to harsh conditions of confinement solely because of his religion, race, or national origin and for no "legitimate penological interest." Ashcroft (D) and Mueller (D) moved to dismiss the complaint. Their motion claimed that the complaint did not state sufficient allegations to show

---

their own involvement in clearly established unconstitutional conduct. The district court denied their motion and the court of appeals affirmed the denial. The court concluded that the case of *Bell Atlantic v. Twombly*, 550 U.S. 544 (2007), called for a flexible "plausibility standard." That standard would require a pleader to amplify a claim with some factual allegations in contexts in which amplification is needed to render the claim plausible. The court found that Ashcroft (D) and Mueller (D) did not present a context that required amplification.

■ **ISSUE**

Was Iqbal's (P) complaint sufficient to state a cause of action against Ashcroft (D) and Mueller (D)?

■ **DECISION AND RATIONALE**

(Kennedy, J.) No. A complaint will not be dismissed if it contains sufficient factual matter, taken as true, to state a claim for relief that is plausible on its face. But facial plausibility requires the plaintiff to plead factual content that allows the court to draw the reasonable inference that the defendant is liable for the misconduct alleged. Determining whether a claim is plausible is a context-specific inquiry that requires the court to draw on its judicial experience and common sense. Plausibility is not the same as probability, but it requires more than just a possibility that a defendant acted unlawfully. A complaint must plead facts that are more than merely consistent with the defendant's liability. As the Court held in *Twombly*, Rule 8 of the Federal Rules of Civil Procedure does not require a complaint to contain detailed factual allegations, but a complaint still must have more than an unadorned the-defendant-unlawfully-harmed-me accusation. The principle that a court will accept as true the allegations of a complaint does not apply to legal conclusions, even if those conclusions are couched as factual allegations. Legal conclusions may provide the framework of a complaint, but they must be supported by factual allegations.

The decision in *Twombly* illustrates the approach the Court will take here. In that case, the plaintiff alleged that the defendants "ha[d] entered into a contract, combination or conspiracy to prevent competitive entry . . . and ha[d] agreed not to compete with one another." The complaint also alleged that the defendants' "parallel course of conduct . . . to prevent competition" and inflate prices was indicative of the unlawful agreement alleged. The Court held that the plaintiff's complaint was deficient under Rule 8. The allegation of an unlawful agreement was a legal conclusion and not entitled to the assumption of truth. The factual allegations alleged behavior that was consistent with unlawful behavior, but did not suggest an illicit accord. The parallel behavior was compatible with, and more likely explained by, lawful, unchoreographed free-market behavior. Because the well-pleaded facts, accepted as true, did not plausibly suggest an unlawful agreement, the Court held that the complaint must be dismissed.

Applying that framework, Iqbal's (P) complaint does not set out a plausible claim of discrimination. Iqbal (P) made allegations that Ashcroft (D) and Mueller (D) knew of, condoned, and agreed to subject Iqbal (P) to harsh conditions as a matter of policy because of his religion, race, or national origin. The complaint alleged that Ashcroft (D) was the "principal architect" of the policy and that Mueller (D) was instrumental in adopting and executing it. These bare allegations amount to nothing more than a formulaic recitation of the elements of a constitutional discrimination claim. They are conclusory and not entitled to an assumption of truth. They are not rejected as unrealistic or nonsensical, but as conclusory. The factual allegations of Iqbal's (P) complaint allege that the FBI, under the direction of Mueller (D), arrested and detained Muslim men and held them in highly restrictive conditions. If taken as true, these allegations are consistent with the designation of detainees as high interest because of their race, religion, or national origin. Given more likely explanations, however, the allegations do not establish such a purpose. Based on the facts alleged, the arrests were likely lawful and justified by a nondiscriminatory intent to detain aliens who were in the U.S. unlawfully and who had potential connections to those who committed terrorist acts. As between that obvious alternative explanation for the arrests and the purposeful, invidious

Twombly case

discrimination Iqbal (P) asks the Court to infer, discrimination is not a plausible conclusion. Even if Iqbal's (P) complaint gave rise to a plausible inference of discrimination, that inference alone would not entitle him to relief. Iqbal's (P) allegations complain of his detention in the secure unit, not his initial arrest or detention. They do not show that Ashcroft (D) and Mueller (D) purposefully housed detainees in the secure unit due to their race, national origin, or religion.

Iqbal (P) argues that the *Twombly* decision should be limited to pleadings made in antitrust cases. That argument is not supported by *Twombly* and is incompatible with the Federal Rules of Civil Procedure. The pleading standard in *Twombly* applies to antitrust and discrimination suits alike. Iqbal (P) also argues that the Court's construction of Rule 8 should be tempered when the trial court has placed controls on discovery. A motion to dismiss a complaint does not, however, turn on limits placed on discovery. Iqbal's (P) complaint is deficient, so he is not entitled to discovery. Finally, Iqbal (P) claims that Rule 9 allows him to allege discriminatory intent generally, which he equates with a conclusory allegation. The Federal Rules do not require the courts to credit a conclusory statement in a complaint without regard to its factual context. Iqbal's (P) complaint does not plead sufficient facts to state a cause of action. Reversed and remanded.

■ **DISSENT**

(Souter, J.) Although it has no bearing on the instant case, the majority does away with supervisory liability under *Bivens.* Ashcroft (D) and Mueller (P) conceded that an officer may be liable under *Bivens* as a supervisor. They admit that they would be liable if they had actual knowledge of discrimination by their subordinates and exhibited deliberate indifference to that discrimination. The majority ignores that concession. Iqbal's (P) complaint alleges, at a bare minimum, that Ashcroft (D) and Mueller (D) knew of and condoned the discriminatory policy their subordinates carried out. The complaint also alleges that Ashcroft (D) and Mueller (D) affirmatively acted to create the discriminatory detention policy. That should be enough to withstand a motion to dismiss.

Ashcroft (D) and Mueller (D) argued that the allegations in Iqbal's (P) complaint fail the plausibility test of *Twombly* because high-ranking officials "tend not to be personally involved in the specific actions of lower-level officials down the bureaucratic chain of command." *Twombly* does not require the court to consider, at the motion to dismiss stage, whether the factual allegations are probably true. On the contrary, the court must take the allegations as true, no matter how skeptical the court may be. The sole exception to this rule is with allegations that are sufficiently fantastic to deny reality as we know it: claims about little green men, or the plaintiff's recent trip to Pluto, or experiences with time travel.

The majority discards the bulk of the allegations with regard to Ashcroft (D) and Mueller (D) as conclusory, and is left considering only the statements in the complaint regarding the arrest and detention of "thousands of Arab Muslim men," and regarding the policy of holding post-September-11th detainees in highly restrictive conditions of confinement until they were "cleared" by the FBI. These allegations suggest only that Ashcroft (D) and Mueller (D) "sought to keep suspected terrorists in the most secure conditions available until the suspects could be cleared of terrorist activity," and that this produced "a disparate, incidental impact on Arab Muslims." The two allegations selected by the majority, standing alone, do not state a plausible entitlement to relief for unconstitutional discrimination. But these allegations do not stand alone as the only significant, nonconclusory statements in the complaint, for the complaint contains many allegations linking Ashcroft (D) and Mueller (D) to the discriminatory practices of their subordinates. Viewed in light of these supervisory allegations, the allegations singled out by the majority as "conclusory" are no such thing.

■ **DISSENT**

(Breyer, J.) The need to prevent unwarranted litigation from interfering with the proper execution of the work of the Government does not justify the majority's interpretation of

Twombly. A trial court could structure discovery in ways that diminish the risk of unwarranted burdens.

Analysis:

Rule 8 of the Federal Rules of Civil Procedure says that a complaint must contain "a short and plain statement of the claim showing that the pleader is entitled to relief." The Rule does not contain any factual plausibility requirement. Courts have long held that the factual accuracy of a party's claim is not something that is decided before trial, but is part of the fact finder's consideration of a case.

■ **CASE VOCABULARY**

BIVENS ACTION: A lawsuit seeking to redress a federal official's violation of a constitutional right, based on the case of *Bivens v. Six Unknown Named Agents of the Federal Bureau of Narcotics,* 403 U.S. 388 (1971). A *Bivens* action subjects federal officials to liability in a manner similar to that set forth at 42 U.S.C. § 1983 for state officials who violate a person's constitutional rights under color of state law.

Stradford v. Zurich Insurance Co.

(Dentist) v. (Insurance Company)

2002 WL 31027517 (S.D.N.Y. 2002)

GENERAL FACTUAL STATEMENTS ARE INSUFFICIENT TO SUPPORT A FRAUD CLAIM

■ **INSTANT FACTS** After Stradford's (P) insurance policy lapsed and was reinstated, Stradford (P) filed a large claim under the policy, prompting the defendant to file a counterclaim for fraud.

■ **BLACK LETTER RULE** Claims of fraud or mistake must be asserted with particularity to provide the party against whom such claims are made fair notice of the claim and the grounds on which it is based.

■ **PROCEDURAL BASIS**

Consideration of the plaintiff's motion to dismiss for failure to state claims with reasonable particularity.

■ **FACTS**

Stradford (P) is a dentist with an office in New York. On August 18, 1999, Stradford (P) took out an insurance policy on his office from Northern (D), an insurance company affiliated with Zurich Insurance Co. (D). From October 10, 1999 to December 13, 1999, however, Stradford (P) failed to pay the necessary policy premiums and Northern (D) cancelled the policy. After Stradford (P) delivered a "no claims" letter indicating that he had no losses during the period of interruption, Northern (D) reinstated the policy on December 14, 1999 and notified Stradford (P) of the reinstatement on January 9, 2000. Shortly thereafter, Stradford (P) filed a claim under the policy seeking coverage of $151,154.74 in damage to his personal property and inventory as a result of a water leak occurring on January 17, 2000. After Northern (D) paid the claim, Stradford (P) submitted an amended claim seeking $1,385,456.70 for damage to personal property and business interruption. Northern (D) investigated the claim and concluded that the loss occurred during the period that the policy had lapsed, and it therefore denied the claim. Stradford (P) sued Northern (D) in federal district court. Northern (D) filed a counterclaim for the return of the money paid on the initial claim and punitive damages for Stradford's (P) willful attempts to defraud the defendants. Stradford (P) moved to dismiss the counterclaim for failure to state claims of fraud with particularity as required by Federal Rule of Civil Procedure 9(b).

■ **ISSUE**

Do general statements of fraud, without specific claims of the time, place, and manner of the alleged fraud, state a claim for fraud with particularity?

■ **DECISION AND RATIONALE**

(Buchwald, J.) No. Federal Rule of Civil Procedure 9(b) requires all allegations of fraud or mistake to be asserted with particularity, while malice, intent, knowledge, and other states of mind may be asserted generally. The rule ensures that a party against whom fraud or mistake is alleged will receive "fair notice of the claim and the factual ground upon which it is based." Here, the counterclaim sufficiently asserts general facts to allow the inference that Stradford (P) intended to defraud Northern (D). However, the counterclaim does not set forth with

---

particularity the allegations of fraud. Particularity requires an affirmative allegation of the time, place, and manner in which the fraud occurred. The defendant's counterclaim lacks these details, relying instead on general allegations of untruthfulness and fraud. Without a showing of the specific acts of fraud, the counterclaim fails to provide Stradford (P) fair notice of the claims against him. However, when a defendant has not previously had an opportunity to amend its pleading, leave to amend should be granted to provide a party the opportunity to assert its claims with particularity as required by the rule. Motion denied with leave to amend.

Analysis:

Rule 9(b) is a stated exception to the "short and plain statement" requirement under Rule 8 notice pleading. Under this heightened standard, it is insufficient to merely place an opposing party on notice that a claim of fraud is asserted. Rather, a party must specifically identify each instance and the particular details of the alleged fraud.

■ **CASE VOCABULARY**

FRAUD: A knowing misrepresentation of the truth or concealment of a material fact to induce another to act to his or her detriment.

NOTICE PLEADING: A procedural system requiring that the pleader give only a short and plain statement of the claim showing that the pleader is entitled to relief, and not a complete detailing of all the facts.

Jones v. Bock

(Prisoner) v. (Warden)

549 U.S. 199, 127 S.Ct. 910 (2007)

PRISONERS MUST EXHAUST THEIR REMEDIES THROUGH THE PRISON SYSTEM
BEFORE BRINGING A LAWSUIT

■ **INSTANT FACTS** A prisoner brought suit for violation of his rights under 42 U.S.C. § 1983, and the Supreme Court consolidated his case with those of other prisoners to determine the pleading requirements applicable to their complaints.

■ **BLACK LETTER RULE** Failure to exhaust administrative remedies is an affirmative defense in prisoner lawsuits, and inmates are therefore not required to specially plead or demonstrate exhaustion in their complaints.

■ **PROCEDURAL BASIS**

Supreme Court consideration of consolidated cases to determine pleading requirements in prisoner litigation.

■ **FACTS**

Jones (P), a prisoner in a Michigan prison, claimed that after he suffered injuries in the prison, the prison staff refused to reassign him to lighter duty work, which allegedly aggravated his injuries. He sued for damages under 42 U.S.C. § 1983, and the Supreme Court consolidated his case with those of other prisoners to decide the issue of whether the requirement of exhausting administrative remedies within the prison system before filing suit is a pleading requirement, which must be satisfied in the plaintiff's complaint, or an affirmative defense, which the defendant must plead and prove.

■ **ISSUE**

Is the failure to exhaust administrative remedies an affirmative defense in prisoner litigation?

■ **DECISION AND RATIONALE**

(Roberts, C.J.) Yes. Failure to exhaust administrative remedies is an affirmative defense in prisoner lawsuits, and inmates are therefore not required to specially plead or demonstrate exhaustion in their complaints. Prisoner litigation accounts for an unrepresentative share of cases in federal court. Many of these cases, alleging violations of civil rights or intolerable prison conditions, have no merit, but our legal system remains committed to guaranteeing that prisoner claims be fairly handled. Congress addressed the challenge of weeding out unmeritorious complaints in the Prisoner Litigation Reform Act, 42 U.S.C. § 1997e *et seq.*, which provides that no § 1983 action may be brought to challenge prison conditions until all administrative remedies have been exhausted. Most courts view the failure to exhaust as an affirmative defense that must be raised by the defendant in its answer, and we agree with the majority. A line of recent decisions confirms that courts should generally not depart from the usual pleading practices of the Federal Rules of Civil Procedure, which regard exhaustion as an affirmative defense. We are not insensitive to the challenges of lower courts in managing their dockets, but adopting different and more onerous pleading rules to deal with particular categories of cases should be done through established rulemaking procedures, not on a case-by-case basis by the courts.

Analysis:

The exhaustion-of-administrative-remedies doctrine is the doctrine providing that, if an administrative remedy is provided by statute or rule, a claimant must first seek relief from the appropriate administrative body before judicial relief becomes available. The purposes of the doctrine are to maintain comity between the courts and administrative agencies, and to ensure that courts will not be burdened by frivolous litigation or suits in which judicial relief is unnecessary. A related doctrine is the exhaustion-of-state-remedies doctrine, which provides that available state remedies must be exhausted in certain types of cases before parties can gain access to the federal courts. A state prisoner, for instance, must exhaust all state remedies before a federal court will hear his petition for a writ of habeas corpus.

■ **CASE VOCABULARY**

ADMINISTRATIVE REMEDY: A nonjudicial remedy provided by an administrative agency. Ordinarily, if an administrative remedy is available, it must be exhausted before a court will hear the case.

AFFIRMATIVE DEFENSE: A defendant's assertion of facts and arguments that, if true, will defeat the plaintiff's or prosecution's claim, even if all the allegations in the complaint are true. The defendant bears the burden of proving an affirmative defense. Examples of affirmative defenses are duress (in a civil case) and insanity and self-defense (in a criminal case).

WRIT OF HABEAS CORPUS: A writ employed to bring a person before a court, most frequently to ensure that the party's imprisonment or detention is not illegal. In addition to being used to test the legality of an arrest or commitment, the writ may be used to obtain review of (1) the regularity of the extradition process, (2) the right to or amount of bail, or (3) the jurisdiction of a court that has imposed a criminal sentence.

Walker v. Norwest Corp.

(Minor) v. (Bank)

108 F.3d 158 (8th Cir. 1997)

THE FAILURE TO ASSERT THE CITIZENSHIP OF ALL DEFENDANTS IN A COMPLAINT
CALLS FOR SANCTIONS

■ INSTANT FACTS The plaintiffs' complaint was dismissed and sanctions were imposed because the plaintiffs failed to assert the citizenship of all defendants necessary to establish diversity jurisdiction.

■ BLACK LETTER RULE Sanctions are appropriate when an attorney, through court submissions, raises allegations or factual contentions that are not supported by evidence or likely to be supported upon reasonable discovery.

■ PROCEDURAL BASIS

Appeal to review a decision of the district court awarding sanctions against the plaintiffs' attorney.

■ FACTS

Walker (P), through his attorney James Harrison Massey, filed a complaint against Norwest Corp. (D) and others in federal district court concerning a dispute over a minor's trust fund. In the complaint, Massey alleged diversity jurisdiction and stated that "the Plaintiff and some of the Defendants are citizens of different states." Specifically, the complaint alleged that all plaintiffs were South Dakota citizens and that Norwest Corp. (D) was a Minnesota corporation, but failed to allege the citizenship of the other defendants. After alerting Massey that the complaint failed to properly allege diversity jurisdiction and requesting his voluntary dismissal of the complaint, Norwest (D) filed a motion to dismiss and a request for sanctions. The federal district court granted the motion to dismiss and ordered Massey to pay $4800 in attorneys' fees and costs as a sanction.

■ ISSUE

Are monetary sanctions appropriate when an attorney fails to assert the citizenship of all defendants in a complaint in order to establish diversity jurisdiction?

■ DECISION AND RATIONALE

(Gibson, J.) Yes. Under Federal Rule of Civil Procedure 11, a court may impose sanctions upon an attorney if it determines that the allegations and factual contentions raised in any pleading, motion, or court submission are not supported by evidence or, with a reasonable opportunity to investigate, are not likely to be supported by evidence. The plaintiffs contend that Rule 11 does not require the level of investigation required to determine the true citizenship of each defendant before filing their complaint. However, it is the plaintiffs' burden to plead the citizenship of each defendant when asserting diversity jurisdiction. While plaintiffs need not definitively establish the citizenship of each defendant, plaintiffs at a minimum must allege in their complaint that none of the defendants share a common citizenship with the plaintiffs, which would destroy the court's diversity jurisdiction. Because the plaintiffs failed to allege the citizenship of all defendants, the court did not abuse its discretion by imposing sanctions.

Nor did the court err in denying the plaintiffs the opportunity to amend their complaint by dismissing those defendants who would destroy diversity jurisdiction. Although Massey raised this argument before the court, Massey again failed to establish the citizenship of all defendants and demonstrate to the court which defendants would destroy jurisdiction. The court "is not obliged to do Massey's research for him." Monetary sanctions were appropriate. Affirmed.

Analysis:

Courts have broad discretion with regard to Rule 11 sanctions. Rule 11, however, is not a rule of ethics. A trial court may not place restrictions on an attorney's authority to practice law or otherwise represent his or her clients. Instead, Rule 11 sanctions are a tool to preserve fairness in the judicial process.

■ CASE VOCABULARY

RULE 11: In federal practice, the procedural rule requiring the attorney of record or the party (if not represented by an attorney) to sign all pleadings, motions, and other papers filed with the court and—by this signing—to represent that the paper is filed in good faith after an inquiry that is reasonable under the circumstances.

SANCTION: A penalty or coercive measure that results from failure to comply with a law, rule, or order.

Christian v. Mattel, Inc.

(Doll Designer) v. (Toy Company)

286 F.3d 1118 (9th Cir. 2003)

NOT ALL LAWYER MISCONDUCT IS SUBJECT TO RULE 11 SANCTIONS

■ **INSTANT FACTS** Christian (P) sued Mattell, Inc. (D) for copyright infringement in federal court over the creation and distribution of a doll.

■ **BLACK LETTER RULE** Rule 11 sanctions are appropriate only when an attorney, through court submissions, raises allegations or factual contentions that are not supported by evidence or likely to be supported with an opportunity to conduct reasonable discovery.

■ **PROCEDURAL BASIS**

Appeal to review a decision of the district court awarding sanctions against the plaintiff's attorney.

■ **FACTS**

Christian (P) created and marketed a doll resembling a college cheerleader, on which she held a copyright. Six years later, Mattell, Inc. (D) created a similar-looking Barbie doll, which Mattell (D) had been producing for several decades. Christian (P), through her attorney James Hicks, sued Mattell (D) in federal district court for copyright infringement, seeking $2.4 million in damages and injunctive relief. Two months later, Mattell (D) moved for summary judgment, demonstrating that it had obtained the copyright for the sculpture of its doll's head years before Christian (P) obtained her copyright. In a follow-up meeting between Hicks and Mattell's (D) attorneys, Mattell (D) attempted to persuade Hicks to dismiss the complaint as frivolous. Hicks refused. Mattell (D) thereafter served Hicks with a motion for Rule 11 sanctions. The court granted Mattell's (D) motion for summary judgment and found that Hicks had filed a meritless complaint without any factual foundation. The court held that a reasonable investigation would have indicated that Mattell's (D) dolls did not infringe upon Christian's (P) copyright and further found Hicks guilty of attorney misconduct, including being sanctioned in prior litigation with Mattell (D), throwing a doll during a meeting with opposing counsel, making discourteous comments to his client during deposition, and making misrepresentations of fact and law during oral arguments. The court ordered Hicks to pay Mattell (D) $501,565 in attorneys' fees as a sanction.

■ **ISSUE**

Did the court abuse its discretion by imposing sanctions, in part, for discovery abuses, past conduct, oral misrepresentations, and other attorney misconduct?

■ **DECISION AND RATIONALE**

(McKeown, J.) Yes. Under Federal Rule of Civil Procedure 11, a court may impose sanctions upon an attorney if it determines that the allegations and factual contentions in any pleading, motion, or other court submission are not supported by evidence or, with a reasonable opportunity to investigate, are not likely to be supported by evidence. As the rule suggests, however, it is limited to court documents signed by an attorney. A court may not impose Rule

---

11 sanctions for misconduct not involving signed court submissions. Accordingly, the court did not abuse its discretion in imposing sanctions related to Hicks's failure to investigate the status of Mattell's (D) copyright, but it did err in considering other instances of misconduct. While the court maintains the inherent power to impose sanctions against those appearing in the courtroom, it may do so only upon "an explicit finding that counsel's conduct constituted or was tantamount to bad faith." Since the court failed to make such a finding, it abused its discretion by imposing sanctions on the totality of Hicks's conduct. On remand, the court must set forth the proper legal and factual basis to support its sanctions order. Remanded.

Analysis:

Under Rule 11, sanctions may be appropriate for improper or frivolous filings in the court. Similarly, a court has the inherent power to sanction courtroom conduct upon a finding of bad faith. Discovery violations are sanctionable under Rule 26(g), including awarding attorneys' fees to an opposing party.

■ **CASE VOCABULARY**

FRIVOLOUS: Lacking a legal basis or legal merit; not serious; not reasonably purposeful, as in a frivolous claim.

FRIVOLOUS CLAIM: A claim that has no legal basis or merit, especially one brought for an unreasonable purpose such as harassment.

FRIVOLOUS SUIT: A lawsuit having no legal basis, often filed to harass or extort money from the defendant.

Zielinski v. Philadelphia Piers, Inc.

(Injured Victim) v. (Alleged Tortfeasor)

139 F.Supp. 408 (E.D.Pa.1956)

ABUSE OF GENERAL DENIAL BACKFIRES WHEN THE COURT EQUATES IT WITH A PRESUMED GENERAL ADMITTANCE

■ **INSTANT FACTS** A man who was hit by a forklift claims that it was owned by large company which denies owning it at the time of the accident.

■ **BLACK LETTER RULE** A general denial will not be valid if any of the allegations being denied have been admitted by both parties as true.

■ **FACTS**

Zielinski (P) suffered physical injuries on February 9, 1953 when his forklift was struck by another forklift. In his complaint for injuries, filed on April 23, 1953, Zielinski named Philadelphia Piers, Inc. (D) as the defendant because the forklift which collided with his had "PPI" written on its side. Thus, Zielinski (P) presumed an agency relationship existed between Johnson, the driver (who would have no money to go after), and Philadelphia Piers (D) (who would have money) as his employer at the time. After the complaint was served, Philadelphia Piers (D) answered it and referred to themselves as "defendant" within the answer. Furthermore, the complaint was also forwarded to Philadelphia Piers, (D) insurance company and they acknowledged responsibility as well. However, at a pretrial conference, information surfaced which made it clear that the business of moving freight on the pier had been sold by Philadelphia Piers (D) to Carload Contractors and Johnson and was switched over to the latter's payroll. In other words, Philadelphia Piers (D) does not believe it shared an agency relationship with Johnson and should, therefore, not be held accountable for any injury caused by him. Thus, Philadelphia Piers (D) generally denied the allegations of Zielinski's complaint. Zielinski (P) responded by filing this motion for a ruling by the court that an agency relationship did exist between Johnson and Philadelphia Piers (D) and that Zielinski (P) was therefore suing the correct defendant.

■ **ISSUE**

Is a general denial valid when at least some of the allegations being denied have been admitted by both parties as true?

■ **DECISION AND RATIONALE**

(Van Dusen, J.) No. A general denial is ineffective when at least some of the claims being denied are clearly true and not at issue. In such a circumstance, the defendant must make a more specific answer. Thus, when Zielinski (P) stated in the pleadings that he was hit and injured by a forklift operated by an agent of Philadelphia Piers (D), a general denial is plainly erroneous. It implies not only the intended denial that the forklift was operated by an agent of Philadelphia Piers (D) but also that Zielinski was injured, which cannot be denied because it was previously admitted as true fact. This finding is supported by two major policy considerations. First, Philadelphia Piers (D) knows that the statute of limitations to file another complaint on a different defendant has already run for Zielinski. Thus, dismissing this complaint would effectively deprive him of any opportunity at redress in violation of established principles of equitable estoppel. Second, when an improper and ineffective answer has been filed knowingly after the plaintiff's statute of limitations has run, an allegation of agency will be instructed to the jury as presumptively admitted by both parties for the purpose of the litigation. Therefore, plaintiff's motion to instruct the jury of the agency relationship between Johnson and Philadelphia Piers (D) is granted.

Analysis:

A defendant has three options when answering a complaint. He can either admit, deny, or plead insufficient information to answer at all. The admissions and denials can either be general, referring to every claim in the complaint, or specific, referring to particular claims as admitted and others as denied. A defendant who chooses to deny any of the claims must be very careful to understand everything that is actually being claimed. Otherwise, the defendant will find himself like Philadelphia Piers (D), where he is denying parts that are debatable as to their truth and parts that have clearly been established as truth. As a result of such an ineffective and erroneous denial, a defendant may be presumed to admit even those facts that he could have effectively denied. While courts are not especially eager to punish defendants for procedural errors and will often allow them to amend the mistakes, there are times when such "punishment" is in the interests of justice, such as in the case of *Zielinski*.

■ **CASE VOCABULARY**

DEPOSITION: Legally admissible witness testimony taken outside court either in the form of oral questioning or written questionnaire.

EQUITABLE ESTOPPEL: The concept of justice which precludes a party from exercising what he would be entitled to if not for some voluntary act of his own which would make it unjust to grant him those rights.

Beeck v. Aquaslide 'N' Dive Corp.

(Slide Victim) v. (Alleged Slide Manufacturer)

562 F.2d 537 (8th Cir.1977)

AN ADMISSION IN A PLEADING CAN BE CHANGED TO A DENIAL IN THE COURT'S DISCRETION

■ **INSTANT FACTS** Defendant admits manufacturing the defective water slide at issue in the case but a year later moves the court to amend the answer to deny manufacture.

■ **BLACK LETTER RULE** A court does not abuse its discretion by allowing an amendment to an answer which initially admitted responsibility for the manufacture of the product at issue but now seeks to deny manufacturing it.

■ **FACTS**

During a company sponsored gathering, Beeck (P) was severely injured at Kimberly Village while using a water slide he claims was negligently manufactured by Aquaslide (D). Kimberly investigated the accident and soon thereafter sent a notice to Aquaslide (D) informing them that one of their Queen Model slides was involved [a kind term for "implicated"]. Aquaslide (D) forwarded this notice to its insurer and an adjuster came out to investigate the slide and question persons who ordered and assembled the slide. The insurance adjuster, as well as investigators for Kimberly Village, indicated that the slide was definitely manufactured by Aquaslide (D). Beeck (P) filed the personal injury complaint which Aquaslide (D) answered, admitting that it "designed, manufactured, assembled and sold" the slide. About six months after the statute of limitations for Beeck's claim had run out (he was on time, though) and a total of one year after the filing of the complaint and answer, the president and owner of Aquaslide visited the sight of the accident himself. From his inspection, he determined that the slide was not Aquaslide's (D) product and then moved the court for leave to amend the answer to deny the slide's manufacture. The court granted the motion and Beeck (P) appealed. Then the court granted a separate jury trial to decide the issue of manufacture which Beeck (P) lost and Beeck (P) appealed this too.

■ **ISSUE**

Is it an abuse of trial court discretion to allow an amendment to an answer from admitting to denying responsibility for the manufacture of the product at issue?

■ **DECISION AND RATIONALE**

(Benson, J.) No. A court does not abuse its discretion by allowing an amendment to an answer which initially admitted responsibility for the manufacture of the product at issue but now seeks to deny manufacturing it. There is substantial authority for this decision both in case law and in the Federal Rules. In *Foman v. Davis* the Supreme Court held that, in the absence of bad faith or dilatory motive on the part of the movant, leave to amend is fully within the discretion of the District court. This holding is rooted in FRCP 15(a) which declares that leave to amend should be "freely given when justice so requires." Applying these principles to the case at hand, the trial court did not abuse its discretion by allowing either the amendment or the trial on the issue. The trial court searched the record for evidence of bad faith and rightfully found none. After all, Aquaslide (D) legitimately relied on the findings of separate

---

insurance adjustors until its president made his own belated investigation and arrived at a contrary conclusion. As to Beeck's (P) contention of prejudice because the statute of limitations had already run prior to the motion to amend, it is unfounded. This presumes that the trial court should have known that Beeck (P) would have lost on the issue at trial or at the mini trial on this particular issue. That is an unreasonable expectation. If anything, to prevent the defendant from denying a disputed factual issue would be prejudicial to it more than to Beeck (P). (Aquaslide would be forced into the ludicrous position of arguing that the slide was not manufactured negligently when it did not manufacture the slide at all!) The blame for this gross error should be shared equally. Thus, the district court ruling is affirmed.

Analysis:

Beeck (P) was not really deprived of a fair trial here—he was just deprived of a trial on the issue of negligence. This is not necessarily a bad thing, because going to trial on all the issues when manufacture was really the essential one would have been a waste of judicial resources. While a day in court belongs to everyone who has a legitimate complaint, it should not be afforded at the expense of other parties. As great as the need may be to insure accountability for negligence, the greater injustice must be to hold the wrong party accountable for it. Many states allow a plaintiff to allege a cause of action against fictitiously named defendants (such as "Doe 1") and later to amend the complaint to substitute a true name. If a fictitious defendant had been named in this case, there probably would be no problem.

■ **CASE VOCABULARY**

NEGLIGENCE: Tort term for the failure to use such standard of care as a reasonable person would in the same circumstances.

STRICT LIABILITY: Tort doctrine of imposing liability for any adverse consequences of a product or act, even when it was not negligent (applies to inherently dangerous products).

AN AMENDMENT TO A PLEADING WILL NOT RELATE BACK UNLESS THERE WAS ENOUGH IN THE ORIGINAL PLEADING TO GIVE NOTICE

■ **INSTANT FACTS** A patient who was disabled after an operation sued the doctor for violation of the informed consent law, and later tried to amend the complaint to include allegations of negligence.

■ **BLACK LETTER RULE** In order to relate back to the time of the original complaint, a proposed amendment must have its basis in the same facts that are alleged in the original complaint.

■ **PROCEDURAL BASIS**

Appeal from a denial of a motion to amend a complaint.

■ **FACTS**

Dr. Baker (D) performed surgery on Judith Moore (P) to remove a blockage of her carotid artery. Baker (D) warned Moore (P) about the surgery and its risks, and Moore (P) signed a consent form. The operation went badly and Moore (P) was permanently and severely disabled. Moore (P) filed her complaint on the last day permitted by the state's statute of limitations, alleging that Baker (D) had violated the state's informed consent law by failing to advise Moore (P) of alternative therapy. Moore (P) later moved to amend her complaint to include allegations of negligence against Baker (D). The district court denied the motion.

■ **ISSUE**

Will the amendment to the complaint relate back to the date of filing the original complaint?

■ **DECISION AND RATIONALE**

(Morgan) No. The statute of limitations will bar Moore's (P) claim of negligence asserted in her amended complaint unless it can be made to relate back to the time of the original complaint, which was filed just before the statute of limitations was about to run. Rule 15(c) permits an amended pleading to relate back to the date of the original pleading whenever the claim or defense asserted in the amended pleading arose out of the conduct, transaction, or occurrence set forth or attempted to be set forth in the original pleading. Thus, *the question is whether the original complaint gave notice to the defendant of the claim that is now being asserted.* We find that it does not. The original complaint focused on Baker's (D) actions before the surgery, whereas the amendment seeks to focus on his actions during and after the surgery. There is nothing in the original complaint that would put Baker (D) on notice that Moore (P) might claim that he was negligent. In order to recover on her negligence claim. Moore would have to prove completely different facts than would otherwise have been required for the informed consent claim of the original complaint. We conclude that Moore's (P) negligence claim does not arise out of the same conduct, transaction, or occurrence as the claims in the original complaint. Therefore, the proposed new claims are barred by the statute of limitations. Affirmed.

Analysis:

Notice that the plaintiff is attempting to get the amendment to relate back to the date of the filing of the original pleading in order to beat the statute of limitations. If the statute of limitations had not run, the plaintiff would be able to simply amend the complaint without a problem. Why didn't Moore (P) just file sooner to avoid the whole problem? Sometimes the applicable statute of limitations is very short, and it will start to run before the plaintiff even discovers the problem, and some people hesitate to contact a lawyer or don't even realize until too late that they have a legal right to compensation for damages that they've suffered. Even after a lawyer has been contacted, if there is some time until the statute of limitations will run, the lawyer will try to settle the case without filing suit. For example, in a medical malpractice case the attorney will talk directly to the doctor's insurer to try to negotiate a settlement without going to court.

■ CASE VOCABULARY

INFORMED CONSENT: The duty of a doctor to fully warn the patient about all of the risks involved in a surgery and get the patient's consent before performing an operation.

PROFESSIONAL NEGLIGENCE: When a professional, such as a doctor or lawyer, does not perform his or her professional duties with the same amount of care that a reasonable, prudent professional would use in that particular case.

RELATION BACK: When the amendment to a pleading is treated as if it were filed on the same date as the original pleading was filed.

RELATION BACK IS FAIR IF THE OPERATIONAL FACTS IN THE ORIGINAL CLAIM PUT DEFENDANT ON NOTICE THAT THE AMENDED CLAIM COULD BE BROUGHT

■ **INSTANT FACTS** Patient originally sued the Rehab Center for negligent maintenance of its basketball court, and later tried to amend the complaint to include a claim for counseling malpractice.

■ **BLACK LETTER RULE** A claim will relate back if the operational facts set out in the original complaint are sufficient to put the defendant on notice that the amended claim could be brought.

■ **PROCEDURAL BASIS**

Motion to amend the complaint.

■ **FACTS**

Bonerb (P) was a patient in the Richard J. Caron Foundation's ("the Foundation") (D) drug and alcohol rehabilitation facility. Bonerb was injured when he slipped and fell while playing basketball as part of the Foundation's (D) mandatory exercise program. Bonerb (P) claimed that the Foundation (D) negligently maintained that basketball court. A year after the complaint was filed, and after the statute of limitations had run, Bonerb (P) has filed a motion to amend his complaint to include a cause of action for counseling malpractice. The Foundation (D) objects, claiming that the counseling malpractice claim does not relate back to the original pleading and will therefore be barred by the statute of limitations.

■ **ISSUE**

Does the malpractice claim relate back to the original negligence claim?

■ **DECISION AND RATIONALE**

(Heckman) Yes. Rule 15(a) provides that leave to amend a complaint should be freely granted absent undue prejudice to the other party, undue delay by the moving party, or bad faith. However, amendment to add a time-barred claim would be futile unless it will relate back to the date of the original complaint. A claim will relate back if the operational facts set out in the original complaint are sufficient to put the defendant on notice that the amended claim could be brought. The principle for this is that one who has been given notice of litigation concerning a given transaction or occurrence has been provided with all the protection that statutes of limitation are designed to afford. In this case, the allegations in the original and amended complaints derive from the same operative facts involving injury suffered by Bonerb (P). The original complaint alleged that participation in the exercise program was mandatory and that Bonerb's (P) injury was caused by the Foundation's (D) failure to properly supervise and instruct Bonerb (P). These allegations are sufficient to alert the Foundation (D) to the possibility of a claim based on negligent performance of professional duties. That is all that is required for relation back under Rule 15(c). Motion granted.

Analysis:

A statute of limitations is a harsh incentive for bringing actions in a timely fashion—claims are barred if the statute of limitations has run. The purpose of the statute of limitations is to prevent the burden of litigating stale claims, forcing a defendant to defend long after memories have faded, witnesses have died or disappeared, and evidence has been destroyed. In the case of a proposed amendment, since the case is ongoing anyway, the purpose of preventing a stale claim has been satisfied. However, a defendant still needs to have notice so that he can build a defense. Also, consider the tension between Rule 15(a) [freely granting leave to amend] and Rule 15(c) [relation back only under certain circumstances]. These rules could be seen as inconsistent—one being liberal in granting leave to amend and the other being very stingy in granting leave to amend. Under Rule 15(a), amendment is usually done very early in the proceeding—before the answer or sometime during discovery. On the other hand, under 15(c), the real problem arises after some discovery has been done, a new claim has been discovered, but the statute of limitations has run. It may be that Rule 15(c) is less favorable to plaintiffs because it is also less favorable to defendants by allowing otherwise time-barred claims to be brought. The court here allowed amendment.

■ CASE VOCABULARY

OPERATIONAL FACTS: Facts that, if different or absent, would affect the outcome of the case; facts giving rise to the claim.

CHAPTER 7

Discovery

Davis v. Precoat Metals

Instant Facts: Davis (P) and others sought discovery of past discrimination complaints lodged against the defendant in the plaintiffs' workplace.

Black Letter Rule: A party may seek discovery of any matter, not privileged, that is relevant to the claim or defense of any party so long as the request cannot be obtained from a more convenient, less burdensome source.

Steffan v. Cheney

Instant Facts: A naval officer refused to answer deposition questions about his sexual conduct in his suit challenging an administrative board's recommendation that he be discharged based on his admission that he was a homosexual.

Black Letter Rule: Evidence is not relevant if it does not relate to a matter pertinent to the decision of the case.

Silvestri v. General Motors Corp.

Instant Facts: Silvestri (P) was injured in a crash when the airbag in the car he was driving failed to deploy, but the car was repaired before suit was filed, so there was no evidence as to whether the airbag was defective, and the court therefore dismissed the case.

Black Letter Rule: Sanctionable spoliation is the destruction or material alteration of evidence or the failure to preserve property for another's use as evidence in pending or reasonably foreseeable litigation.

Hickman v. Taylor

Instant Facts: Hickman (P) sought to obtain copies of written statements and descriptions of oral interviews acquired by Fortenbaugh, the opposing counsel.

Black Letter Rule: A party is not entitled, without a showing of good cause, to obtain copies of an opposing attorney's notes and memoranda acquired from interviews with witnesses.

Thompson v. The Haskell Co.

Instant Facts: An employee suing an employer for sexual harassment seeks to protect a psychologist's report regarding the employee.

Black Letter Rule: A party cannot compel discovery of the opinions or findings of a non-testifying expert hired by the opposing party in preparation of litigation unless there are no other practical means to obtain the facts and opinions contained in that report.

Chiquita International Ltd. v. M/V Bolero Reefer

Instant Facts: A carrier, sued by a shipper for loss and damage to a cargo of bananas, sought to depose and discover any documents held by a non-testifying expert witness hired by the shipper to examine the cause of the damage.

Black Letter Rule: Discovery of an opposing party's non-testifying expert cannot be permitted under the exceptional circumstances exception where the party seeking discovery had an opportunity to examine the subject of the expert's opinion.

Stalnaker v. Kmart Corp.

Instant Facts: An employee, who was sued by a former co-worker for sexual harassment, sought a protective order preventing the co-worker from deposing four non-party witnesses in order to determine whether they had any romantic conduct or sexually related activities with the co-worker.

Black Letter Rule: A party seeking a protective order must establish good cause for the order by submitting a particular and specific demonstration of fact.

Zubulake v. UBS Warburg LLC

Instant Facts: An employee suing her employer for gender discrimination sought an "adverse inference" instruction after she learned that the employer failed to preserve e-mails that she alleged would support her claim.

Black Letter Rule: A party seeking an adverse inference instruction must meet three requirements: it must establish that the party having control over the evidence had an obligation to preserve it when it was destroyed, that the records were destroyed with a culpable state of mind, and that the destroyed evidence was relevant to the party's claim or defense.

PAST DISCRIMINATON ALLEGATIONS ARE RELEVANT

■ **INSTANT FACTS** Davis (P) and others sought discovery of past discrimination complaints lodged against the defendant in the plaintiffs' workplace.

■ **BLACK LETTER RULE** A party may seek discovery of any matter, not privileged, that is relevant to the claim or defense of any party so long as the request cannot be obtained from a more convenient, less burdensome source.

■ **PROCEDURAL BASIS**

Consideration of the plaintiffs' motion to compel discovery.

■ **FACTS**

Davis (P) and others sued Precoat Metals (D) for discrimination on the basis of race and national origin in violation of Title VII of the Civil Rights Act of 1964. The plaintiffs alleged that while employed by Precoat Metals (D), they were subjected to racial comments by management-level employees; suffered discrimination in their job placement, work assignments, promotions and discipline; and endured retaliation after complaining about the discrimination. During discovery, the plaintiffs requested that the defendant disclose any past racial or national origin discrimination complaints asserted against it by employees at the same plant in which the plaintiffs worked. The defendants refused to disclose information pertaining to past discrimination, arguing that the request was overbroad and any complaints were not relevant to the plaintiffs' claims. The plaintiffs filed a motion to compel discovery.

■ **ISSUE**

Are the plaintiffs' discovery requests relating to past race and national origin discrimination complaints against the defendants relevant to their claims?

■ **DECISION AND RATIONALE**

(Nolan, Mag. J.) Yes. Under Federal Rule of Civil Procedure 26(b)(1), a party may seek discovery of "any matter, not privileged, that is relevant to the claim or defense of any party," and it need not be admissible at trial. Information is relevant when it is "reasonably calculated to lead to the discovery of admissible evidence." However, when relevant evidence is unreasonably cumulative or duplicative, when it could be obtained from a more convenient, less burdensome, and less expensive source, or when the burden on the opposing party outweighs the likely benefit of the evidence, the court may preclude or limit discovery. Here, the evidence sought by the plaintiffs may be relevant to establish pretext, an element of their Title VII claims. The plaintiffs' request is restricted to a specific period of time, limited to complaints of race and national origin discrimination, and confined to the specific plant in which the plaintiffs work. Because the plaintiffs' request is relevant to their claims and has been narrowly tailored to specific discoverable information, the defendants must disclose the information. Motion granted.

Analysis:

The discovery rules of the Federal Rules of Civil Procedure operate independently of the evidentiary rules of the Federal Rules of Evidence. To be discoverable, information need not be admissible at trial. Instead, information is properly discoverable if it is likely to lead to other discoverable or admissible evidence. In this sense, the Federal Rules of Civil Procedure are broader than the Federal Rules of Evidence.

■ CASE VOCABULARY

MOTION TO COMPEL DISCOVERY: A party's request that the court force the party's opponent to respond to the party's discovery request (as to answer interrogatories or produce the documents).

RELEVANT: Logically connected and tending to prove or disprove a matter in issue; having appreciably probative value—that is, rationally tending to persuade people of the probability or possibility of some alleged fact.

(Naval Officer) v. (United States Secretary of Defense)

920 F.2d 74 (D.C.Cir. 1990)

EVIDENCE IS NOT RELEVANT IF IT DOES NOT RELATE TO A MATTER PERTINENT TO THE DECISION OF THE CASE

■ **INSTANT FACTS** A naval officer refused to answer deposition questions about his sexual conduct in his suit challenging an administrative board's recommendation that he be discharged based on his admission that he was a homosexual.

■ **BLACK LETTER RULE** Evidence is not relevant if it does not relate to a matter pertinent to the decision of the case.

■ **PROCEDURAL BASIS**

An appeal of a district court ruling dismissing the plaintiff's cause of action for failure to comply with a discovery order.

■ **FACTS**

Joseph C. Steffan (P) was a naval officer who resigned from the military in 1987 after an administrative board recommended his discharge after Steffan's (P) admission that he was a homosexual. He was not discharged for any homosexual conduct. In 1988, Steffan (P) filed an action against the government (D), represented by then Secretary of Defense, Dick Cheney, to challenge the constitutionality of the regulations that required the discharge of admitted homosexuals. During the discovery phase, Steffan (P) [who decided to resort to his own "don't ask, don't tell" policy] refused to answer deposition questions regarding whether he engaged in homosexual conduct while in the Navy and asserted his Fifth Amendment privilege against self-incrimination. The district court, after issuing a prior warning, dismissed Steffan's (P) case for failure to comply with the discovery order. Steffan (P) appealed to the appellate court.

■ **ISSUE**

Is evidence relevant if it does not speak to a matter pertinent to the decision of the case?

■ **DECISION AND RATIONALE**

(Court) No. The district court acknowledged that "the record is clear that [Steffan] was separated from the naval academy based on his admission that he is a homosexual rather than on any evidence of his conduct". However, the district court found that questions about his homosexual conduct were "highly relevant" because the navy could discharge individuals engaged in homosexual conduct. The district court held that "in seeking reinstatement and award of his diploma, [Steffan] through his claims has placed in issue whether he is qualified for such relief." [Any judicial review of an administrative action, including administrative actions by the military, is confined to "the grounds upon which the record discloses that [the] action was based"]. *SEC v. Chenery Corp.*, 318 U.S. 80, 87 (1943). In this case, Steffan (P) is challenging the Navy's administrative action finding him unfit for military service because he stated he was a homosexual. Since this was the basis for his discharge, the issue of whether he engaged in potentially disqualifying conduct is not relevant. Evidence is not relevant if it does not relate to a matter pertinent to the decision of the case. Therefore, the district court

---

erred in finding the issue of homosexual conduct to be relevant in this case. The judgment of the district court is reversed and remanded for further proceedings consistent with this opinion.

Analysis:

This opinion rests on whether the disputed evidence is relevant to a fact of consequence in the case. If a person is being sued for employment discrimination, evidence of the employer's propensities for pedophilia would not be relevant. This is because the pedophilia is not a fact of consequence in the case. The important issue is whether the employer discriminated against the plaintiff in the hiring process. Similarly, in this case, Steffan (P) was recommended for discharge for admitting he was a homosexual, not for homosexual conduct. The record clearly stated that his admission was the basis of the government's (D) decision. His admission was a fact of consequence. Therefore, while evidence of homosexual conduct may prove that Steffan (P) was a homosexual, this was not at issue because he was not discharged for such conduct.

■ **CASE VOCABULARY**

CONSTRUCTIVE DISCHARGE: A discharge not necessarily in fact, but by law.

VEL NON: Literally "or not"; or the absence of it. "This case does not hinge on the issue of sexual conduct vel non".

AN ACCIDENT VICTIM CLAIMING A DEFECTIVE AIRBAG HAD A DUTY TO PROVIDE THE MANUFACTURER WITH AN OPPORTUNITY TO INSPECT

■ **INSTANT FACTS** Silvestri (P) was injured in a crash when the airbag in the car he was driving failed to deploy, but the car was repaired before suit was filed, so there was no evidence as to whether the airbag was defective, and the court therefore dismissed the case.

■ **BLACK LETTER RULE** Sanctionable spoliation is the destruction or material alteration of evidence or the failure to preserve property for another's use as evidence in pending or reasonably foreseeable litigation.

■ **PROCEDURAL BASIS**

Federal appellate court review of a district court judgment dismissing the action.

■ **FACTS**

Silvestri (P) was involved in a single-vehicle crash when he was driving his landlord's Chevrolet Monte Carlo, which was manufactured by General Motors. He was intoxicated and driving too fast when he lost control of the car and it struck a utility pole. The airbag did not deploy on impact, and, although Silvestri (P) was wearing his seatbelt, he suffered severe facial lacerations and bone fractures, permanently disfiguring his face. While he was still in the hospital, Silvestri's (P) parents engaged two accident reconstructionists, who concluded that the airbag was defective, but neither Silvestri (P) nor his attorney contacted General Motors (D) as the constructionists advised until filing suit three years later, prior to which time the vehicle had been repaired. The federal district court dismissed the case, finding that the vehicle in an unrepaired state would have been the only evidence from which General Motors (D) could construct a defense, and the plaintiff appealed.

■ **ISSUE**

Did Silvestri's (P) conduct in failing to preserve the car in its unrepaired state constitute spoliation of evidence subject to the sanction of dismissal?

■ **DECISION AND RATIONALE**

(Niemeyer, J.) Yes. Sanctionable spoliation is the destruction or material alteration of evidence or the failure to preserve property for another's use as evidence in pending or reasonably foreseeable litigation. The right to impose sanctions for spoliation arises from the court's inherent power to control the judicial process, but the power is limited to that necessary to redress conduct that *abuses* the judicial power. The plaintiff argues that he was not responsible for any spoliation here because the car was not his, and that even if he were, dismissal was too harsh a sanction. We disagree. Although the court must find some degree of fault before imposing sanctions, and dismissal should be avoided if a lesser sanction will suffice, we find that dismissal was appropriate in this case. Silvestri (P) may not have owned the vehicle, but he still had an obligation to inform General Motors (D) and provide it with an opportunity to inspect the evidence before filing suit, and breaching this duty constitutes spoliation. Moreover, the spoliation in this case was highly prejudicial to General Motors (D), denying it access to the only evidence from which it could prepare a defense. Under those circumstances, and even though the degree of Silvestri's (P) fault is not entirely certain, we find that the district court did not err in dismissing the case. Affirmed.

Analysis:

Note that the parties here argued that the law of New York—where the accident occurred—governed the consideration of spoliation concepts in this case, but the court concluded that federal law applied, because the right to sanction for spoliation derives from the inherent power of the court, not substantive law. The court is applying the Erie doctrine, pursuant to which a federal court exercising diversity jurisdiction over a case that does not involve a federal question must apply the substantive law of the state where the court sits. Because a procedural, rather than substantive, question was before the court, federal law applied.

■ **CASE VOCABULARY**

SPOLIATION: The intentional destruction, mutilation, alteration, or concealment of evidence, usually a document. If proved, spoliation may be used to establish that the evidence was unfavorable to the party responsible.

(Representative of Decedent) v. (Tugboat Owners)

329 U.S. 495, 67 S.Ct. 385 (1947)

ABSENT A SHOWING OF NEED, AN ATTORNEY'S WORK PRODUCT IS BEYOND THE SCOPE OF DISCOVERY

■ **INSTANT FACTS** Hickman (P) sought to obtain copies of written statements and descriptions of oral interviews acquired by Fortenbaugh, the opposing counsel.

■ **BLACK LETTER RULE** A party is not entitled, without a showing of good cause, to obtain copies of an opposing attorney's notes and memoranda acquired from interviews with witnesses.

■ **PROCEDURAL BASIS**

Writ of certiorari reviewing reversal of order for contempt and order to respond to discovery request.

■ **FACTS**

This suit arises out of the mysterious sinking of the tugboat "J.M. Taylor," an accident which killed five crew members. Hickman (P), the representative of a deceased crew member, brought suit against the tug owners and the Baltimore & Ohio Railroad, whose cars were being tugged at the time of the accident. The tug owners were represented by Fortenbaugh, an attorney who privately interviewed the survivors and other witnesses prior to the institution of the lawsuit. Hickman (P) submitted interrogatories to the tug owners seeking the production of written statements and other memoranda acquired by Fortenbaugh, as well as detailed accounts of any oral statements made to Fortenbaugh. The tug owners, through Fortenbaugh, declined to answer some interrogatories or produce the documents, claiming that the requests called for privileged matter and constituted an attempt to obtain Fortenbaugh's private files. The District Court, sitting en banc, held that the requested matters were not privileged. Accordingly, the Court ordered the tug owners and Fortenbaugh to answer the interrogatories and produce the documents.

■ **ISSUE**

Are all of an attorney's files related to an incident open to discovery by the opposing party?

■ **DECISION AND RATIONALE**

(Murphy, J.) No. Even with liberal discovery rules, not all of an attorney's files are open to discovery by the opposing party. Rule 26(b) provides necessary limitations on discovery when the inquiry encroaches upon the recognized domains of privilege. In the case at hand, the memoranda, statements and mental impressions in issue and in Fortenbaugh's possession fall outside the scope of the attorney-client privilege. Nevertheless, they are not freely discoverable by Hickman (P). Hickman (P) had an adequate opportunity to seek discovery of the same basic facts, through inquiries and production requests propounded on Fortenbaugh and on the parties to the lawsuit, and through direct interviews with the witnesses themselves. Hickman (P) showed no compelling reason why he should be entitled to the information in

---

Fortenbaugh's files, and he did not indicate that the denial of such production would unduly prejudice the preparation of his case. An attorney's work product may be discovered where relevant and non-privileged facts remain hidden in an attorney's file and where production of those facts is essential to the preparation of the opposing party's case. However, the policy against invading the privacy of an attorney's work product is so essential that the party seeking the production must bear the burden. Hickman (P) failed to make the requisite showing. Further, as to the oral statements made by witnesses to Fortenbaugh, no showing of necessity is sufficient to justify production. It should be noted that procedural irregularities existed in Hickman's (P) discovery requests, although these irregularities are insufficient in themselves to deny production. Hickman was incorrect in propounding Rule 33 interrogatories and seeking the production of documents, and Rule 34 could not have been used to obtain documents from a non-party such as Fortenbaugh. Hickman (P) should have taken Fortenbaugh's deposition under Rule 26 and attempted to force Fortenbaugh to produce the materials by way of a subpoena duces tecum in accordance with Rule 45. Regardless, Hickman (P) would have had no unqualified right to discovery of Fortenbaugh's private files. Affirmed.

■ **CONCURRENCE**

(Jackson, J.) Hickman (P) has no right to receive a detailed account of any oral statements made to Fortenbaugh. In arguing that such discovery is permissible, Hickman (P) erroneously maintains that the Rules were created to do away with the "battle of wits" between counsel, effectively placing all counsel on equal footing. Discovery was never intended to diminish the adversarial nature of common law trials. Requiring an attorney to recount every statement a witness has uttered would create severe hardship for that attorney. It is almost impossible to accurately record the exact accounts of a witness, and whenever a witness's testimony at trial differed slightly from the attorney's account, the opposing counsel could impeach the witness using the attorney's account. Moreover, in the situation at hand, Hickman (P) gives no reason why he cannot interview the witnesses himself. In addition, Hickman (P) has no right to use the signed statements acquired by Fortenbaugh in the case at hand. Production of such statements is governed by Rule 34, which requires the party seeking discovery to show good cause. Hickman (P) did not make such an application here. Thus, I agree to the affirmance of the Court of Appeals.

Analysis:

This case analyzes the extent to which a party has access to an opposing attorney's "work product," information obtained by counsel in preparation for trial. The literal language of the initial Federal Rules allowed virtually unlimited access to the discovery of such information. However, this case creates an exception to the unlimited access approach, requiring the party to show a need for obtaining an opposing counsel's work product. And as the opinion states, this need must be substantial. A party who can question the same witnesses, and obtain much the same information in other ways, has no right to reap the benefits of another party's or another attorney's hard work. Notice that this work-product exemption applies only to materials prepared in anticipation of trial. Thus, statements of witnesses taken in the ordinary course of business, outside of pending litigation, remain open to discovery.

■ **CASE VOCABULARY**

WORK PRODUCT: Materials prepared and statements obtained in preparation of a lawsuit for trial.

Thompson v. The Haskell Co.

(Employee) v. (Employer)

65 Fair Empl.Prac.Cas. (BNA) 1088 (M.D.Fla.1994)

A PARTY CANNOT COMPEL DISCOVERY OF THE OPINIONS OR FINDINGS OF THE OPPOSING PARTY'S NON-TESTIFYING EXPERT UNLESS THERE ARE EXCEPTIONAL CIRCUMSTANCES

■ **INSTANT FACTS** An employee suing an employer for sexual harassment seeks to protect a psychologist's report regarding the employee.

■ **BLACK LETTER RULE** A party cannot compel discovery of the opinions or findings of a non-testifying expert hired by the opposing party in preparation of litigation unless there are no other practical means to obtain the facts and opinions contained in that report.

■ **PROCEDURAL BASIS**

A motion to shield from discovery documents relating to a psychological report.

■ **FACTS**

Thompson (P) sued her employer, Haskell Company (D1), and her supervisor, Zona (D2), for sexual harassment after being fired on June 5, 1992. Thompson (P) alleged she was fired because she did not "acquiesce to the advances of [Zona]" and her termination reduced her "to a severely depressed emotional state". Thompson (P) hired an attorney who retained a psychologist, Dr. Lucas, to perform a diagnostic review and personality profile of Thompson (P). On June 15, 1992, Dr. Lucas prepared a psychological report. Haskell Company (D1) sought discovery of Dr. Lucas' report. On May 13, 1994, Thompson (P) filed a motion for a protective order to prevent Haskell Company (D1) from discovering the report. Thompson (P) argued that Rules 26(b)(3)-(4) of the Federal Rules of Civil Procedure protected the psychological report from discovery. Rule 26(b)(4)(B) provides that opinions and facts held by a non-testifying expert who has been retained or employed by the opposing party in anticipation of litigation cannot be discovered except as provided for under Rule 35(b) or if there is a showing of exceptional circumstances where it is impracticable for the party seeking discovery to obtain the same facts or opinions on the same subject by other means.

■ **ISSUE**

Can a party compel discovery of the opinions or findings of a non-testifying expert's report, retained by the opposing party in preparation of litigation, where there are no other means to obtain the facts and opinions contained in that report?

■ **DECISION AND RATIONALE**

(Snyder) Yes. Dr. Lucas' psychological report was made just ten days after her termination from the Haskell Company (D1) and is "highly probative" of Thompson's (P) depressed emotional state. This report is still discoverable under Rule 26(b)(4) because the information contained in the report cannot be obtained by other means. Under Rule 26(b)(4), an opposing party's expert's opinions or facts retained in anticipation of litigation cannot be discovered unless exceptional circumstances make it impracticable for the party to discover the facts or opinions by other means. In this case, there exists no other report regarding Thompson's (P) state of mind made during the weeks immediately following her termination. In a similar case, the court found that "independent examinations . . . pursuant to Rule 35 would not contain equivalent information". *Dixon v. Capellini,* 88 F.R.D. 1, 3 (M.D. Pa. 1980). Therefore, with these facts, there exist exceptional circumstances allowing for the disclosure of Dr. Lucas' report. The motion is denied.

Analysis:

Experts hired by parties are not independent experts, but are usually retained by attorneys to prove certain facts or opinions that are essential to their case. Thus, these experts are acting, in a sense, as agents of the attorney. Therefore, it would seem logical to expand the work product rule to these experts, because often they are a mere extension of the attorney's legal theory regarding the case. This is especially true if the attorney decides the expert should not testify, such as when the expert develops a finding or opinion that is unfavorable to the attorney's case. The disclosure in court of such an adverse finding could destroy the case of the party who employed that expert. However, if an expert retained by the party does not testify at trial, the opposing party does not have the opportunity to discover relevant information. The opposing party may find the information that this expert holds by other means, but a difficult situation arises if the information sought is simply not discoverable by other means. In such a situation, Rule 26(b)(4) opens the door and makes the expert's work product discoverable.

■ **CASE VOCABULARY**

ARGUENDO: For the sake of argument.

Chiquita International Ltd. v. M/V Bolero Reefer

(Shipper) v. (Carrier)

1994 WL 177785 (S.D.N.Y.1994)

THE EXCEPTIONAL CIRCUMSTANCES EXCEPTION DOES NOT APPLY WHERE THE PARTY SEEKING DISCOVERY HAD AN OPPORTUNITY TO EXAMINE THE SUBJECT OF THE EXPERT'S OPINION

■ **INSTANT FACTS** A carrier, sued by a shipper for loss and damage to a cargo of bananas, sought to depose and discover any documents held by a non-testifying expert witness hired by the shipper to examine the cause of the damage.

■ **BLACK LETTER RULE** Discovery of an opposing party's non-testifying expert cannot be permitted under the exceptional circumstances exception where the party seeking discovery had an opportunity to examine the subject of the expert's opinion.

■ **PROCEDURAL BASIS**

A hearing on a motion to prohibit a discovery request.

■ **FACTS**

Chiquita International (P) employed International Reefer Services (D) ("International Reefer") to ship 154,660 boxes of bananas from Ecuador to Germany aboard the ship Bolero Reefer. However, Chiquita International (P) alleged that the ship's loading cranes and side-ports were defective and allowed only 111,660 boxes to be loaded. The remaining 43,000 boxes of bananas were left in Ecuador and were thrown away. The cargo that did arrive in Germany arrived in poor condition. Shortly after the ship arrived in Germany, Chiquita International (P) hired Joseph Winer, a marine surveyor, to inspect the ship and the loading gear. After the inspection, Chiquita International (P) [went bananas] and sued International Reefer (D). International Reefer (D) sought to depose Mr. Winer as a witness and compelled disclosure of documents he prepared in connection to his inspection. Chiquita objected on the ground that Mr. Winer is a non-testifying expert who is protected from discovery under Rule 26(b)(4)(B). International Reefer (D) claims that Mr. Winer is not an expert but a witness, and, even if he is an expert, discovery is warranted because he was the only surveyor who inspected the vessel shortly after it arrived in Germany.

■ **ISSUE**

Can discovery of an opposing party's non-testifying expert be permitted under the exceptional circumstances exception where the party seeking discovery had an opportunity to examine the subject of the expert's opinion?

■ **DECISION AND RATIONALE**

(Francis) No. A non-testifying expert is immune from discovery except where there are exceptional circumstances that make it impossible or highly impracticable for the party seeking the information to obtain facts or opinions on the same subject by other means. Mr. Winer qualifies as a non-testifying expert because he is a marine engineer who was hired by Chiquita (P) to inspect the vessel in question, and Chiquita (P) is not calling him as a witness. He is an expert because he used his technical knowledge and background to offer an opinion

---

to Chiquita (P). While Mr. Winer learned "facts" firsthand and not from the observations of others, this does not disqualify him as an expert. The Federal Rules understand that experts may base their opinions on their own firsthand investigations. In addition, the Federal Rules specifically protect the "facts known or opinions held" by a non-testifying expert. Therefore, distinguishing between fact and opinion is irrelevant and Rule 26(b)(4)(B) applies. International Reefer (D) further argues that discovery still should be permitted under the exceptional circumstances clause of Rule 26(b)(4)(B). However, this argument has no merit since International Reefer (D) had an opportunity to send its own expert to the scene when the ship arrived in Germany. There were no forces beyond its control that would have prevented such an inspection by International Reefer (D). Furthermore, during the three week trip to Germany, International Reefer's (D) employees had the exclusive opportunity to inspect the ship and its cranes. Therefore, permitting discovery where International Reefer (D) failed to hire, in a timely manner, its own marine surveyor to investigate "would permit the exceptional circumstances exception to swallow Rule 26(b)(4)(B)". Finally, International Reefer (D) argues that if it is prohibited from deposing Mr. Winer, it should be given access to the documents he prepared as result of its inspection. However, Rule 26(b)(4)(B) also applies to document discovery of non-testifying experts as well. Nevertheless, International Reefer (D) may discover information provided to Mr. Winer by others provided that this information does not reflect Mr. Winer's own observations or opinions. International Reefer's (D) request to take the deposition of Joseph Winer is denied and Chiquita (P) will produce information from Mr. Winer's files that do not contain his observations and opinions or are otherwise privileged.

Analysis:

The exceptional circumstances clause was included in Rule 26(b)(4)(B) in fairness to parties who were unable to examine a critical piece of evidence before it was lost, destroyed, or altered. However, this exception carries with it a notion of responsibility on the party seeking discovery. If the party seeking discovery did in fact have an opportunity to inspect the evidence in question and failed to do so in a timely fashion, then permitting the exception to apply would effectively allow the party seeking discovery to obtain expert testimony and information. Thus, if the party seeking discovery passed on an opportunity that it could have used to examine the evidence in question, it cannot later conveniently benefit by capitalizing on the fruits of the opposing party's efforts.

■ **CASE VOCABULARY**

FORECLOSED: Stopped or prevented from doing something.

Stalnaker v. Kmart Corp.

(Employee) v. (Corporation and Co-Worker)

71 Fair Empl. Prac. Cas. (BNA) 705 (1996)

A PARTY SEEKING A PROTECTIVE ORDER MUST ESTABLISH GOOD CAUSE FOR THE ORDER

■ **INSTANT FACTS** An employee, who was sued by a former co-worker for sexual harassment, sought a protective order preventing the co-worker from deposing four non-party witnesses in order to determine whether they had any romantic conduct or sexually related activities with the co-worker.

■ **BLACK LETTER RULE** A party seeking a protective order must establish good cause for the order by submitting a particular and specific demonstration of fact.

■ **PROCEDURAL BASIS**

Consideration of a protective order filed by the defendant to prohibit the plaintiff from deposing certain non-party witnesses.

■ **FACTS**

Stalnaker (P) was an employee of Kmart (D1) corporation. She filed suit against both Kmart (D1) and a fellow employee, Donald Graves (D2), alleging that he created a hostile working environment and sexually harassed her by engaging in inappropriate touching. [Apparently Stalnaker (P) wasn't the only woman whom Graves (D2) tried to work his charms on], so Stalnaker (P) issued depositions for four non-party witnesses who had relationships with Graves (D2). Graves (D2) moved for a protective order protecting these witnesses from discovery, especially regarding any voluntary romantic conduct or any sexually related activities with Graves (D2). Stalnaker (P) opposed Graves' (D2) motion.

■ **ISSUE**

Can the discovery of information potentially embarrassing and annoying to a party or non-party be limited?

■ **DECISION AND RATIONALE**

(Judge) Yes. While Rule 26 of the *Federal Rules of Civil Procedure* "permits a broad scope of discovery", a court may issue protective orders to either totally prohibit or limit the scope of discovery on certain matters. According to *Federal Rules of Civil Procedure* Rule 26(c), a court has the discretion to issue a protective order upon good cause where "justice requires to protect a party or person from annoyance, embarrassment, oppression, or undue burden or expense" or where the inquiry reaches "into areas that are clearly outside the scope of appropriate discovery". *Caldwell v. Life Ins. Co. of N. Am.*, 165 F.R.D. 633, 637 (D. Kan. 1996). The party seeking a protective order must establish good cause showing "a particular and specific demonstration of fact, as distinguished from stereotyped and conclusory statements." *Gulf Oil Co. v. Bernard*, 452 U.S. 89, 102 n. 16 (1981). In addition, the *Federal Rules of Evidence*, Rule 412, provides that ["[e]vidence offered to prove that any alleged victim has engaged in other sexual behavior" or "to prove the any alleged victim's sexual predisposition" is not admissible in criminal or civil actions involving sexual misconduct]. Rule 412 was designed to protect the victim of sexual abuse against invasion of privacy,

---

embarrassment, and stereotyping that can be associated with the public disclosure of intimate sexual practices and encourages victims to initiate and participate in legal proceedings against the their abusers. However, Rule 412 does not apply in this case because Graves (D2) is not the victim of sexual misconduct. Nevertheless, Graves (D2) has shown good cause to limit discovery of voluntary romances and sexual activities of the non-party witnesses to the extent they have no relationship to the allegations against Kmart (D1). Graves (D2) asserts that the witnesses were not involved in the creation of the hostile work environment, the sexual harassment claim, or otherwise wronged Stalnaker (P). In addition, none of these witnesses have complained about sexual harassment. Furthermore, inquiry into such activities will also constitute an invasion of their privacy. Stalnaker (P) argues that these witnesses may possess relevant information about sexual harassment at Kmart (D1); however, she would agree to a protective order preventing disclosure to any third party. Consequently, discovery is limited to inquiry about "any voluntary romantic or sexual activities with Mr. Graves (D2) to the extent they show any conduct on his part to encourage, solicit, or influence any employee of Graves (D2) to engage or continue in such activities." The parties will utilize such discovery only for the purposes of litigation and the information will not be disclosed any third parties. The court grants in part and overrules in part the Graves' (D2) motion for a protective order.

Analysis:

This opinion shows that, while certain evidence may have relevance, its value may be outweighed by the embarrassment, annoyance, or invasion of privacy the disclosure may cause. A witness in a sexual harassment claim may not be willing to testify if her entire sexual history is brought out in the open. Therefore, the protective order under Rule 26 encourages the introduction of evidence by attempting to eliminate relevant, but tangential, issues that may be sensitive to the witness or party. Second, protective orders also prevent the opposing party from harassing the other side. Since discovery is a powerful tool, courts have realized a need to prevent overzealous attorneys from intimidating their opponents by seeking to disclose every conceivably relevant piece of evidence. In this case, the opinion struck a balance by closing the door on voluntary sexual activities, but leaving open on those sexual activities that may have some bearing on the sexual harassment claim.

■ CASE VOCABULARY

PROBATIVE VALUE: The value of a piece of evidence in terms of proving or disproving a fact.

Zubulake v. UBS Warburg LLC

(Former Employee) v. (Employer)

217 F.R.D. 309 (S.D.N.Y. 2003)

IF DESTROYED EVIDENCE WOULD NOT HELP THE PLAINTIFF'S CASE, THE SANCTIONS WILL BE LIMITED

■ **INSTANT FACTS** An employee suing her employer for gender discrimination sought an "adverse inference" instruction after she learned that the employer failed to preserve e-mails that she alleged would support her claim.

■ **BLACK LETTER RULE** A party seeking an adverse inference instruction must meet three requirements: it must establish that the party having control over the evidence had an obligation to preserve it when it was destroyed, that the records were destroyed with a culpable state of mind, and that the destroyed evidence was relevant to the party's claim or defense.

■ **PROCEDURAL BASIS**

Federal district court consideration of the plaintiff's motion for sanctions against the defendant.

■ **FACTS**

Zubulake (P) was an equity trader who earned $650,000 a year working for UBS Warburg (D). She sued UBS (D) for gender discrimination, failure to promote, and retaliation, and argued that the evidence she needed to prove her case existed in e-mail correspondence exchanged among various UBS (D) employees and stored on UBS's (D) computers. When UBS (D) failed to produce requested backup tapes, the plaintiff sought sanctions against UBS for its failure to preserve the e-mails and tapes that would have helped her prove her case. She sought, among other sanctions, an adverse inference instruction against UBS with respect to the backup tapes that were missing.

■ **ISSUE**

Was the plaintiff entitled to an adverse inference instruction with regard to the missing e-mails?

■ **DECISION AND RATIONALE**

(Scheindlin, J.) No. A party seeking an adverse inference instruction must meet three requirements: it must establish that the party having control over the evidence had an obligation to preserve it when it was destroyed, that the records were destroyed with a culpable state of mind, and that the destroyed evidence was relevant to the party's claim or defense. The spoliation of evidence germane to proof of an issue at trial can, in appropriate cases, support an inference that the evidence would have been unfavorable to the party responsible for its destruction, but whether such an instruction to the jury is an appropriate sanction for spoliation is within the discretion of the trial judge. When a jury is instructed that it may infer that the party who destroyed potentially relevant evidence did so out of a realization that the evidence was unfavorable to its position, the party suffering this instruction will be hard-pressed to prevail.

Before there can be spoliation, there must be a duty to preserve that evidence. Once a party reasonably anticipates litigation, it must suspend its routine document retention/destruction policy and put in place a "litigation hold" to ensure the preservation of relevant documents. Here, everyone associated with Zubulake (P) understood there was a reasonable possibility she may sue, so the duty to preserve the e-mails attached at the time that litigation was reasonably anticipated. That duty encompasses all evidence that could have been required in the litigation, and it extends to all employees likely to have relevant information, as well as all methods of storage, including backup tapes. In this case, there was a duty, and it was breached.

With regard to the second factor, a culpable state of mind includes ordinary negligence. And third, when evidence is destroyed in bad faith, that fact alone is sufficient to demonstrate relevance, but when the spoliation arises from negligence, the party seeking the instruction must prove relevance. Here, we have already established that UBS (D) had a duty to preserve the backup tapes, and it was negligent if not reckless in failing to do so. Because its actions were negligent and not willful, however, the plaintiff must establish the relevance of the spoliated evidence. Nowhere in the tapes that *were* produced was there evidence that UBS's (D) dislike of Zubulake (P) was based on her gender, so it is unlikely the other tapes would have substantiated that claim. Thus, the plaintiff has failed to establish relevance, and she is therefore not entitled to an adverse inference instruction. Even so, the e-mails should have been produced, so UBS (D) must bear the additional discovery costs necessitated by its negligence.

Analysis:

In practice, a plaintiff may be hard-pressed to establish that missing evidence would be relevant to her case, because if the evidence has been destroyed, how would she establish whether or not the evidence would be relevant? Here, the fact that the e-mails that *were* produced did not reflect gender discrimination does not necessarily indicate that those *not* produced were of similar quality. If an employer were to hide any intra-company e-mails in a case like this, wouldn't they more likely be the incriminating ones? Another rule similar to the adverse-inference rule is the adverse-interest rule, which is based on the principle that if a party fails to produce a witness who is within its power to produce, and who should have been produced, the judge may instruct the jury to infer that the witness's testimony would be unfavorable to that party's position in the case.

■ CASE VOCABULARY

ADVERSE INFERENCE: A detrimental conclusion drawn by the factfinder from a party's failure to produce evidence that is within the party's control.

CHAPTER 8

Resolution without Trial

Peralta v. Heights Medical Center

Instant Facts: The guarantor of hospital debt sought to set aside a default judgment on the grounds that service was a nullity under state law due to delay; but the state court in spite of the defective service required the guarantor to show he had a meritorious defense before the it would set aside the judgment.

Black Letter Rule: The fact that a defendant suffers no harm from a default judgment does not alter the rule holding that a default judgment entered without notice or service to the defendant violates the Due Process Clause of the Fourteenth Amendment.

Matsushita Elec. Industrial Co. v. Epstein

Instant Facts: Although a state court approved a settlement whereby the class-action plaintiffs agreed to release all present and future state and federal claims, the federal appeals court before which the class-plaintiff's federal securities claim was pending held that a state court-approved settlement cannot release those claims within the exclusive jurisdiction of federal courts.

Black Letter Rule: Federal courts must give full faith and credit to state court judgments approving settlements that release claims within the exclusive jurisdiction of federal courts.

Kalinauskas v. Wong

Instant Facts: A casino being sued for sexual discrimination by a former employee sought to avoid the deposition of another former employee with whom the casino had previously settled a sexual discrimination suit.

Black Letter Rule: In order to avoid repetitive discovery, courts may modify protective orders or settlement agreements to allow for the discovery of facts otherwise held confidential under the agreement.

Ferguson v. Countrywide Credit Industries, Inc.

Instant Facts: Ferguson (P), an employee of Countrywide (D), filed sexual harassment, retaliation and hostile work environment complaints in district court against Countrywide (D) and her supervisor, despite having signed an arbitration agreement as a condition of her employment that required arbitration of any claims against Countrywide (D).

Black Letter Rule: Under California law, there must be both a procedural and substantive element of unconscionability in order to render a contract unenforceable under the unconscionability doctrine, although the elements need not be present in the same degree.

AT&T Mobility LLC v. Concepcion

Instant Facts: The Concepcions (P) filed a class action suit against AT&T Mobility (D) for false advertising and fraud, and AT&T (D) moved to enforce a contractual clause requiring that disputes be submitted to individual arbitration.

Black Letter Rule: The Federal Arbitration Act will preempt state laws on the unconscionability of contracts if those laws single out arbitration and make private agreements to arbitrate unenforceable.

Ferguson v. Writers Guild of America, West

Instant Facts: A screenwriter sought court review of the arbitration proceeding that granted him the screenplay credit and not the story-line credit to a movie he had written.

Black Letter Rule: Courts are limited in their power to review the final decision of arbitration panels.

Celotex Corp. v. Catrett

Instant Facts: Charged with several claims for asbestos poisoning that lead to the death of Mr. Catrett, Celotex (D) moved for summary judgment on the grounds that Mrs. Catrett (P) failed to produce evidence to support the claims.

Black Letter Rule: In a summary judgment motion, a moving party may meet its burden of persuasion by demonstrating that the nonmoving party failed to supply sufficient evidence of a genuine dispute of material fact.

Bias v. Advantage International, Inc.

Instant Facts: Bias's estate (P) sued his sports agency for failing to obtain a life insurance policy before his death.

Black Letter Rule: Upon a summary judgment movant's showing of an absence of genuine issues of material fact, the nonmoving party must come forward with specific facts to demonstrate a genuine issue for trial.

Peralta v. Heights Medical Center

(Guarantor) v. (Hospital)

485 U.S. 80, 108 S.Ct. 896 (1988)

THE DUE PROCESS CLAUSE IMPOSES LIMITS ON A COURT'S ABILITY TO ENTER DEFAULT JUDGMENTS AGAINST DEFENDANTS WHO HAVE NOT RECEIVED ADEQUATE NOTICE

■ **INSTANT FACTS** The guarantor of hospital debt sought to set aside a default judgment on the grounds that service was a nullity under state law due to delay; but the state court—in spite of the defective service—required the guarantor to show he had a meritorious defense before the it would set aside the judgment.

■ **BLACK LETTER RULE** The fact that a defendant suffers no harm from a default judgment does not alter the rule holding that a default judgment entered without notice or service to the defendant violates the Due Process Clause of the Fourteenth Amendment.

■ **PROCEDURAL BASIS**

Appeal to the United States Supreme Court from the decision of the Texas Court of Appeals affirming summary judgment.

■ **FACTS**

In 1982, Heights Medical Center (Heights) (D) initiated a law suit against Mr. Peralta (P), the guarantor of a hospital debt of $5600. Peralta (P) was personally served 90 days after the summons was issued, a delay which nullified the service of process under state law. Peralta failed to answer and a default judgment was entered against him. The judgment was abstracted and recorded, clouding his title to real property that was eventually sold to satisfy the judgment. In 1984, Peralta (P) began a bill of review proceeding in the Texas courts to set aside the judgment on the grounds that service was defective, and as a result the judgment and subsequent sale were void. Heights (D) filed a motion for summary judgment asserting that Peralta (P) was required to show that he had a meritorious defense to the action in which judgment was entered. The defective service notwithstanding, the Texas courts agreed with Heights (D) and granted summary judgment. The court reasoned that without a meritorious defense, the same judgment would have been entered on retrial, and thus Peralta (P) suffered no harm.

■ **ISSUE**

May a default judgment be sustained against a defendant who has not been properly served or notified on the ground that the defendant was not harmed because he had no defense to the action?

■ **DECISION AND RATIONALE**

(White, J.) No. Where a person has been deprived of property in a manner inconsistent with due process, it is no answer to say that due process would have led to the same result because he had no defense on the merits. We have held that for a proceeding to be accorded preclusion, due process requires notice reasonably calculated, under the circumstances, to apprise parties of the action and afford them the opportunity to be heard. Yet, the Texas courts held that Peralta (P) was required to show that he had a meritorious defense, apparently, on the ground that the same judgment would be entered against him on retrial, and hence, he suffered no harm. This reasoning is untenable. Had Peralta (P) been notified, he might have impleaded the original debtor, worked out a settlement, or paid the debt. This judgment carried with it serious consequences including a lien encumbering Peralta's (P) property and the property's eventual sale below market value, all without notice. Here, we assume that the judgment entered against Peralta (P) and its ensuing consequences occurred without notice. Therefore, we hold that the holding of the Texas courts violated the Due Process Clause of the Fourteenth Amendment. Reversed.

Analysis:

This case demonstrates that rather than enter a default judgment, courts prefer to see the parties engage on the merits of the dispute. The Court here holds, as it had in previous cases, that due process requires a defendant to be notified of a proceeding against him before he may be deprived of property. The ease with which the case is disposed of relies on the assumption that Peralta (P) received no actual notice. This assumption is based on a legal fiction. Although actual notice was given, Texas law nullified any service of process not effectuated within ninety days of its issuance. Had the Court assumed that Peralta (P) received actual—although invalid—service, the outcome of the case may have been different.

■ CASE VOCABULARY

BILL OF REVIEW: A procedure used to start a suit to set aside a previous final judgment.

WRIT OF ATTACHMENT: An order to seize property in satisfaction of a debt or judgment.

Matsushita Elec. Industrial Co. v. Epstein

(Acquiring Corporation) v. (Shareholders of Acquired Corporation)

516 U.S. 367, 116 S.Ct. 873 (1996)

FEDERAL COURTS ARE REQUIRED TO GIVE FULL FAITH AND CREDIT TO STATE COURT JUDGMENTS APPROVING SETTLEMENTS, EVEN IF THEY RELEASE A CLAIM WITHIN THE EXCLUSIVE JURISDICTION OF FEDERAL COURTS

■ **INSTANT FACTS** Although a state court approved a settlement whereby the class-action plaintiffs agreed to release all present and future state and federal claims, the federal appeals court—before which the class-plaintiff's federal securities claim was pending—held that a state court-approved settlement cannot release those claims within the exclusive jurisdiction of federal courts.

■ **BLACK LETTER RULE** Federal courts must give full faith and credit to state court judgments approving settlements that release claims within the exclusive jurisdiction of federal courts.

■ **PROCEDURAL BASIS**

Appeal to the United States Supreme Court, challenging the decision of the Ninth Circuit Court of Appeals which refused give full faith and credit to a state court-approved settlement.

■ **FACTS**

The shareholders of MCA (P), an entertainment company acquired by Matsushita (D), brought two sets of class-action suits against Matsushita (D). The first set were federal actions arising under the federal securities laws. The second, filed in Delaware Chancery Court, alleged violations of state fiduciary responsibilities. While the federal cases were on appeal before the Ninth Circuit, the parties to the state action entered into a settlement releasing all claims—state and federal—arising out of the Matsushita-MCA acquisition. The Delaware court approved of the settlement, and entered a judgment incorporating its terms. Matsushita (D) then asserted that the Delaware judgment was a bar to the federal actions before the Ninth Circuit. The Ninth Circuit disagreed, holding that Delaware's approval of the settlement could not preclude litigation of claims within the sole jurisdiction of federal courts.

■ **ISSUE**

May a federal court withhold full faith and credit from a state-court judgment approving a class-action settlement simply because the settlement releases claims within the exclusive jurisdiction of the federal courts?

■ **DECISION AND RATIONALE**

(Thomas, J.) No. Pursuant to 28 U.S.C. §1738 (the federal statute requiring courts to give state judgments full faith and credit) a federal court must give the judgment the same effect that it would have in the courts of the State in which it was rendered. This act directs federal courts to treat state court judgments with the same respect the judgment would receive in the courts of the rendering state. An examination of Delaware law indicates that these federal claims would be barred in Delaware. In providing for exclusive jurisdiction over federal securities laws, Congress did not impliedly repeal §1738. Thus, pursuant to §1738, the judgment must be given full faith and credit. The shareholders (P) additionally claim that the

---

HIGH COURT CASE SUMMARIES

settlement proceedings should not be accorded full faith and credit because the judgment did not satisfy due process due to inadequate class representation. We first note that the Delaware Chancery Court held that the class was adequately represented. Without determining the accuracy of this finding, we do not address the due process issue because it is outside the scope of the issue presented. Reversed and remanded.

■ CONCURRENCE AND DISSENT

(Ginsburg, J.) Under §1738, a state court judgment is not entitled to full faith and credit unless the requirements of the Due Process Clause are satisfied. As the shareholders (P) point out, adequate representation is one of those very requirements. Because the lower court decided the case on other grounds, the due process inquiry remains open for consideration.

Analysis:

The issue in this case arises out of the conflict created by the mandate of the Full Faith and Credit Act, which requires federal courts to give state court judgments the same preclusive effect those judgments would have within the state, and the grant of exclusive subject matter jurisdiction to federal courts over federal securities claims. Matsushita argued before the Court of Appeals that the Full Faith and Credit Act barred the pending claim. The question raised was: how could a state court judgment bar federal claims that the state court had no authority to hear? The Supreme Court held that Congress did not intend to repeal the Full Faith and Credit Act by granting federal courts exclusive jurisdiction over certain claims. The shareholders alternatively argued that this particular judgment should not be given full faith and credit because the Delaware court failed to abide by due process. The Court suggests—but does not hold—that the Delaware court had decided the issue, and even if it had not, the Court notes the due process issue was not properly before it.

■ CASE VOCABULARY

CHANCERY COURT: Court of equity. In Delaware the Chancery Court hears all cases arising under corporate law.

Kalinauskas v. Wong

(Fired Employee) v. (Casino)

151 F.R.D. 363 (D. Nev. 1993)

THE PUBLIC POLICIES FAVORING BROAD DISCOVERY IN FEDERAL CIVIL CASES
TRUMP SETTLEMENT AGREEMENTS THAT PROHIBIT A PARTY FROM DISCLOSING ANY
ASPECT OF A SETTLED CASE

■ **INSTANT FACTS** A casino being sued for sexual discrimination by a former employee sought to avoid the deposition of another former employee with whom the casino had previously settled a sexual discrimination suit.

■ **BLACK LETTER RULE** In order to avoid repetitive discovery, courts may modify protective orders or settlement agreements to allow for the discovery of facts otherwise held confidential under the agreement.

■ **PROCEDURAL BASIS**

Decision by the Federal District Court denying a Motion for a Protective Order.

■ **FACTS**

Ms. Lin T. Kalinauskas (P), a former employee of Caesar's Palace (D), sued the casino for sexual discrimination. As part of discovery, Kalinauskas (P) sought to depose Donna Thomas, another former employee who had settled a sexual discrimination suit with Caesar's (D). The settlement, which the court had sealed upon stipulation by the parties, provided that Thomas was not to discuss any aspect of her employment at Caesar's (D). Ceaser's (D) sought a Protective Order to prevent Thomas' deposition. The District Court denied the motion.

■ **ISSUE**

Does a settlement agreement, entered into by private litigants, prevent the future discovery of materials or testimony held confidential by the agreement?

■ **DECISION AND RATIONALE**

(Johnston, M.J.) No. Courts are permitted to modify settlement agreements to place private litigants in a position they would otherwise reach only after a repetition of another's discovery; such modification can be denied only where it prejudices substantial rights of the opposing party, and the prejudice outweighs the benefits of the modification. This case presents a direct conflict between the policies behind the liberal discovery rules and the interest in protecting the secrecy of settlements. To allow full discovery of sealed agreements would discourage such settlements in the future. Because these settlements resolve disputes quickly—serving both public and private interests—they deserve court protection. On the other hand, to prohibit any discovery would condone buying the silence of a witness and would lead to repetitive and wasteful discovery. In the case at hand, Caesar's (D) has not demonstrated any potential injury or prejudice which could arise from allowing the deposition. We also reject Caesar's (D) contention that Kalinauskas (P) must intervene in the Thomas case and seek modification of the order. First, requiring intervention would be wasteful since no live controversy exists in which Kalinauskas (P) can intervene. Moreover, the confidentiality agreement itself provides that a court may order the disclosure of information. The argument that Kalinauskas (P) must show a compelling need to obtain discovery only applies to the specific terms of the

---

settlement, not to the factual circumstances surrounding the case. Accordingly, this court will allow the deposition of Ms. Thomas, but such deposition may not disclose the substantive terms of the agreement. The penalties imposed upon Ms. Thomas by the agreement are inapplicable to the deposition. Motion granted in part and denied in part.

Analysis:

In this case the district court holds that the ability of private litigants to enter into confidential settlement agreements must yield to the policies supporting broad discovery whenever the two come into conflict. The opinion recognizes the importance of confidential settlements in an era where courts seek to encourage alternatives to litigation. Nevertheless, the court thought that, in general, the benefits of allowing discovery outweigh the need to encourage settlements. The court does recognize an exception whenever discovery would prejudice the opposing party, and that injury would outweigh the benefits of discovery. But because Caesar's (D) failed to demonstrate any prejudice, the court does not state what kind of prejudice is necessary to prevent the discovery.

■ CASE VOCABULARY

PROTECTIVE ORDER: An order issued for the protection of a party, usually as a limit on discovery.

Ferguson v. Countrywide Credit Industries, Inc.

(Employee) v. (Employer)

298 F.3d 778 (9th Cir. 2002)

AN AGREEMENT TO ARBITRATE EMPLOYMENT CLAIMS IS UNCONSCIONABLE

■ **INSTANT FACTS** Ferguson (P), an employee of Countrywide (D), filed sexual harassment, retaliation and hostile work environment complaints in district court against Countrywide (D) and her supervisor, despite having signed an arbitration agreement as a condition of her employment that required arbitration of any claims against Countrywide (D).

■ **BLACK LETTER RULE** Under California law, there must be both a procedural and substantive element of unconscionability in order to render a contract unenforceable under the unconscionability doctrine, although the elements need not be present in the same degree.

■ **PROCEDURAL BASIS**

Appeal of district court's decision denying Countrywide's (D) petition to compel arbitration.

■ **FACTS**

Ferguson (P), as a condition of her employment with Countrywide (D), executed a contract that required arbitration of any claims she might have against Countrywide (D). Ferguson (P) later filed a complaint against Countrywide (D) and her supervisor, alleging several causes of action, including sexual harassment, retaliation, and hostile work environment. Countrywide (D) filed a petition for an order compelling arbitration on the ground that the arbitration agreement required arbitration of all claims against Countrywide (D). The district court found that Ferguson (P) could not be compelled to arbitrate her Title VII employment discrimination claims and denied Countrywide's (D) petition on the ground that the arbitration agreement was unenforceable because it was unconscionable under California law.

■ **ISSUE**

Is an agreement to arbitrate employment claims unconscionable?

■ **DECISION AND RATIONALE**

(Pregerson, J.) Yes. Under California law, there must be both a procedural and substantive element of unconscionability in order to render a contract unenforceable under the unconscionability doctrine, although the elements need not be present in the same degree. Procedural unconscionability, which concerns the manner in which the contract was negotiated and the circumstances of the parties at that time, exists here because Ferguson (P) was in a position of unequal bargaining power and was presented with the offending contract terms without an opportunity to negotiate. Substantive unconscionability, which focuses on the agreement's terms and whether they are so one-sided as to shock the conscience, exists because the arbitration agreement compelled arbitration of the employee's claims, but exempted from arbitration Countrywide's (D) claims against its employees. The clause also imposed multiple arbitration fees on employees who elected arbitrate a claim, and created an unfair employer advantage through its discovery provision limitations. Affirmed.

Analysis:

The *Ferguson* contract had both a procedural and substantive element of unconscionability, so that it was unenforceable under the unconscionability doctrine. A court that determines a contract clause is unconscionable has several options. It may enforce the contract without the unconscionable clause or limit the application of any unconscionable clause as to avoid an unconscionable result. However, the court also may refuse to enforce the contract as a whole if the contract is permeated by the unconscionability.

■ **CASE VOCABULARY**

ARBITRATION: A method of dispute resolution involving one or more neutral third parties who are usually agreed to by the disputing parties and whose decision is binding.

FAA: Federal Arbitration Act. A federal statute providing for the enforcement of private agreements to arbitrate disputes related to interstate commercial and maritime matters. Under the Act, arbitration agreements are enforced in accordance with their terms, just as other contracts are. The Act supersedes substantive state laws that frustrate enforcement of arbitration agreements, but it does not apply to matters of procedure.

UNCONSCIONABLE: Showing no regard for conscience; affronting the sense of justice, decency, or reasonableness.

UNCONSCIONABLE AGREEMENT: An agreement that no promisor with any sense, and not under a delusion, would make, and that no honest and fair promisee would accept.

(Telephone Company) v. (Customer)

131 S. Ct. 1740 (2011)

ARBITRATION AGREEMENTS ARE FAVORED BY THE COURT

■ **INSTANT FACTS** The Concepcions (P) filed a class action suit against AT&T Mobility (D) for false advertising and fraud, and AT&T (D) moved to enforce a contractual clause requiring that disputes be submitted to individual arbitration.

■ **BLACK LETTER RULE** The Federal Arbitration Act will preempt state laws on the unconscionability of contracts if those laws single out arbitration and make private agreements to arbitrate unenforceable.

■ **PROCEDURAL BASIS**

Appeal from an order of the Ninth Circuit Court of Appeals affirming a ruling that an arbitration clause was unenforceable.

■ **FACTS**

The Concepcions (P) purchased telephone service from AT&T Mobility (D). The contract provided that any disputes between the parties would be submitted to arbitration. The agreement also provided that claims would be brought in a party's individual capacity, and not as a plaintiff or class member in a class or representative proceeding; AT&T (D) was required to pay the costs of all nonfrivolous claims; arbitration would take place in the county in which the customer was billed for the service; if the claim was for $10,000 or less, the customer could choose whether the arbitration would be in person, by telephone, or based on written submissions; the arbitrator could award any type of relief; either party was allowed to bring a claim in small claims court instead of arbitrating; AT&T (D) was barred from seeking attorney's fees; and if an arbitration award was greater than AT&T's (D) last written settlement offer, AT&T (D) would be required to pay a $7500 minimum recovery, plus twice the amount of the claimant's attorney's fees.

The telephone service the Concepcions (P) purchased was advertised as including free telephones. The Concepcions (P) were not charged for their phones, but were charged $30.22 for sales tax. They filed an action against AT&T (D) in U.S. District Court, and their complaint was later consolidated with a putative class action that alleged, among other things, false advertising and fraud. AT&T (D) moved to compel arbitration and the Concepcions (P) opposed the motion, claiming that the arbitration clause was unconscionable under California law because it disallowed class-wide procedures. The District Court denied the motion, relying on California law. The Ninth Circuit affirmed.

■ **ISSUE**

Was the arbitration clause enforceable?

■ **DECISION AND RATIONALE**

(Scalia, J.) Yes. The Federal Arbitration Act will preempt state laws on the unconscionability of contracts if those laws single out arbitration and make private agreements to arbitrate unenforceable. Section 2 of the Federal Arbitration Act (FAA) provides that written provisions to arbitrate are "valid, irrevocable, and enforceable, save upon such grounds as exist at law or in equity for the revocation of any contract." This language reflects a federal policy favoring arbitration, as well as the principle that arbitration is a matter of contract.

California law, as set out in the case of *Discover Bank v. Superior Court,* 36 Cal. 4th 148 (2005), states that a waiver of the right to bring a class action contained in an arbitration agreement is unconscionable when it is in a consumer contract of adhesion in a setting in which disputes will involve small amounts of damages, and when it is alleged that the party with the superior bargaining power carried out a scheme to deliberately cheat large numbers of consumers out of individually small sums of money. The Concepcions (P) argue that the *Discover Bank* rule is a ground that "exist[s] at law or in equity for the revocation of any contract." They also argue that even if the rule is construed as a prohibition on collective-action waivers instead of simply an application of unconscionability, the rule would still be applicable to all dispute-resolution contracts, since California prohibits waivers of class litigation as well.

When state law prohibits the arbitration of a particular type of claim, the conflicting rule is displaced by the FAA. A court may not rely on the uniqueness of an agreement to arbitrate as a basis for a state-law holding that enforcement would be unconscionable, as this would enable a court to do what a state legislature could not do. An illustration of this point would be a case finding unconscionable or unenforceable arbitration agreements that do not provide for judicially monitored discovery. Because the rule would be applicable to "any" contract and thus preserved by the FAA, in practice the rule would have a disproportionate impact on arbitration agreements. This example is not fanciful, since the judicial hostility towards arbitration that prompted the FAA was shown in numerous declarations that arbitration was against public policy. It is worth noting that California's courts have been more likely to hold contracts to arbitrate unconscionable than other contracts.

The Concepcions (P) admit that the FAA's saving clause should not be construed to include a state's mere preference for procedures incompatible with arbitration. We largely agree. Although the saving clause preserves contract defenses, there is nothing that would preserve state-law rules that are obstacles to the FAA's objectives. We differ with the Concepcions (P) only in the application of this analysis to the instant case. The overarching purpose of the FAA is to ensure the enforcement of arbitration agreements according to their terms. Requiring the availability of class-wide arbitration interferes with fundamental attributes of arbitration and thus creates a scheme inconsistent with the FAA. The principal purpose of the FAA is to ensure that private arbitration agreements are enforced according to their terms. Parties may agree to limit the issues subject to arbitration, to arbitrate according to specific rules, and to limit with whom a party will arbitrate. The point of giving parties discretion in designing the process is to allow for efficient, streamlined procedures tailored to the dispute. The informality of arbitration proceedings is itself desirable, reducing the cost and increasing the speed of dispute resolution.

The *Discover Bank* rule interferes with arbitration. Although the rule does not require class-wide arbitration, it allows any party to a consumer contract to demand it. The rule is limited to adhesion contracts, but the times in which consumer contracts were anything other than adhesive are long past. Consumers remain free to bring and resolve their disputes on a bilateral basis, but there is little incentive for lawyers to arbitrate on behalf of individuals when they may do so for a class and reap far higher fees in the process. Companies would likewise have less incentive to continue resolving potentially duplicative claims on an individual basis.

The shift from bilateral arbitration to class-wide arbitration involves fundamental changes. Class-wide arbitration includes absent parties, necessitating additional and different procedures and involving higher stakes. Confidentiality becomes more difficult. In addition, arbitrators are not generally knowledgeable in the often-dominant procedural aspects of certification. The conclusion follows that class arbitration, to the extent it is manufactured by *Discover Bank* rather than consensual, is inconsistent with the FAA. First, the switch from bilateral to class arbitration sacrifices the principal advantage of arbitration—its informality—

and makes the process slower, more costly, and more likely to generate a procedural morass than final judgment. Second, class arbitration requires formality. The American Arbitration Association's rules governing class arbitrations mimic the Federal Rules of Civil Procedure for class litigation. Third, class arbitration greatly increases risks to defendants. The absence of review makes it more likely that errors will go uncorrected. The costs of these errors will be in arbitration, since their impact is limited to the size of individual disputes. But when damages allegedly owed to tens of thousands of potential claimants are aggregated and decided at once, the risk of an error will often become unacceptable. Defendants will thus be pressured into settling questionable claims.

The dissent quotes *Dean Witter Reynolds Inc. v. Byrd*, 470 U.S. 213 (1985), as rejecting the suggestion that the overriding goal of the FAA was to promote the expeditious resolution of claims. That is greatly misleading. After saying that "the overriding goal of the Arbitration Act was [not] to promote the expeditious resolution of claims," but to "ensure judicial enforcement of privately made agreements to arbitrate," *Dean Witter* went on to say that Congress was not "blind to the potential benefit of the legislation for expedited resolution of disputes." Our cases have repeatedly described the Act as embodying a national policy favoring arbitration, and a liberal federal policy favoring arbitration agreements, notwithstanding any state policies to the contrary. The dissent also claims that class proceedings are necessary to prosecute small-dollar claims that might otherwise slip through the legal system. But states cannot require a procedure that is inconsistent with the FAA, even if it is desirable for unrelated reasons. Reversed.

■ DISSENT

(Breyer, J.) The *Discover Bank* rule is consistent with the FAA's language. It applies equally to class-action-litigation waivers in contracts without arbitration agreements and class-arbitration waivers in contracts with such agreements. The majority does not explain where it gets its idea that individual, rather than class, arbitration is a fundamental attribute of arbitration.

Analysis:

Arbitration clauses are ubiquitous and are often found in cell phone contracts, credit card agreements, and consumer loan contracts. Critics point out that these clauses are often unfair to consumers, in that they impose onerous costs or restrictions. The arbitration clause at issue in this case was a particularly generous one, minimizing the financial risk and inconvenience to the customer. It is possible that this "easy" arbitration agreement influenced the Court's thinking.

■ CASE VOCABULARY

ARBITRATION: A method of dispute resolution involving one or more neutral third parties who are usually agreed upon by the disputing parties, and whose decision is binding.

Ferguson v. Writers Guild of America, West

(Screenwriter) v. (Writers Guild)

226 Cal.App.3d 1382 (1991)

PARTIES WHO AGREE TO ARBITRATE THEIR DISPUTES ARE FREE TO ADOPT A WIDE RANGE OF PROCEDURAL RULES THAT DIFFER DRAMATICALLY FROM THOSE ADOPTED BY COURTS

■ **INSTANT FACTS** A screenwriter sought court review of the arbitration proceeding that granted him the screenplay credit and not the story-line credit to a movie he had written.

■ **BLACK LETTER RULE** Courts are limited in their power to review the final decision of arbitration panels.

■ **PROCEDURAL BASIS**

Appeal to the California Court of Appeal from a judgment of the superior court denying a petition for a writ of mandate.

■ **FACTS**

Larry Ferguson (P), a screenwriter, was hired to write a screenplay for the movie "Beverly Hills Cop II." The Writers Guild (D) awarded Ferguson (P) partial screenplay credit, but gave the story-line credit to two others. The process for determining writing credits was governed by a 369-page agreement entered into by various entities in the entertainment industry, and the Writers Guild West's credits manual. The process is summarized as follows. After each party to the proceeding peremptorily disqualified a reasonable number of arbitrators from a list of 400, a Writers Guild secretary selected the arbitrators to hear the case. The arbitrators were then provided with all written material used in the creation of the screenplay. The arbitrators held no hearing, and they deliberated independently of each other. In fact, their identity remained undisclosed to the parties throughout the procedure, and even thereafter. Within 24 hours after the arbitrators reached their decision, Ferguson requested the convening of the policy review board to determine whether the "proceedings" substantially deviated from the policy of the Writers Guild (D). The board was not empowered to review the judgment. The policy review board approved the credit determination, a final decision. In support of his challenge, Ferguson asserted several procedural defects in the process, and as error, the rulings of the superior court denying his requests to (1) depose the writer awarded shared screenplay credit, and (2) compel the Writers Guild (D) to reveal the name of the arbitrators.

■ **ISSUE**

May a court review the appropriateness of procedural rules adopted in an arbitration proceeding?

■ **DECISION AND RATIONALE**

(Klein, J.A.) No. Judicial review of arbitration proceedings is limited to whether the parties agreed to submit the issue to arbitration and whether the arbitrator exceeded the power granted by the agreement. Under the agreement establishing the arbitration process, disputes over writing credits for movies are nonjusticiable. The writers who constitute the Writers Guild (D) have decided that the credit-determination process can be handled more skillfully and

---

efficiently by arbitration committees than by courts. We note that the procedures adopted in the challenged arbitration have been reviewed for correctness by the policy review board. Because of their expertise, we accord the policy review board considerable deference. Ferguson (P), did not specify to the review board the errors argued before this court. Consequently, Ferguson (P) did not preserve for judicial review the contentions he has made. Even if we were to decide on Ferguson's claims, we find them without merit. Judicial review of the credit determination is restricted to considering whether there was a material and prejudicial departure from the procedures specified in the agreement. No such departure exists in this case. We also reject Ferguson's challenge of the decision of the superior court. Deposition of the writer awarded shared credit would add nothing to Ferguson's claim of sole credit. With respect to the identity of the arbitrators, the Writers Guild has important and legitimate reasons for withholding their identity, including the need to have arbitrators free of pressure, retaliation, and litigation. Although it is unusual for an arbitration to be conducted without an in-person hearing before the arbitrators, discovery of the names in this case would serve no function. Even in arbitration conducted under more familiar rules, the parties have no right to inquire into the arbitrators reasons for reaching a particular decision. Affirmed.

Analysis:

Judicial review of arbitration is severely limited. In this case the court bases its decision on two factors: (1) the parties agreed to arbitrate this issue, and (2) the arbitration was held in accordance with rules fashioned by the agreement. The court's reliance on the two agreements is important because freedom of contract forms the basis for allowing parties to submit their disputes to arbitration. The court analogizes the decision of the policy review board with decisions reached by administrative agencies, and hints that they should be accorded similar deference. Extending the analogy, the court "refuses" to entertain Ferguson's procedural contentions because they were not presented to the board. The court finally notes that the particular procedures adopted by the Writers Guild are a deviation from the norm (of courts and other arbitration proceedings), but that there are substantial interests supporting the procedural peculiarities, which must be respected.

■ **CASE VOCABULARY**

WRIT OF MANDATE: A court order or command; also *writ of mandamus.*

Celotex Corp. v. Catrett

(Product Manufacturer) v. (Wife of Decedent)

477 U.S. 317, 106 S.Ct. 2548 (1986)

SUMMARY JUDGMENT MAY BE APPROPRIATE EVEN IF THE MOVING PARTY FAILS TO PRODUCE EVIDENCE DEMONSTRATING A LACK OF A FACTUAL DISPUTE

■ **INSTANT FACTS** Charged with several claims for asbestos poisoning that lead to the death of Mr. Catrett, Celotex (D) moved for summary judgment on the grounds that Mrs. Catrett (P) failed to produce evidence to support the claims.

■ **BLACK LETTER RULE** In a summary judgment motion, a moving party may meet its burden of persuasion by demonstrating that the nonmoving party failed to supply sufficient evidence of a genuine dispute of material fact.

■ **PROCEDURAL BASIS**

Writ of certiorari reviewing reversal of granting of summary judgment against a party claiming damages for negligence, breach of warranty and strict liability.

■ **FACTS**

Mrs. Catrett (P) sued Celotex Corp. (D) and others for negligence, breach of warranty, and strict liability, alleging that her husband's death was caused by exposure to products containing asbestos manufactured by Celotex (D) and the other defendants. Celotex (D) moved for summary judgment on the grounds that Catrett (P) failed to produce any evidence that any Celotex (D) product caused the injuries. In response, Catrett (P) produced three documents which she claimed demonstrated that a genuine factual dispute existed. Celotex (D) argued that the three documents, including the husband's deposition and two letters, were inadmissible hearsay. The District Court granted Celotex's (D) motion for summary judgment because there was no showing that Mr. Catrett was exposed to Celotex's (D) product. The Court of Appeals reversed since Celotex (D) made no effort to adduce any evidence, in the form of affidavits or otherwise, in support of its motion for summary judgment. The Supreme Court granted certiorari.

■ **ISSUE**

Must a party moving for summary judgment supply evidence or affidavits showing the absence of a genuine dispute about a material fact?

■ **DECISION AND RATIONALE**

(Rehnquist, J.) No. A party moving for summary judgment does not necessarily bear the burden of supplying evidence or affidavits showing the absence of a genuine dispute about a material fact. The plain language of Rule 56(c) of the Federal Rules of Civil Procedure mandates the entry of summary judgment, after adequate time for discovery, against a party who fails to establish the existence of an element essential to that party's case, and on which that party will bear the burden of proof at trial. The Court of Appeals misconstrued the holding in *Adickes v. S.H. Kress & Co.* [the party moving for summary judgment must establish the absence of a genuine issue, when viewed in a light most favorable to the opposing party]. This holding should not be construed to mean that the burden is always on the moving party to produce evidence showing the absence of a material fact in dispute. Rather, a summary

---

judgment motion may properly be made in reliance solely on the pleadings, depositions, answers to interrogatories, and admissions on file. Thus, the moving party does not have to submit supporting evidence, as the plain language of Rules 56(a) and (b) indicate. The moving party only bears the initial responsibility of informing the court of the basis for its motion. This responsibility may be met by showing the court that there is an absence of evidence to support the nonmoving party's case. The amendment to Rule 56(e), precluding a party opposing summary judgment from referring only to its pleadings, was intended to broaden the scope of summary judgment motions. However, the Court of Appeal's reasoning tends to make summary judgments more difficult to obtain. In the case at hand, the parties had an adequate opportunity to conduct discovery and establish the evidence needed to prove their cases. The Court of Appeals declined to address whether Catrett (P) had made an adequate showing to carry her burden of proof at trial. For this reason, and based on the foregoing analysis, the judgment of the Court of Appeals is reversed for such a determination. Reversed and remanded.

■ **CONCURRENCE**

(White, J.) I agree that a moving party must not always support a summary judgment motion with evidence or affidavits showing the absence of a genuine dispute of a material fact. However, the movant may not simply discharge his burden by asserting that the opposing party has no evidence to prove his or her case. The case should be reversed for the Court of Appeals to consider whether Catrett (P) revealed enough evidence to defeat the motion for summary judgment.

■ **DISSENT**

(Brennan, J.) The Court has not clearly explained what is required of a moving party seeking summary judgment on the ground that the nonmoving party cannot prove its case. I believe that Celotex (D) has failed to meet its burden of production. The burden on the party seeking summary judgment has two components. First, the party bears the initial burden of production, which shifts to the nonmoving party if satisfied by the moving party. Second, the moving party bears the ultimate burden of persuasion. The decision as to whether the moving party has discharged its initial burden of production depends upon which party will bear the burden of persuasion on the challenged claim at trial. If the moving party will bear the burden of persuasion, it must support its motion with credible evidence that would entitle it to a directed verdict if not controverted at trial. On the other hand, if the burden of persuasion at trial would be on the nonmoving party, then the party moving for summary judgment may satisfy its burden of production in two ways. First, it may submit affirmative evidence that negates an essential element of the nonmoving party's claim. Second, it may demonstrate that the nonmoving party's evidence itself is insufficient to establish an essential element of the nonmoving party's claim. However, the moving party in this scenario may not simply assert a conclusory statement that the nonmoving party's evidence is insufficient. Rather, it must affirmatively show the absence of evidence in the record to support a judgment for the nonmoving party. Based on the facts of this case, Celotex (D) failed to discharge its initial burden of production. Thus, summary judgment is improper.

Analysis:

The majority, led by Justice Rehnquist, clearly desired to expand the scope of summary judgment motions following the restrictive holding in *Adickes v. S.H. Kress & Co.* As a result of this holding, a moving party meets its burden by simply alerting the court that the nonmoving party has failed to establish evidence sufficient to prove its claims. Indeed, this holding furthers the general goals of the Federal Rules of Civil Procedure, which were designed to secure speedy and inexpensive determinations of controversies. However, as Justice Brennan's well-reasoned dissent mentions, the Court failed to establish just what is required of a moving party.

■ CASE VOCABULARY

BURDEN OF PERSUASION: A party's obligation to establish evidence sufficient to convince the trier of fact that each element of the party's claim or defense is correct.

BURDEN OF PRODUCTION: A party's obligation to produce evidence sufficient to avoid an adverse ruling on an issue, even if this falls short of persuasion.

Bias v. Advantage International, Inc.

(Basketball Player's Estate) v. (Sports Agency)

905 F.2d 1558 (D.C.Cir. 1990)

SUMMARY JUDGMENT MUST BE GRANTED WHEN THERE ARE NO GENUINE ISSUES FOR TRIAL

■ **INSTANT FACTS** Bias's estate (P) sued his sports agency for failing to obtain a life insurance policy before his death.

■ **BLACK LETTER RULE** Upon a summary judgment movant's showing of an absence of genuine issues of material fact, the nonmoving party must come forward with specific facts to demonstrate a genuine issue for trial.

■ **PROCEDURAL BASIS**

On appeal to consider the district court's grant of summary judgment to the defendants.

■ **FACTS**

Bias, a star basketball player at the University of Maryland, entered into a representation agreement with Advantage International, Inc. (D) and A. Lee Fentress (D) and was later drafted in the first round by the Boston Celtics. Two days after the draft, Bias died of a cocaine overdose. Bias's estate (P) sued the defendants, alleging breach of contract by not obtaining a one-million-dollar life insurance policy on Bias's life, misrepresenting that they had obtained such a policy, and thereby preventing Bias's parents from securing the necessary insurance coverage. The district court granted the defendants' motion for summary judgment because the evidence showed that no insurance company would have insured Bias because of his past cocaine use. Bias's estate (P) appealed.

■ **ISSUE**

Did the estate (P) carry its burden on summary judgment by asserting specific facts to demonstrate a genuine issue for trial?

■ **DECISION AND RATIONALE**

(Sentelle, J.) No. For summary judgment purposes, the moving party bears the burden of demonstrating to the court the absence of a genuine issue of material fact. The nonmoving party must then provide specific evidence tending to show that material facts are in dispute to preclude summary judgment. Mere doubt or speculation will not carry the nonmoving party's burden. Regardless of the movant's burden, however, summary judgment is appropriate when a party fails to come forward with evidence to support an essential element of the case on which that party bears the burden of proof at trial.

The district court based its decision upon a finding that there was no genuine issue of material fact as to whether Bias was a drug user or whether Bias could have obtained a life insurance policy. As to the first issue, the defendants offered the specific testimony of two eyewitnesses, who stated that they witnessed Bias use cocaine on numerous occasions prior to his death. Rather than impeaching the defendants' witnesses, the estate (P) offered general statements from Bias's parents and basketball coach, as well as drug test-results, that suggested no knowledge of any drug use. This rebuttal evidence, however, failed to contradict the specific

---

evidence that two witnesses saw Bias using drugs at various times before his death. Bias's parents and coach had no knowledge concerning the specific instances in which the defendants' witnesses claim to have seen Bias using cocaine. In order to sufficiently challenge the defendants' witnesses' testimony, the estate (P) could have deposed those witnesses or otherwise offered testimony from those familiar with the instances in which Bias is alleged to have used cocaine. Without direct evidence to the contrary, there is no genuine issue of material fact as to Bias's past drug use.

Concerning the availability of a life insurance policy, the defendants offered evidence that every insurance company inquired regarding the applicant's drug use at some point in the process. In response, the estate (P) offered evidence that some insurance companies did not inquire about drug use at certain stages of the process. The estate (P) failed, however, to come forward with specific facts to demonstrate that some insurance company would have insured Bias without inquiring about his past drug use at some point in the process. Because the defendants met their burden of demonstrating an absence of a genuine issue of material fact, the plaintiff was required to assert specific facts in rebuttal. Having failed to do so, summary judgment was appropriate. Affirmed.

Analysis:

On a motion for summary judgment, a court must refrain from considering the credibility of the witnesses and must consider the evidence, and all inferences arising therefrom, in the light most favorable to the non-moving party. If there are no genuine issues for trial, summary judgment must be granted. Here, the evidence offered by the plaintiff, even taken as true, did not conflict with the evidence offered by the defendants. Accordingly, the defendants were entitled to judgment in their favor.

■ CASE VOCABULARY

GENUINE ISSUE OF MATERIAL FACT: In the law of summary judgments, a triable, substantial, or real question of fact supported by substantial evidence.

MATERIAL FACT: A fact that is significant or essential to the issue or matter at hand.

SUMMARY JUDGMENT: A judgment granted on a claim about which there is no genuine issue of material fact and upon which the movant is entitled to prevail as a matter of law.

CHAPTER 9

The Trier and the Trial

McKey v. Fairbairn

Instant Facts: In a negligence suit against a landlord, the tenant's attorney moved to introduce housing regulations as proof of negligence, but the court denied the motion because the regulations were not contained in the pretrial order.

Black Letter Rule: Trial judges have justifiably large discretion in refusing parties to change their theory during the trial, after a pre-trial order.

Reid v. San Pedro, Los Angeles & Salt Lake Railroad

Instant Facts: Reid (P) sued Railroad (D) for negligence after her cattle was hit by a train, and the jury found negligence without direct evidence of how the animal entered onto the tracks.

Black Letter Rule: There is insufficient evidence to support a verdict where two equal inferences exist to prove a fact, but only one of which can establish liability.

Thompson v. Altheimer & Gray

Instant Facts: Thompson (P) moved for a new trial on appeal, alleging a juror should have been stricken for cause after indicating that her experiences could cloud her judgment.

Black Letter Rule: A juror should be stricken for cause when he or she demonstrates bias against any party.

Caperton v. A.T. Massey Coal Co.

Instant Facts: The president of A.T. Massey Coal Co. (D) made large campaign contributions to a judicial candidate shortly before a case involving Massey (D) was to be heard, and after he was elected, that judge refused to recuse himself from the case.

Black Letter Rule: Objective factors that show a risk of actual bias may require a judge to recuse himself from consideration of a particular case.

Pennsylvania Railroad v. Chamberlain

Instant Facts: Action for negligence by train brakeman's heir against railroad contending that certain rail cars collided killing brakeman based upon indirect evidence of hearing collision.

Black Letter Rule: Where the facts give equal support to each of two inconsistent inferences, a party has not sustained her burden of proving facts by a preponderance of the evidence.

Lind v. Schenley Industries

Instant Facts: Liquor company sales manager obtained jury verdict for breach of contract and liquor company moved for j.n.o.v., and alternatively new trial.

Black Letter Rule: A trial judge abuses his discretion in granting a new trial where he substitutes his judgment for that of the jury concerning the weight of the evidence.

Peterson v. Wilson

Instant Facts: Employee of University successfully obtained a jury verdict, but new trial was ordered based upon statements made by jurors to judge and employee thereafter lost on re-trial.

Black Letter Rule: It is error to grant a new trial based upon post verdict statements from jurors relating to the mental processes of the jurors during their deliberations.

McKey v. Fairbairn

(Tenant) v. (Landlord's Agent)

345 F.2d 739 (D.C. Cir. 1965)

COURTS MAY HOLD LITIGANTS TO THE ISSUES IDENTIFIED IN A PRETRIAL ORDER

■ **INSTANT FACTS** In a negligence suit against a landlord, the tenant's attorney moved to introduce housing regulations as proof of negligence, but the court denied the motion because the regulations were not contained in the pretrial order.

■ **BLACK LETTER RULE** Trial judges have justifiably large discretion in refusing parties to change their theory during the trial, after a pre-trial order.

■ **PROCEDURAL BASIS**

Appeal to the D.C. Circuit Court of Appeals, challenging the District Court's directed verdict.

■ **FACTS**

Levi McKey rented a dwelling house from Kenneth Fairbairn (D), agent for the property's owner. Fairbairn was made aware of a leak in one of the house's bedrooms. Shortly thereafter, McKey's mother-in-law (Littlejohn) entered the room, and despite knowing the condition of the floor proceeded to slip and fall, sustaining injuries. After initiating a suit for negligence, Littlejohn died from causes unrelated to the fall, and Helen McKey (P), her administratrix, was substituted as plaintiff. The pretrial order contained McKey's (P) theory of the case. It stated that Littlejohn's injuries were a result of Fairbairn's negligence in failing to repair the roof and eliminate the leak after notice thereof and Fairbairn's promise to repair, all in breach of a duty owed under the lease. During the trial McKey's (P) attorney became aware of housing regulations requiring roofs to be leak-proof. Counsel moved to amend the pretrial order to permit these regulations to be entered into evidence. The court denied the motion and directed verdict for Fairbairn (D).

■ **ISSUE**

Does a court abuse its discretion when it refuses to amend the pretrial order so that pertinent evidence, which came to light during trial, may be admitted; particularly where the other party was aware of the evidence?

■ **DECISION AND RATIONALE**

(Miller, J.) No. A judge has justifiably large discretion in refusing to permit a party to change its theory during the trial. We need not decide whether the proffered regulations are pertinent to this case. The trail judge acted within his discretion in refusing to admit them. There is also a further reason for upholding the directed verdict. Mainly, Mrs. Littlejohn admitted she knew of the floor's condition and yet failed exercise proper care. Thus, the trial judge would have been justified in instructing the jury that Mrs. Littlejohn was contributorily negligent as a matter of law. Affirmed.

■ **DISSENT**

(Fahy, J.) There are cases when judges should use their discretion to depart from the pretrial order. The Federal Rules of Procedure provide that the pretrial order controls the course of the action "unless modified at trial to prevent manifest injustice." In deciding the matter of "manifest

---

injustice" the court must weigh the failure of counsel to bring forth this new theory of liability until trial against the possible prejudice to the defendant. The failure in this case was inadvertent. Any prejudice to the defendant could have been obviated by a continuance. Manifest injustice is more likely to occur when the applicable law is precluded from consideration because not referred to in the pretrial order than when the preclusion is of evidentiary matter that takes the adversary by surprise. The court should also not rely on any theory of contributory negligence because the trial court did not rule on the issue.

Analysis:

The pre-trial order issued pursuant to Rule 16 of the Federal Rules of Civil Procedure narrows the issues, guides the trial, and supplants the pleadings. As the court points out, the trial judge has the discretion to hold the litigants to the issues identified in the order. The dissent argues that the trial court should have weighed the benefits of amending the pre-trial order against the detriment to the defendant. This makes sense, but unfortunately for Mrs. McKey (P), trial courts are given wide latitude in decisions relating to the management of the trial.

Reid v. San Pedro, Los Angeles & Salt Lake Railroad

(Cattle Owner) v. (Railroad)

39 Utah 617, 118 P. 1009 (1911)

THE COURT HAS THE POWER TO DIRECT A VERDICT IF, BY LOOKING AT THE EVIDENCE PRESENTED, IT DETERMINES THAT THE INFERENCES MADE BY THE JURY FROM THE EVIDENCE ARE NOT RATIONAL

■ **INSTANT FACTS** Reid (P) sued Railroad (D) for negligence after her cattle was hit by a train, and the jury found negligence without direct evidence of how the animal entered onto the tracks.

■ **BLACK LETTER RULE** There is insufficient evidence to support a verdict where two equal inferences exist to prove a fact, but only one of which can establish liability.

■ **PROCEDURAL BASIS**

Appeal from a judgment following jury verdict in negligence action seeking damages.

■ **FACTS**

Reid (P) filed suit against San Pedro, Los Angeles & Salt Lake Railroad (Railroad) (D) for damages when her cattle was killed by Railroad's (D) train. Reid (P) contended that Railroad (D) negligently maintained the fence along the railroad so that it was down in certain areas and negligently allowed a gate along the railroad to be opened, so that in either event her heifer strayed onto the railroad tracks and was hit by a train. [Test your farm animal knowledge—Is a heifer a calf, bull, cow, cattle steer, bovine, all of the above or none of the above?] Reid (P) kept the cattle on private land owned by another and located next to the train tracks. Railroad (D) provided the gates for the convenience of the land owner. It was not contended at trial that Railroad (D) left the gate open. The evidence showed that the animal was killed in the immediate vicinity of the open gate and about a mile from the downed portion of the fence. However, there was no direct evidence as to which passage the animal used to reach the tracks. There was no evidence that the train operated negligently. The jury returned a verdict in favor of Reid (P) and Railroad (D) appealed based upon insufficient evidence to support the verdict.

■ **ISSUE**

Is there sufficient evidence to support a verdict where liability is established based upon two equal inferences, one which could establish liability and the other which could not?

■ **DECISION AND RATIONALE**

(McCarty) No. Reid (P) cannot meet her burden of proof to establish liability by a preponderance of the evidence where there are two equal inferences, only one of which can establish liability. Railroad (D) asserts on appeal that there is insufficient evidence to support the verdict because it cannot be determined where and under what circumstances the cattle got onto the tracks. Statutory law provides that if a railroad company provides gates at private crossings for the convenience of the land owners, the gates must be closed at all times when not in use, and if the owner fails to do so, and his animals stray onto the tracks, the owner cannot recover damages for killed or injured animals. Railroad (D) contends that since the cattle could have passed through the open gate and onto the tracks, resulting in no liability to Reid (P), the verdict must be set aside. The evidence showed that the animal was killed in the

---

immediate vicinity of the gate, and about one mile from the downed fence. However, there was no direct evidence as to how the cattle got onto the tracks. [Maybe it jumped the fence!] The inference is just as strong, if not stronger, that the animal entered through the gate. Reid (P) has the burden of proof to establish liability by a preponderance of the evidence. It is well established that if there are two equal inferences, one which establishes liability and the other which does not, the plaintiff has not met his burden and cannot prevail. In this matter, it was essential for Reid (P) to show by a preponderance of the evidence that the animal entered onto the railroad tracks through the downed fence. Reid (P) did not prove this and thus the verdict is not supported by the evidence. The trial court should have directed a verdict for Railroad (D). [Answer—a heifer is a cow that has not had a calf.]

Analysis:

A jury's verdict may be set aside when there is insufficient evidence to support the verdict. There was no direct evidence to prove how the animal got onto the tracks in this case, only indirect evidence based upon inferences. The holding of the case exemplifies that where there are two equal inferences, only one of which can support liability, there is no preponderance of the evidence. Reid (P) did not produce evidence to permit the jury to rationally conclude that it was more probable than not that the Railroad's (D) negligence caused the death of the animal. There must be a preponderance of evidence to support the verdict, and the judge has the power to set aside the jury's verdict where the evidence presented at trial does not satisfy the burden of proof.

■ CASE VOCABULARY

DIRECT EVIDENCE: Proof of precise fact in question by direct means, such as where a witness sees or hears something.

DIRECTED VERDICT: Judge entering judgment for one party before return of jury verdict.

PREPONDERANCE OF THE EVIDENCE: Proving something by the greater, not just equal, weight of the evidence.

(Employee) v. (Employer)

248 F.3d 621 (7th Cir.2001)

A TRUE BELIEF IS NOT JUROR BIAS WITHOUT AN INDICATION THAT THE BELIEF CLOUDS THE JUROR'S JUDGMENT

■ **INSTANT FACTS** Thompson (P) moved for a new trial on appeal, alleging a juror should have been stricken for cause after indicating that her experiences could cloud her judgment.

■ **BLACK LETTER RULE** A juror should be stricken for cause when he or she demonstrates bias against any party.

■ **PROCEDURAL BASIS**

On appeal to review a judgment for the defendant.

■ **FACTS**

Thompson (P) sued her employer, Altheimer & Gray (D), for racial discrimination. After the case was tried and a verdict for the defendant delivered, Thompson (P) appealed, alleging a juror named Leiter should have been stricken for cause, entitling her to a new trial. During voir dire, Leiter informed the judge that as a business owner, Leiter's decision would be swayed toward the defendant. Leiter also informed the judge that she would do her best to properly apply the law to the case, but that her judgment would be influenced by her experiences. In response to questioning from Thompson's (P) lawyer, Leiter further stated that she was often faced with decisions based on benefits to be afforded to employees and that she believed that sometimes employees file lawsuits simply because they did not get their way. Ultimately, Leiter promised to be as fair as she could, given her experiences. After the court denied Thompson's (P) request to strike Leiter for cause, the jury was impaneled. Each juror, including Leiter, affirmatively indicated that he or she was capable of following the court's instructions and would be able to withhold judgment until all evidence had been considered.

■ **ISSUE**

Should a juror in an employment case be stricken for cause after expressing a belief that some employees file frivolous suits against their employers?

■ **DECISION AND RATIONALE**

(Posner, J.) No. It is true that all parties are entitled to have their claims heard by a fair, unbiased jury. Thus, when a juror expresses manifest bias against any party, the juror should be stricken for cause and replaced with an alternate juror. The expression of a true, realistic belief, however, does not of itself establish juror bias. Here, Leiter expressed her true belief that some employees sue their employers merely because they have been denied benefits to which they believe they are entitled. This belief alone, true as it may be, is insufficient to establish bias without taking the next step, to question whether the belief would impair the juror's judgment. This inquiry was not made here. Although the judge asked the jury as a whole whether it could be faithful to his instructions, his line of questioning to Leiter should have been followed by an individual assurance that her belief did not amount to juror bias. Reversed and remanded for a new trial.

■ CONCURRENCE

(Wood, J.) While Thompson (P) is entitled to a new trial because of the court's failure to properly eliminate potential juror bias, such may not always be the case. When a party fails to exhaust all of his or her peremptory challenges, such a failure may amount to a waiver of the right to challenge juror bias on appeal.

Analysis:

All jurors likely have preconceived notions concerning the subject matter of a case. Whether motivated by experience, political affiliation, gender attitudes, or racial perspective, the particular viewpoints of jurors are the fundamentally important aspect of the right to trial by jury. Only when those viewpoints rise to the level of bias should a juror be disqualified.

■ CASE VOCABULARY

CHALLENGE FOR CAUSE: A party's challenge supported by a specified reason, such as bias or prejudice, that would disqualify that potential juror.

PEREMPTORY CHALLENGE: One of a party's limited number of challenges that need not be supported by any reason, although a party may not use such a challenge in a way that discriminates on the basis of race, ethnicity, or gender.

VOIR DIRE: A preliminary examination of a prospective juror by a judge or lawyer to decide whether the prospect is qualified and suitable to serve on a jury.

Caperton v. A.T. Massey Coal Co.

(Coal Company President) v. (Supplier)

556 U.S. 868 (2009)

THE APPEARANCE OF JUDICIAL BIAS MAY VIOLATE DUE PROCESS

It's not enough to be good, it has to also look good, or people won't swallow it.

stus.com

■ **INSTANT FACTS** The president of A.T. Massey Coal Co. (D) made large campaign contributions to a judicial candidate shortly before a case involving Massey (D) was to be heard, and after he was elected, that judge refused to recuse himself from the case.

■ **BLACK LETTER RULE** Objective factors that show a risk of actual bias may require a judge to recuse himself from consideration of a particular case.

■ **PROCEDURAL BASIS**

Certiorari to the West Virginia Supreme Court of Appeals.

■ **FACTS**

Caperton (P) obtained a $50 million verdict in West Virginia state court against A.T. Massey Coal Co. (D) and its affiliates (D) for fraudulent misrepresentation, concealment, and tortious interference with existing contractual relations. After the verdict in the case, but before the appeal was filed, West Virginia held judicial elections. Blankenship, the chairman, CEO, and president of Massey (D), gave a $1000 campaign contribution (the maximum permitted by law) to Benjamin, a candidate for the Supreme Court of Appeals. Blankenship also donated almost $2.5 million to a tax-exempt organization that supported Benjamin, and spent $500,000 on independent expenditures supporting Benjamin. Blankenship's contributions were more than the total amount spent by all of Benjamin's other supporters, and three times the amount spent by Benjamin's own campaign committee. Benjamin was elected to the court.

After an appeal was filed, Caperton (P) moved to disqualify Benjamin under the Due Process Clause and the West Virginia Code of Judicial Conduct. Caperton (P) based his motion on the conflict caused by Blankenship's campaign involvement. Benjamin denied the motion, stating that he found "no objective information . . . to show that this Justice has a bias for or against any litigant, that this Justice has prejudged the matters which comprise this litigation, or that this Justice will be anything but fair and impartial." The Supreme Court of Appeals reversed the jury verdict. The majority opinion was authored by Chief Justice Davis, and joined by Justices Benjamin and Maynard. Justice Starcher and Justice Albright dissented. Caperton (P) moved for rehearing, and the parties moved to disqualify three of the five judges who decided the appeal. Justice Maynard granted the recusal motion after photographs surfaced of him vacationing with Blankenship on the French Riviera. Justice Starcher granted Massey's (D) recusal motion, apparently based on his public criticism of Blankenship. Benjamin again refused to recuse himself. Rehearing was granted, and Justice Benjamin, as acting Chief Justice, appointed two judges to replace the recused Justices. The court reversed the jury verdict again, by a three-to-two vote.

■ **ISSUE**

Was Justice Benjamin required to recuse himself?

■ **DECISION AND RATIONALE**

(Kennedy, J.) Yes. Objective factors that show a risk of actual bias may require a judge to recuse himself from consideration of a particular case. Although questions of judicial recusal usually do not rise to a constitutional level, experience teaches that there are circumstances in which the probability of actual bias is too high to be constitutionally tolerable. A fair trial in a fair tribunal is a basic requirement of due process. The Court has considered two categories of cases that require judicial disqualification. In *Tumey v. Ohio,* 273 U.S. 510 (1927), the Court concluded that the Due Process Clause incorporated the common-law rule that a judge must recuse himself or herself when the judge has a "direct, personal, substantial, pecuniary interest" in a case. Personal bias or prejudice alone did not rise to the level of a due process violation. The *Tumey* case involved a mayor who had the authority to try cases involving possession of alcoholic beverages, alone and without a jury. The mayor received a salary supplement for trying cases, and that supplement came from fines paid by those who were convicted. No supplement was paid if a defendant was acquitted. The village also received some of the funds from the fines. The Court held that the Due Process Clause required disqualification due to the mayor's direct pecuniary interest in the outcome, and because of his official motive to convict to help the financial needs of the village. Similarly, in *Ward v. Monroeville,* 409 U.S. 57 (1972), the Court invalidated a conviction from another mayor's court. The mayor in that case received nothing from the fines, but the money went to the town's finances. The Court held that the fact that the mayor received no money directly did not matter. What was important was the possible temptation the mayor might face. The proper constitutional inquiry is whether a case offers a possible temptation to the average judge to lead him or her "not to hold the balance nice, clear and true." The degree or kind of interest that would require disqualification cannot be defined with precision, but the test should have an objective component.

The second type of case involved criminal contempt, and the conflict that arose from a judge's participation in an earlier proceeding. In that first proceeding, the judge examined witnesses to determine whether charges should be brought. The judge determined that one witness lied, and charged him with perjury. The second witness declined to answer questions, and the judge charged him with contempt. The Court held that due process required disqualification, based on the maxim that "no man can be a judge in his own case." Having been a part of the earlier process, a judge cannot be wholly disinterested in the outcome. A judge will not always be barred from hearing contempt charges when the contempt was directed against him or her, but the question is whether the average judge is likely to be neutral, or whether there is an unconstitutional potential for bias.

The instant case arises in the context of judicial elections. Although Blankenship's contributions were not bribes or criminal influence, Justice Benjamin would nevertheless feel a debt of gratitude for the extraordinary efforts to get him elected. That temptation, Caperton (P) claims, is strong and inherent in human nature. Based on the facts presented by Caperton (P), Justice Benjamin conducted a probing search into his actual motives and inclinations. He found none to be improper. The Court does not question his findings of impartiality and propriety, and there is no determination as to whether there was actual bias. Judges often inquire into their subjective motives and purposes in the ordinary course of deciding a case. There are instances when inquiry may reveal that what the judge had assumed to be a proper, controlling factor is not the real one at work. If the judge discovers that some personal bias or improper consideration may undermine neutrality, the judge may think it necessary to consider withdrawing from the case. The difficulties of inquiring into actual bias, and the fact that the inquiry is often a private one, underscore the need for objective rules. Otherwise there may be no adequate protection against a judge who misreads or misapprehends the real motives behind a decision. In lieu of exclusive reliance on personal inquiry, or on appellate review of the judge's determination respecting bias, the Due Process Clause does not require proof of actual bias. Instead, the Court asks whether, "under a realistic appraisal of psychological tendencies and human weakness," the interest "poses such a risk of actual bias or prejudgment that the practice must be forbidden if the guarantee of due process is to be adequately implemented."

Not every campaign contribution by a litigant or attorney creates a probability of bias that requires a judge's recusal. This, however, is an exceptional case. There is a serious risk of actual bias—based on objective and reasonable perceptions—when a person with a personal stake in a particular case had a significant and disproportionate influence in placing the judge on the case. The inquiry centers on the contribution's relative size in comparison to the total amount of money contributed to the campaign, the total amount spent in the election, and the apparent effect such contribution had on the outcome of the election. Applying this principle, Blankenship's efforts had a significant and disproportionate influence in placing Justice Benjamin on the case. The proper inquiry is not whether Blankenship's campaign contributions were a necessary and sufficient cause of Benjamin's victory. Due process requires an objective inquiry into whether the contributor's influence on the election under all the circumstances "would offer a possible temptation to the average . . . judge to . . . lead him not to hold the balance nice, clear and true."

This decision addresses an extraordinary situation. Massey (D) and its supporting amici predict consequences that range from a flood of recusal motions to unnecessary interference with judicial elections. It is worth noting the effects, or lack thereof, of the Court's prior recusal decisions. The Court was not flooded with recusal motions after those cases. That is perhaps due in part to the extreme facts those cases addressed. States have also implemented reforms designed to eliminate even the appearance of partiality. Codes of judicial conduct are the "principal safeguard against judicial campaign abuses." States may choose to adopt more rigorous standards for recusal than those required by the Due Process Clause, so most disputes over disqualification will be resolved without resort to the Constitution. Reversed.

■ DISSENT

(Roberts, C.J.) Until today, the Court has recognized exactly two situations in which the Federal Due Process Clause requires disqualification of a judge: When the judge has a financial interest in the outcome of the case; and when the judge is trying a defendant for certain criminal contempts. Vague notions of bias or the appearance of bias were never a basis for disqualification. Those issues were addressed by legislation or court rules. Now, the Due Process Clause is used to overturn a judge's failure to recuse because of a "probability of bias." The Court's new "rule" provides no guidance to judges and litigants about when recusal will be constitutionally required. This will inevitably lead to an increase in allegations that judges are biased. The majority says that the present case is an "extreme" one, so there is no need to worry about other cases. But this is just so much whistling past the graveyard. Claims that have little chance of success are nonetheless frequently filed.

■ DISSENT

(Scalia, J.) This decision will erode public confidence in the judicial system. Public confidence is eroded by the perception that litigation is just a game. The majority's decision will reinforce that perception, adding to the vast arsenal of lawyerly gambits what will come to be known as the *Caperton* claim.

Analysis:

The importance of the *Caperton* case is not that it dealt with explicit expressions of judicial bias, but the temptation of bias posed by hefty campaign contributions. Some commentators on this case have said that it creates a potential "constitutional crisis." Candidates for judicial office have the First Amendment right to make their opinions known to the electorate, even if those opinions would seem to bind them when deciding future cases, but litigants have a Due Process right not to have a case heard by a biased judge.

Pennsylvania Railroad v. Chamberlain

(Railroad) v. (Deceased Brakeman's Heir)

288 U.S. 333, 53 S.Ct. 391 (1933)

COURT MAY REFUSE TO SUBMIT CASE TO THE JURY, AND INSTEAD DIRECT A VERDICT, WHERE PARTY HAS NOT SUSTAINED HER BURDEN OF PROOF

■ **INSTANT FACTS** Action for negligence by train brakeman's heir against railroad contending that certain rail cars collided killing brakeman based upon indirect evidence of hearing collision.

■ **BLACK LETTER RULE** Where the facts give equal support to each of two inconsistent inferences, a party has not sustained her burden of proving facts by a preponderance of the evidence.

■ **PROCEDURAL BASIS**

Appeal to the United States Supreme Court from a judgment in a negligence action seeking damages for wrongful death.

■ **FACTS**

The heir of a deceased brakeman, Chamberlain (P), brought a negligence action against Pennsylvania Railroad (Railroad) (D) for the brakeman's wrongful death in the train yard. The decedent was riding on a string of two rail cars while trying to move them onto a certain track. Chamberlain (P) contends that the Railroad's (D) employees were negligent in that they caused another set of rail cars to collide with those ridden by the decedent, causing him to be thrown onto the track, run over by the cars and killed. The evidence at trial established that there were a string of seven cars in front of the decedent's string of two cars, and behind him were a string of nine cars. The basis for the claim of negligence is that the string of nine cars behind the decedent collided with the cars ridden by him. However, the testimony from the Railroad (D) employees riding the nine car string, as well as others close by, was that no such collision occurred. The one witness who testified for Chamberlain (P) was also an employee. He testified that he saw the decedent riding the rail cars, and also saw another string of cars that were placed onto another track, and this was followed by the nine car string. He did not pay further attention but when he looked again, decedent was still on his string of cars directing them to a track, and the string of nine cars was behind him and the speed had increased. While looking away again, he heard a loud crash, but did not immediately look in the direction of the noise since it was not uncommon to hear this kind of noise in train yards. [They must crash a lot of trains in train yards.] When he did turn to look, the decedent was no longer in sight. His distance from where the decedent's body was found was approximately 900 feet. This witness did not testify that a collision occurred, but inferred it because he heard a crash, and thereafter saw the two strings of cars moving together. At the conclusion of the evidence, the trial judge directed the jury to find in favor of Railroad (D). The trial judge believed that all of the testimony, being circumstantial evidence, was so insubstantial and insufficient that it did not justify submission to the jury. The court of appeals reversed the judgment and Railroad (D) appealed to the United States Supreme Court.

■ **ISSUE**

Has a party sustained her burden of proving facts by a preponderance of the evidence where the facts give equal support to each of two inconsistent inferences?

■ DECISION AND RATIONALE

(Sutherland) No. A party has not sustained her burden of proving facts by a preponderance of the evidence where the facts give equal support to each of two inconsistent inferences. In these circumstances, it is proper to not submit the matter to the jury and enter a directed verdict against the party who has the burden of proof. Where there is a direct conflict in the testimony concerning a factual matter, the jury must determine which testimony should be believed. In this case, there is no conflict in testimony concerning the facts. The witnesses for the Railroad (D) testified that there was no collision between the nine car string and the decedent's two car string. The witness for Chamberlain (P) did not testify that there was a collision, rather, he said that he heard a loud crash. It was not unusual for him to hear this type of noise in the train yard, and he did not immediately turn to look when he heard the noise. Thus, there is no direct evidence that the crash by the two strings of cars occurred. At most there was an inference to that effect. However, there is equal support to the opposite inference that a collision occurred between either other strings of cars away from the scene of the accident, or a collision between the cars ridden by the decedent and the seven car string in front of him. Thus, the evidence gives equal support to each of two inconsistent inferences. It does not matter that Chamberlain's (P) sole witness has concluded from what he saw that the string of nine cars was involved in a collision with the decedent. His testimony is considered suspicious and incredible. [Although we are not supposed to weigh the credibility of witnesses, we can't resist.] The distance and angle of vision, near dusk, make it practically impossible of seeing whether the front of the nine car string was in contact with the back of the decedent's two car string. Thus, Chamberlain (P) has not sustained her burden of proof. Accordingly, since neither of the inferences can be established, judgment, as a matter of law, must be against Chamberlain (P), the party who has the burden of proof. Judgment of the court of appeals is reversed and that of the district court affirmed.

Analysis:

In this case, the court did not even allow the case to be submitted to a jury for determination. Instead, the court directed a verdict in favor of the Railroad (D). The Supreme Court agreed with the trial judge, and reversed the court of appeals, holding that there were two inconsistent inferences that could be drawn from the testimony. On the one hand, there could be an inference that the collision involved the nine car string, and on the other hand, it could have involved the seven car string or other cars entirely. In fact, it was at best an inference that a collision occurred, since the witness for Chamberlain (P) only heard a loud noise sounding like a crash. In this case, there was no direct evidence that a collision occurred. The indirect, or circumstantial evidence from Chamberlain's (P) witness was not sufficient because there were two inconsistent inferences that could be drawn from his testimony. The testimony gives equal support to each of two inconsistent inferences. Accordingly, the court decided, as a matter of law, that Chamberlain (P) could not sustain her burden of proof by a preponderance of the evidence.

■ CASE VOCABULARY

BURDEN OF PROOF: Obligation of proving each necessary element of the cause of action or defense.

CIRCUMSTANTIAL EVIDENCE: Indirect evidence from which inferences from the facts are drawn.

Lind v. Schenley Industries

(Liquor Sales Manager) v. (Liquor Company Employer)

278 F.2d 79 (3d Cir.1960)

A VERDICT MAY BE SET ASIDE BY WAY OF MOTION FOR J.N.O.V. OR IN THE ALTERNATIVE NEW TRIAL

■ **INSTANT FACTS** Liquor company sales manager obtained jury verdict for breach of contract and liquor company moved for j.n.o.v., and alternatively new trial.

■ **BLACK LETTER RULE** A trial judge abuses his discretion in granting a new trial where he substitutes his judgment for that of the jury concerning the weight of the evidence.

■ **PROCEDURAL BASIS**

Appeal from judgment following granting of motion notwithstanding the verdict and alternative motion for new trial after jury verdict in breach of contract action.

■ **FACTS**

Lind (P), a liquor company sales manager, brought an action against his employer Schenley Industries (Schenley) (D), a liquor company, for breach of oral contract. Lind (P) and his secretary testified as to certain promises made by the company and agents for Schenley (D) [not surprisingly] testified that they did not make such promises. The jury found in favor of Lind (P) and awarded him damages. The trial judge granted Schenley's (D) motion for judgment notwithstanding the verdict and, in the alternative, a new trial. The order granting a new trial was made because the judge concluded that the verdict in favor of Lind (P) was against the weight of the evidence. Lind (P) appealed.

■ **ISSUE**

Does a trial judge abuse his discretion in granting a new trial where he substitutes his judgment for that of the jury concerning the weight of the evidence?

■ **DECISION AND RATIONALE**

(Biggs) Yes. A trial judge may not substitute his judgment for that of the jury concerning the weight of the evidence. If he does so and grants a new trial, an abuse of discretion occurs. In order to overturn the granting of a new trial on the ground that the verdict was against the weight of the evidence, there must be a clear showing that the trial judge abused his discretion in so doing. There is a closer degree of scrutiny and supervision by the appellate court when the ground for granting a new trial is on the basis of the verdict being against the weight of the evidence, as opposed to other permitted grounds for granting new trials. If the appellate court believes that an injustice may result, it may reverse the trial court. The trial judge has wide discretion in determining whether or not a new trial ought to be granted, but he may not set aside the verdict merely because he would have come to a different conclusion than that reached by the jury. It is only upon finding that the jury reached a seriously erroneous result that the verdict should be set aside. In this case, the subject matter for the jury's consideration was simple and straight forward. Its main function, as trier of fact, was to determine whether or not the witnesses were telling the truth. We conclude [luckily for Lind (P)] that the trial judge substituted his judgment for that of the jury and therefore abused his legal discretion. We

---

reverse and remand the case with direction to reinstate the verdict and judgment in favor or Lind (P).

■ DISSENT

(Hastie) This court has never before reversed an order of a trial judge granting a new trial because of his conclusion that the jury had reached an unjust result. Once a trial judge reaches this conclusion, the appellate court's only function is to see whether there was any basis in reason for the judge's conclusion. In this case, there was sharp conflict in testimony. The trial judge may have reasoned that the amount claimed to have been promised to Lind (P) was so abnormally large, and his concern over nonpayment so unnaturally small, as to make it incredible that the promise ever was made. If so, the conclusion of the judge was neither arbitrary nor an abuse of discretion. I think that the appellate court, rather than the trial judge, has usurped the function of the jury.

Analysis:

Following a jury's verdict, alternative motions may be made for judgment notwithstanding the verdict ("j.n.o.v.") or, in the alternative, for a new trial. The grounds for the motion for j.n.o.v. are the same as for a motion for directed verdict, i.e., insufficient evidence to support the verdict. The only differences lie in when the motions are made—one before the verdict and one following. One ground for making a motion for new trial is that the verdict is against the weight of the evidence. There is a fine line between the permissible granting of the motion on this ground and the erroneous substituting of the court's judge's opinion in place of the jury's opinion. This case examines that fine line. The majority opinion reviews the standard to be applied by trial judges in ruling on a motion for new trial on the ground that the verdict is against the weight of evidence. It also discusses the standard that the appellate court should apply in reviewing the order granting the new trial.

■ CASE VOCABULARY

ABUSE OF DISCRETION: A standard of review used by the appellate courts, indicating that a judge has come to a clearly erroneous decision.

J.N.O.V.: Latin initials for judgment non obstante veredicto; otherwise known as judgment notwithstanding the verdict.

MOTION FOR JUDGMENT NOTWITHSTANDING THE VERDICT: Motion made post verdict to have judgment rendered in favor of one party notwithstanding a verdict in favor of the other party.

MOTION FOR NEW TRIAL: Motion made post verdict or post decision by court to have the matter tried again.

Peterson v. Wilson

(Fired Employee) v. (Person Who Fired)

141 F.3d 573 (5th Cir.1998)

JURORS' COMMENTS WHICH REVEAL LACK OF UNDERSTANDING OF THE INSTRUCTIONS CANNOT BE USED TO IMPEACH VERDICT

■ **INSTANT FACTS** Employee of University successfully obtained a jury verdict, but new trial was ordered based upon statements made by jurors to judge and employee thereafter lost on re-trial.

■ **BLACK LETTER RULE** It is error to grant a new trial based upon post verdict statements from jurors relating to the mental processes of the jurors during their deliberations.

■ **FACTS**

Peterson (P) brought suit for federal statutory and constitutional claims after being fired, allegedly arbitrarily and capriciously, from Texas Southern University where he worked as a grant director. The jury returned a verdict in Peterson's (P) favor and awarded him damages. Following the verdict, Wilson (D), the person who made the decision to terminate Peterson (P), renewed his motion for judgment as a matter of law, and supplemented it with an alternative motion for new trial. Four months later, the judge granted the new trial for the following specified reason: "The court concludes, based on the jury's verdict and *comments the jurors made to the court after returning the verdict* [and outside the presence of the parties and their respective counsel], that the jury completely disregarded the Court's instructions. Instead, it appears that the jury considered improper factors in reaching its verdict. Accordingly, the Court deems it in the interest of justice to grant a new trial (emphasis added)." Peterson (P) unsuccessfully moved for reconsideration. The case was re-tried and a jury verdict was rendered in favor of Wilson (D). [This is why jury trials are similar to flipping a coin, you never can predict the verdict.] Peterson (P) appealed.

■ **ISSUE**

Is it error to grant a new trial based upon post verdict statements from jurors relating to the mental processes of the jurors during their deliberations?

■ **DECISION AND RATIONALE**

(Wiener) Yes. It is improper to impeach a verdict based upon the jurors' mental processes during deliberations. It is clearly apparent that the trial judge relied upon information he obtained from the jurors post verdict, and outside the presence of the parties and counsel. Meeting with the jurors alone was impermissible. [But it did not end there. The judge did more.] The judge relied upon the jurors' comments to grant a new trial. The Federal Rules of Evidence govern impeachment of jury verdicts. Rule 606(b) provides that when inquiring into the validity of a verdict, a juror may not testify concerning matters or statements made during the jury's deliberations, such as another juror's mind or emotions influencing a juror to vote a certain way, or the mental processes involved in the deliberations. An exception exists for extraneous prejudicial information or outside influence which is improperly brought to the jury's attention. It is also well settled in case law that juror testimony may not be used to impeach a jury verdict. [Obviously the trial judge didn't know the law on how not to impeach a verdict.] In Robles v. Exxon Corp. we held that receiving testimony from jurors after they had returned

---

their verdict, for the purpose of ascertaining whether the jury misunderstood the jury instructions is prohibited by Rule 606(b). It is clear in the case before us that the jurors' statements to the judge related directly to matters that transpired in the jury room, and that these matters comprehended the mental processes of the jurors in their deliberations. These statements formed the foundation of the court's impeachment of the verdict. Such conduct clearly violates *Robles*. We therefore must reverse the trial court's grant of a new trial, vacate the court's judgment rendered on the basis of the jury verdict in the second trial, and reinstate the results of the first trial. We remand the case to the district court for entry of judgment in favor of Peterson (P) and against Wilson (D).

Analysis:

There are express rules, both federal and state, that set forth the specific grounds for impeaching a verdict. Since this was a federal case, Rule 606(b) of the Federal rules applied. It was error to impeach the verdict because it was based upon the *deliberation process* of the jurors. If, however, a juror had brought something into the jury room from the outside, such as a dictionary, and it was used as part of the deliberation process, the verdict could be impeached. Note that the judge obtained the information from the jurors outside the presence of the parties and their counsel. The court of appeals referred to this as "impermissible". This case also examines appellate procedure. When a motion for new trial is granted, the order granting the new trial is not immediately appealable because it is not a final judgment. Peterson (P) tried, unsuccessfully, to have the judge reconsider his granting of Wilson's (D) motion for new trial. When that failed, Peterson (P) had to wait for the outcome of the second trial. Since he lost and judgment was entered on the verdict in favor of Wilson (D), Peterson (P) appealed from the judgment in the second trial.

■ CASE VOCABULARY

EX PARTE: Application made by one party [in this case it was the judge] without notice to the other.

INTERROGATORY: A written question.

MOTION FOR J.M.L.: Name used in federal court for motion for judgment as a matter of law. Formerly called motion for judgment notwithstanding the verdict.

QUA: Indicating in the capacity "as" or by virtue of being "as".

SUA SPONTE: Acting in a voluntary manner.

CHAPTER 10

Appeal

Liberty Mutual Insurance Co. v. Wetzel

Instant Facts: Liberty Mutual Insurance Co. (D) appealed the grant of partial summary judgment against it, and the Supreme Court now considers the jurisdiction of the appellate court.

Black Letter Rule: A grant of partial summary judgment on the issue of liability is an interlocutory order and is not appealable.

Lauro Lines s.r.l. v. Chasser

Instant Facts: An interlocutory order denying an Italian company's motion to dismiss, based on a contractual forum-selection clause, is held not to come within the collateral order doctrine exception to the final judgment rule, and therefore cannot be immediately appealed.

Black Letter Rule: Passengers on a cruise ship bring suit against the owner of the ship for deaths caused by terrorists. The cruise ship (D) claims suit must be filed in Italy according to the ticket.

Anderson v. City of Bessemer City

Instant Facts: The appellate court conducted a new review of the district court's findings of fact in a discrimination case, reversing the district court's ruling.

Black Letter Rule: An appellate court must utilize a "clearly erroneous" standard rather than an "de novo" review when reviewing findings of fact.

Harnden v. Jayco, Inc.

Instant Facts: Harnden (P) sued Jayco (D) after several attempts to repair an RV he purchased from Jayco (D) failed to fix it, but the court granted the defendant's motion for summary judgment on the basis of an expert report that Harnden (P) argued was inadmissible.

Black Letter Rule: Even if a court's consideration of inadmissible evidence is in error, such error is harmless it if does not affect any party's substantial rights.

Liberty Mutual Insurance Co. v. Wetzel

(Employer) v. (Employee)

424 U.S. 737, 96 S.Ct. 1202 (1976)

THE SUPREME COURT REAFFIRMS THE FINAL JUDGMENT RULE

■ **INSTANT FACTS** Liberty Mutual Insurance Co. (D) appealed the grant of partial summary judgment against it, and the Supreme Court now considers the jurisdiction of the appellate court.

■ **BLACK LETTER RULE** A grant of partial summary judgment on the issue of liability is an interlocutory order and is not appealable.

■ **PROCEDURAL BASIS**

Writ of certiorari reviewing jurisdiction of Court of Appeals following affirmance of partial summary judgment finding liability for violations of the Civil Rights Act.

■ **FACTS**

Wetzel (P) sued Liberty Mutual Insurance Co. (D) in federal district court, alleging that Liberty Mutual's employee insurance benefits and maternity leave provisions violated Title VII of the Civil Rights Act of 1964. Wetzel (P) sought a declaratory judgment, an injunction, and damages. The District Court granted Wetzel (P) partial summary judgment on the issue of liability, holding that the policies did indeed violate Title VII. However, the judgment did not provide any of the relief sought by Wetzel (P). Liberty Mutual (D) appealed this grant of partial summary judgment. The Third Circuit Court of Appeals held that it had jurisdiction and affirmed the judgment. The Supreme Court granted certiorari, and the Supreme Court now analyzes the jurisdiction of the Court of Appeals.

■ **ISSUE**

Does a Court of Appeals have jurisdiction to review the granting of partial summary judgment.

■ **DECISION AND RATIONALE**

(Rehnquist, J.) No. A Court of Appeals does not have jurisdiction to review the granting of partial summary judgment. Such orders are interlocutory in nature, and thus are not final judgments within the meaning of 28 U.S.C. §1291. Moreover, §1292 is not applicable as a basis for jurisdiction in the instant action. If the District Court had granted injunctive relief, this interlocutory order would have been appealable under §1292(a)(1). However, the District Court granted no relief whatsoever when it decided on the issue of Liberty Mutual's (D) liability. In addition, Rule 54(b) does not apply to cases like this, which are actions on a single claim, and the requirements of §1292(b) are not satisfied. Were we to allow the Court of Appeals to exercise jurisdiction over cases like this, we would condone the procedure whereby any district court could render an interlocutory decision on liability which would be immediately appealable. Although Congress has provided for exceptions to the "final judgment" rule, none are applicable in the case at hand. Vacated and remanded, with instructions to dismiss Liberty Mutual's (D) appeal.

Analysis:

As a general rule, only final decisions are appealable to higher federal courts although there are numerous exceptions. According to many commentators, a final judgment is one rendered after all possible issues have been determined by a trial court. Stated differently, a final judgment ends the litigation on the merits and leaves nothing for the court to do but execute the judgment. Thus, a decision addressing only liability but not considering possible remedies, as in this case, is not a final judgment. Consider briefly the rationale for the final judgment rule. Trial courts make several decisions, ranging from minor orders to grants of summary judgment, throughout the course of the trial. It would obviously cause a substantial disruption in the trial process if each decision were appealable. On the other hand, if one of these decisions is erroneous, it appears to be a tremendous waste of judicial resources to litigate the case to conclusion only to have the entire case reversed on appeal and retried. As the Supreme Court mentions in this opinion, Congress has attempted to reconcile these two arguments by providing limited exceptions to the final judgment rule.

■ **CASE VOCABULARY**

INTERLOCUTORY: An order occurring during a proceeding which is not final and does not ultimately resolve the issues in dispute.

Lauro Lines s.r.l. v. Chasser

(Yacht Owner) v. (Passengers)

490 U.S. 495, 109 S.Ct. 1976 (1989)

EXCEPT IN RARE CIRCUMSTANCES, AN APPEAL CAN ONLY BE MADE AFTER A
JUDGMENT IS FINAL; CLAIMS THAT THE SUIT WAS REQUIRED TO BE FILED IN A
DIFFERENT COURT ARE NO EXCEPTION

■ **INSTANT FACTS** An interlocutory
order denying an Italian company's motion
to dismiss, based on a contractual forum-
selection clause, is held not to come
within the collateral order doctrine
exception to the final judgment rule, and
therefore cannot be immediately appealed.

■ **BLACK LETTER RULE** Passengers on
a cruise ship bring suit against the owner
of the ship for deaths caused by terrorists.
The cruise ship (D) claims suit must be
filed in Italy according to the ticket.

■ **PROCEDURAL BASIS**

Certification to the United States Supreme Court of an interlocutory order by the United States
District Court denying a motion to dismiss.

■ **FACTS**

On October 1985, the cruise ship Achille Lauro, owned by Lauro Lines s.r.l (Lauro) (D), an
Italian company, was hijacked by terrorists in the Mediterranean. Plaintiffs, who were the
passengers, or represent the estate of passengers who were aboard the Achille Lauro at the
time, filed suit against Lauro (D) in the District Court for the Southern District of New York, for
injuries sustained and for the wrongful death of Leon Klinghoffer. Lauro (D) moved before trial
to dismiss the actions, pursuant to the forum clause printed on the back of each passenger
ticket. This clause stated that all passengers were obligated to institute any suit arising in
connection with the contract in Naples, Italy, and renounce the right to sue elsewhere. The
District court denied Lauro's (D) motion to dismiss, holding that the ticket did not give
reasonable notice to passengers that they were waiving the opportunity to sue in a domestic
forum. Lauro (D) then sought to appeal the District Court's order. The Court of Appeals for the
Second Circuit denied Lauro's (D) appeal on the ground that the District Court's orders
denying petitioner's motions to dismiss were interlocutory and could be appealed according to
section 1291 [which provides that appeals to the court of appeals may only be from final
decisions handed down by the district courts]. Furthermore, the Court held that the orders did
not fall within an exception to the final judgment rule. The Supreme Court granted certiorari.

■ **ISSUE**

Is an interlocutory order denying a motion to dismiss based on a contractual forum-selection
clause, appealable under the collateral order doctrine exception to the final judgment rule?

■ **DECISION AND RATIONALE**

(Brennan, J.) No. An interlocutory order denying a motion to dismiss based on the right to be
sued elsewhere, cannot be appealed under the collateral order doctrine exception to the final
judgment rule. A "final judgment" in general, is a decision that ends litigation on the merits and
leaves nothing for the court to do but execute judgment. An order denying a motion to dismiss
based on a contractual forum-selection clause is not a decision on the merits that ends
litigation. It in fact ensures that litigation will continue in the District Court. Therefore, section

---

1291 will only permit an appeal if the order falls within the narrow exception to the final judgment rule, the collateral order doctrine, as held in Cohen v. Beneficial Industries Loan Corporation [which stated that an exception applies to orders that finally determine claims separable and collateral to rights asserted in the action, too important and too independent of the cause itself to be deferred until the whole case is settled]. The three requirements of this exception are: 1). The order must conclusively determine the disputed question, 2) resolve an important issue completely separate from the merits of the action, and 3) be effectively unreviewable on appeal from a final judgment. The order in this case fails to satisfy the third requirement. An order is unreviewable only when the order involves an asserted right which would be destroyed if it were not vindicated before trial. For instance we have held that the denial of a motion to dismiss, based upon a claim of absolute immunity from suit, is immediately appealable prior to final judgment because of the right of not having to answer for conduct in a civil action. On the other hand, we have held that the collateral order doctrine is not applicable where a district court has denied a claim that the defendant is not properly before the particular court for lack of jurisdiction. In the instant case, Lauro (D) argues their right not to be tried by tribunals outside the agreed forum, cannot be vindicated by appeal after trial in an improper forum. However, an entitlement to avoid suit is different from an entitlement to be sued only in a particular forum. Lauro's (D) claim that it may be sued only in Naples, is as adequately vindicable by appeal after the trial, as the claim that the court lacked personal jurisdiction over the defendant. Therefore the third requirement of the collateral order doctrine has not been fulfilled. Affirmed.

■ CONCURRENCE

(Scalia, J.) The law does view the right to be sued elsewhere, important enough to be vindicated by an injunction against its violation obtained through interlocutory appeal. The collateral order doctrine permits appeal of final interlocutory determinations of claims that are not only collateral to the rights asserted in the action, but that are also too important to be denied review. The right to be sued elsewhere is not important enough to overcome the policies militating against interlocutory appeals.

Analysis:

This case presents the collateral order doctrine, a well-recognized exception to the final judgment rule. The collateral order doctrine is a very narrow exception. As stated in the concurring opinion, final interlocutory determinations of claims must not only be collateral and separable from the rights asserted in the action, the claims must also be too important to be denied review in order to fall within the exception. If the appellate court's review of a claim, after a trial on the merits, would not infringe upon an essential right, then the claim is not appealable until the final judgment of the case has been handed down. In other words, the collateral order doctrine requires that the court necessarily find that a denial of immediate review would most likely preclude any review whatsoever.

■ CASE VOCABULARY

COLLATERAL ORDER DOCTRINE: An exception to the final judgment rule, which allows the appeal of prejudgment orders that finally determine claims of right collateral to rights asserted in the action, and which are too important to be denied immediate review.

Anderson v. City of Bessemer City

(Applicant) v. (Government)

470 U.S. 564, 105 S.Ct. 1504 (1985)

IT IS NOT THE FUNCTION OF APPELLATE COURTS TO DECIDE FACTUAL ISSUES DE NOVO

■ **INSTANT FACTS** The appellate court conducted a new review of the district court's findings of fact in a discrimination case, reversing the district court's ruling.

■ **BLACK LETTER RULE** An appellate court must utilize a "clearly erroneous" standard rather than an "de novo" review when reviewing findings of fact.

■ **PROCEDURAL BASIS**

Writ of certiorari reviewing reversal of finding of discrimination.

■ **FACTS**

Anderson (P) sued Bessemer City (D) for discrimination, alleging that she was overlooked for a position because she was a woman. The District Court found that Anderson (P) was the most qualified candidate, and entered other findings of fact and conclusions of law. The Court of Appeals for the Fourth Circuit reversed, holding that the District Court's findings were clearly erroneous. The Supreme Court granted certiorari.

■ **ISSUE**

When reviewing factual findings, is the function of an appellate court to conduct a de novo review?

■ **DECISION AND RATIONALE**

(Justice Not Stated) No. When reviewing factual findings, the function of an appellate court is not to conduct a de novo review. Rather, the appellate court is bound by the "clearly erroneous" standard. Where there are two permissible views of the evidence, the factfinder's choice between them cannot be clearly erroneous. In the instant action, it was plausible, in light of the entire record, that Anderson (P) was the most qualified candidate for the job. In light of a trial court's capacity to rule on issues of fact, we must give deference to the District Court's finding that Anderson (P) was indeed the most qualified. The Court of Appeals improperly conducted a de novo review of the record. If it had conducted a "clearly erroneous" review, it would have determined that nothing in the record mandates reversal of the District Court's findings. Reversed.

Analysis:

This case presents perhaps the best explanation and rationale for the "clearly erroneous" standard. District court (trial court) findings of fact should be given great deference. When there are two equally plausible views of the evidence, and the lower court has adopted one of them, the appellate court should not conduct an independent review and choose the other. Furthermore, the Court notes that this standard applies even when district court's findings are based on physical or documentary evidence. When the district court's findings rest on

---

credibility determinations, even more deference must be given to the trial judge's findings, since the trial judge was present at the examination of the witnesses.

■ CASE VOCABULARY

DE NOVO: A standard of review where the appellate court conducts a new review of the facts and law of the case.

Harnden v. Jayco, Inc.

(RV Purchaser) v. (RV Seller)

496 F.3d 579 (6th Cir. 2007)

SUMMARY JUDGMENT TESTIMONY MUST GENERALLY BE IN THE FORM OF AN AFFIDAVIT OR SWORN STATEMENT

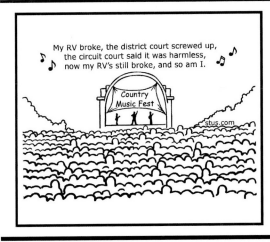

My RV broke, the district court screwed up, the circuit court said it was harmless, now my RV's still broke, and so am I.

Country Music Fest

stus.com

■ **INSTANT FACTS** Harnden (P) sued Jayco (D) after several attempts to repair an RV he purchased from Jayco (D) failed to fix it, but the court granted the defendant's motion for summary judgment on the basis of an expert report that Harnden (P) argued was inadmissible.

■ **BLACK LETTER RULE** Even if a court's consideration of inadmissible evidence is in error, such error is harmless it if does not affect any party's substantial rights.

■ **PROCEDURAL BASIS**

Federal circuit court review of a district court order granting summary judgment to the defendant.

■ **FACTS**

Harnden (P) purchased a recreational vehicle from Jayco (D), but had to return it several times for the repair of defects. When the repairs failed to fix the vehicle, Harnden (P) brought suit against Jayco (D) and others. Jayco (D) moved for summary judgment based in part on an expert report prepared by Zonker, a Jayco (D) employee, and the court granted the defendant's motion. Harnden (P) appealed.

■ **ISSUE**

Did the court's consideration of the report prepared by the defendant's employee constitute reversible error?

■ **DECISION AND RATIONALE**

(Martin, J.) No. Even if a court's consideration of inadmissible evidence is in error, such error is harmless it if does not affect any party's substantial rights. Here, admission of the report was harmless error. Harnden (P) objected to the admissibility of the report because it was not in the form of an affidavit or sworn statement as required by Fed. R. Civ. P. 56(e), the rule for summary judgment motions. Thus, he argued, it constituted inadmissible hearsay. But the defendant had offered to resubmit the expert report in admissible form (although the district court did not take it up on its offer). Sending this case back to the district court would simply result in resubmission of the expert report, ultimately leading to the same result as reached the first time. Moreover, Harnden (P) had advance warning of Zonker's testimony, so he could have prepared to rebut it; therefore, the district court's error in admitting the unsworn testimony did not affect Harnden's (P) substantial rights. Affirmed.

Analysis:

A motion for summary judgment, as brought by the defendant in this case, is essentially a request that the court enter judgment without a trial, because there is no genuine issue of material fact to be decided by a factfinder. In other words, no trial is required because the evidence is legally insufficient to support a verdict in the non-moving party's favor. In federal court, as well as most state courts, when the defendant is the moving party, such as here, it generally must point out in its motion the absence of evidence on an essential element of the plaintiff's claim. The burden then shifts to the non-moving plaintiff to produce evidence raising a genuine fact issue. Harnden (P) was unable to do so. When the plaintiff moves for summary judgment on its own claim, by contrast, it must establish each element of the claim as a matter of law.

■ **CASE VOCABULARY**

HARMLESS ERROR: An error that does not affect a party's substantive rights or the case's outcome. A harmless error is not grounds for reversal.

HEARSAY: In federal law, a statement (either a verbal assertion or nonverbal assertive conduct), other than one made by the declarant while testifying at the trial or hearing, offered in evidence to prove the truth of the matter asserted.

SUMMARY JUDGMENT: A judgment granted on a claim or defense about which there is no genuine issue of material fact and upon which the movant is entitled to prevail as a matter of law. The court considers the contents of the pleadings, the motions, and additional evidence adduced by the parties to determine whether there is a genuine issue of material fact rather than one of law. This procedural device allows the speedy disposition of a controversy without the need for trial.

CHAPTER 11

Respect for Judgments

Frier v. City of Vandalia

Instant Facts: A car owner brought suit against the city in which he lived for multiple towings of a number of cars that he tended to park illegally.

Black Letter Rule: Where the parties and the causes of action in two different suits are identical, the first suit precludes the second under the doctrine of claim preclusion.

Searle Brothers v. Searle

Instant Facts: A partnership brought suit against a recently divorced woman who was, in a divorce decree, awarded ownership of property belonging partly to the partnership.

Black Letter Rule: A person is in privity with another when he is so identified in interest with another that he represents the same legal right as that other person; privity means one whose interest has been legally represented at the time.

Taylor v. Sturgell

Instant Facts: Taylor (P) brought a Freedom of Information Act suit against the Federal Aviation Administration (D), and the suit was dismissed on the grounds of claim preclusion because a nearly identical suit brought by a close associate of Taylor's (P) had been dismissed earlier.

Black Letter Rule: Claim preclusion by virtual representation will not bar a suit by nonparties unless the facts of the virtual representation bring the suit within one of the existing rules that bar suits by nonparties.

Gargallo v. Merrill Lynch, Pierce, Fenner & Smith

Instant Facts: A disgruntled investor brought suit against his broker on grounds of violations of federal securities law.

Black Letter Rule: A final judgment by a state court upon a cause of action over which the adjudicating court had no subject matter jurisdiction does not have claim preclusive effect in any subsequent proceedings.

Illinois Central Gulf Railroad v. Parks

Instant Facts: An accident victim brought a second suit against the railroad company that crashed into his car, after having not been successful in a first suit.

Black Letter Rule: Where a judgment may have been based upon either or any of two or more distinct facts, a party desiring to plead the judgment as an estoppel by verdict or finding upon the particular fact involved in a subsequent suit must show that it was previously decided upon that fact, or else the question will be open to a new contention.

Parklane Hosiery Co. v. Shore

Instant Facts: Shore (P), a stockholder in Parklane Hosiery Co. (D) ("Parklane") brought a class action against the latter alleging that Parklane (D) had issued a materially false and misleading proxy statement in connection with a merger.

Black Letter Rule: Trial courts have broad discretion to apply the doctrine of offensive collateral estoppel, even in cases where the defendant will be deprived of a jury trial.

State Farm Fire & Casualty Co. v. Century Home Components

Instant Facts: Suit regarding the propriety of employing issue preclusion where three cases regarding the negligence of a house builder in starting a fire reached inconsistent results.

Black Letter Rule: Where, in a prior case, there are extant determinations that are inconsistent on the matter in issue with those made in a subsequent case, it is a strong indication that the application of collateral estoppel would work an injustice.

Kovach v. District of Columbia

Instant Facts: A motorist "caught" by a red-light camera brought suit after the District of Columbia realized that the intersection where the camera was installed was confusing to motorists and forgave all unpaid fines, but refused to issue refunds for fines already paid.

Black Letter Rule: Under the doctrine of res judicata, or claim preclusion, a final judgment on the merits precludes relitigation between the same parties concerning the same factual transaction not only as to every ground of recovery or defense actually presented in the action, but also as to every ground that might have been presented.

Durfee v. Duke

Instant Facts: Suit regarding the preclusive effect of a prior decision as to the ownership of certain bottom land on the Missouri River.

Black Letter Rule: A judgment is entitled to full faith and credit, even as to the question of jurisdiction, when the second court's inquiry disclosed that those questions have been fully and fairly litigated and finally decided in the court which rendered the original judgment.

United States v. Beggerly

Instant Facts: A purported land owner sought to reopen a suit over the ownership of a particular piece of land.

Black Letter Rule: Independent actions must be reserved for those cases of injustices which, in certain circumstances, are deemed sufficiently gross to demand a departure from the rigid adherence to the doctrine of res judicata.

Frier v. City of Vandalia

(Car Owner) v. (City Government)

770 F.2d 699 (7th Cir.1985)

A PLAINTIFF CANNOT BRING TWO IDENTICAL SUITS AGAINST ONE DEFENDANT IN TWO DIFFERENT COURTS

■ **INSTANT FACTS** A car owner brought suit against the city in which he lived for multiple towings of a number of cars that he tended to park illegally.

■ **BLACK LETTER RULE** Where the parties and the causes of action in two different suits are identical, the first suit precludes the second under the doctrine of claim preclusion.

■ **PROCEDURAL BASIS**

Certification to the Seventh Circuit Court of Appeals of a district court decision dismissing a citizen's claim against the City of Vandalia (D) for failure to state a claim on which relief can be granted.

■ **FACTS**

Charles Frier (P), a citizen of the small city of Vandalia (D), had a "problem" with parking his cars illegally on a narrow street, which forced others to drive on another citizen's lawn in order to get past Frier's (P) car. During 1983, the police had four of Frier's (P) cars towed to various garages in the city. Frier (P) balked at paying the $10 garage fee, and instead filed suits in Illinois state court seeking replevin. In each suit Frier (P) named as defendants the City of Vandalia (D) and the garage that had towed the car. One of the suits was voluntarily dismissed when Frier (P) got his cars back, but the two other cases were consolidated and litigated. Frier's (P) writ of replevin was denied in each case. After losing in state court, Frier (P) turned to federal court, arguing that the city (D) had not offered him a hearing either before or after it took the cars and that it is the "official policy" of the City (D) not to do so. The complaint invoked the Due Process Clause and 42 U.S.C. §1983, and it sought equitable relief in addition to $100,000.00 in compensatory and $100,000.00 in punitive damages. The district court dismissed Frier's (P) complaint for failure to state a claim on which relief may be granted. Frier (P) appealed.

■ **ISSUE**

Can a plaintiff bring the same suit against the same defendant more than once?

■ **DECISION AND RATIONALE**

(Easterbrook, J.) No. A court ought not resolve a constitutional dispute unless that is absolutely necessary. Here it is not. Frier (P) had his day in court in the replevin action. The City (D) has argued that this precludes further suits. The district court bypassed this argument because, it believed, Frier (P) could not have asserted his constitutional arguments in a replevin action. This is only partially correct. Frier (P) could not have obtained punitive damages or declaratory relief in a suit limited to replevin. But he was free to join one count seeking such relief with another seeking replevin. As such, the law of Illinois, which governs the preclusive effect to be given to the judgment in the replevin actions, would bar this suit. The City (D) is therefore entitled to prevail on the ground of claim preclusion, although the

---

district court did not decide the case on that ground. Illinois recognizes the principles of claim preclusion, also called res judicata or estoppel by judgment. Under that doctrine, one suit precludes a second where the parties and the cause of action are identical. Causes of action are identical where the evidence necessary to sustain a second verdict would sustain the first, i.e., where the causes of action are based on a common core of operative facts. Two suits may entail the same cause of action even though they present different legal theories, and the first suit operates as an absolute bar to a subsequent action, not only as to every matter which was offered and received to sustain or defeat the claim or demand, but as to any other admissible matter which might have been offered for that purpose. In this case the City (D) was a defendant in each replevin action. Frier (P) could have urged constitutional grounds as reasons for replevin. He also could have joined a constitutional claim seeking punitive damages and declaratory relief to his demand for replevin, and therefore he had a full and fair opportunity to litigate. The actions also involve both the same common core of operative facts and the same transactions; the operative facts in the replevin and §1983 actions are therefore the same. The replevin actions diverged from the path of this §1983 suit only because the state judge adjudicated on the merits the propriety of the seizures. Having found the seizures proper, the judge had no occasion to determine whether the City (D) should have offered Frier (P) an earlier hearing. But this divergence does not mean that the two causes of action require a different core of operative facts. The courts of Illinois sometimes put the inquiry as whether the two theories of relief allege the same conduct by the defendant, and Frier (P) has attacked the same conduct in all of his suits. Here the replevin theory contained the elements that make up a due process theory, and we are therefore confident that the courts of Illinois would treat both theories as one case of action. The final question is whether it makes a difference that only two of the replevin actions went to judgment, while here Frier (P) challenges the towing of four cars. Under Illinois law the answer is no. The defendant may invoke claim preclusion when the plaintiff litigated in the first suit a subset of all available disputes between the parties. If Frier (P) had filed the current suit in state court, he would have lost under the doctrine of claim preclusion. Under 28 U.S.C. §1738 [requiring federal courts to follow state claim preclusion rules] he therefore loses in federal court as well. Affirmed.

■ **CONCURRENCE**

(Swygert, J.) In my view, the majority has simply applied the wrong analysis to the problem at hand. Rather than trying to squeeze a res judicata solution into a mold that does not fit, I would review the facts to determine whether Frier's (P) procedural due process claims could withstand a summary judgment motion. Because I believe the City (D) was entitled to summary judgment, I concur in the result. Illinois adheres to a narrow, traditional view of claim preclusion, as opposed to the broader approach codified in the Restatement (Second) of Judgments. Under the modern view, all claims arising from a single transaction—broadly defined to include matters related in time, space, origin, and motivation—must be litigated in a single, initial lawsuit, or be barred from being raised in subsequent litigation. Under that approach, I would agree that Frier's (P) claims are barred, but under the traditional approach that Illinois takes, they are not.

Analysis:

Claim preclusion is designed to impel parties to consolidate all closely related matters into one suit. Doing so "prevents the oppression of defendants by multiple cases, which may be easy to file and costly to defend." Thus, the doctrine of claim preclusion protects potential defendants from both possible harassment and a potentially steep financial burden. The court states that "[t]here is no assurance that a second or third case will be decided more accurately than the first and so there is no good reason to incur the costs of litigation more than once. When the facts and issues of all theories of liability are closely related, one case is enough." Claim preclusion is necessary and proper when the facts, issues, and theories of liability are closely enough related that there is no need for a second or third lawsuit. "Causes of action are identical where the evidence necessary to sustain a second verdict would sustain the first, i.e., where the causes of action are based on a common core of operative facts. Two suits may entail the same cause of action even though they present different legal theories, and the first suit operates as an absolute bar to a subsequent action, not only as to every matter which was offered and received to sustain or defeat the claim or demand, but as to any other admissible matter which might have been offered for that purpose."

■ CASE VOCABULARY

CLAIM PRECLUSION: A doctrine of civil procedure that bars two or more parties from litigating a claim that has already been litigated in a prior suit.

"CORE OF OPERATIVE FACTS": The factual basis for a lawsuit, or the facts that make up the basis of a cause of action under the law.

DUE PROCESS CLAUSE: A portion of the 14%Gth%G Amendment which states that "No state shall . . . deprive any person of life, liberty, or property, without due process of law."

ESTOPPEL BY JUDGMENT: As used in this case, estoppel by judgment is a third name or term for the doctrine of claim preclusion. Other courts, however, have used this same term to refer to issue preclusion.

REPLEVIN: An action brought by one wrongfully deprived of personal property to regain possession of that property.

RES JUDICATA: Another name or term for the doctrine of claim preclusion.

"SAME TRANSACTION": Broadly defined by some to include matters related in time, space, origin, and motivation, a transaction is an occurrence that is the basis for a cause of action under the law. For example, a car accident is a "transaction" for the purposes of claim preclusion.

COLLATERAL ESTOPPEL CAN ONLY BE ASSERTED AGAINST A PARTY WHO WAS A PARTY OR IN PRIVITY WITH A PARTY IN A PRIOR SUIT

■ **INSTANT FACTS** A partnership brought suit against a recently divorced woman who was, in a divorce decree, awarded ownership of property belonging partly to the partnership.

■ **BLACK LETTER RULE** A person is in privity with another when he is so identified in interest with another that he represents the same legal right as that other person; privity means one whose interest has been legally represented at the time.

■ **PROCEDURAL BASIS**

Certification to the Utah Supreme Court of a lower state court judgment barring Searle Brothers' (P) claim against Edlean Searle (Edlean) (D) on grounds of claim and issue preclusion.

■ **FACTS**

In a divorce settlement between Edlean (D) and Woodey Searle, the court gave Edlean (D) a piece of property known as the Slaugh House, which had been recorded in Woodey's name but was considered part of the marital property. Despite Woodey's contention that he only owned half of the property, the entire property was given to Edlean (D). The other half, he claimed, belonged to a partnership known as the Searle Brothers (P), of which he and his sons were members. Following the divorce decree, the Searle Brothers (P) brought suit seeking a return of its portion of the property.

■ **ISSUE**

Are agents and principles in privity with one another for the purposes of claim and issue preclusion?

■ **DECISION AND RATIONALE**

(Ellett, C.J.) No. In general, a divorce decree, like other final judgments, is conclusive as to parties and their privies, and operates as a bar to any subsequent action. In order for res judicata to apply, both suits must involve the same parties or their privies and also the same cause of action. If the subsequent suit involves different parties, those parties cannot be bound by the prior judgment. Collateral estoppel, on the other hand, arises from a different cause of action and prevents parties or their privies from relitigating acts and issues in a second suit that were fully litigated in the first suit. This means that the plea of collateral estoppel can be asserted only against a party in the subsequent suit who was also a party or in privity with a party in a prior suit. The following factors apply in determining whether collateral estoppel applies: [1] Was the issue decided in a prior adjudication identical with the one presented in the action in question? [2] Was there a final judgment on the merits? [3] Was the party against whom the plea is asserted a party or in privity with a party to the prior adjudication? [4] Was the issue in the first case competently, fully, and fairly litigated? With respect to the third factor, it is clear that the Searle Brothers partnership (P) was not a party to the first action; hence, the only way it can be barred from pursuing this second suit is if it were in privity with the parties to the divorce action. The legal definition of a person in privity with another, is a person so identified in interest with another that he represents the same legal right. This includes a mutual or successive relationship to rights in property. Privity means one whose interest has been legally represented at the time. In this case, the Searle Brothers' (P) interest was neither mutual or successive. It claims no part of the interest owned by Woodey Searle, but asserts its own independent partnership interest. The rights are similar, but not identical. The first and fourth tests previously outlined also do not permit the application of collateral estoppel in this case. The partnership interest was not legally represented in the divorce suit, as Woodey Searle was acting in his own individual capacity as the husband of Edlean (D) and not as a representative of the partnership. Edlean (D) argues that Woodey was acting as an agent for the partnership, and therefore the Searle Brothers (P) is bound by the results of the prior action. However, the general rule is that agents and principals do not have any mutual or successive relationship to rights of property and are not, as a consequence, in privity with each other; therefore, a principal is not bound by any judgment obtained against an agent unless the principal became a party or privy thereto by actually and openly defending the action. Further, the right to intervene as a party in a prior suit does not bind the party in the subsequent suit where he failed to so intervene. Based on the foregoing, collateral estoppel is not available to defeat the Searle Brothers' (P) claim. The Searle Brothers (P) cannot be bound by the decree entered in the previous suit, nor is it estopped from litigating its own claim against the property in a subsequent suit. Reversed.

■ DISSENT

(Crockett, J.) I am unable to agree with the majority. Upon a survey of the circumstances, I think that the trial court was justified in its ruling. The property at issue was owned solely in the name of Woodey Searle. The Searle Brothers partnership (P) even admit that he was the managing partner of the claimed partnership and had control of the property in dispute and the income therefrom; he should thus be regarded as representing and protecting whatever interests they and the claimed partnership had therein. Further, the Searle Brothers (P) itself was fully aware of the disputation concerning the ownership of the property. The Searle Brothers (P) actively participated in the lawsuit, but asserted no claim for itself. Instead, it stood by until the determination was made adverse to its interests. Such claim as it has in contesting the record title to the property is based solely on supposed oral declarations made within the family, and self-serving declarations at that. The purpose of collateral estoppel is to protect a party from being subjected to harassment by being compelled to litigate the same controversy more than once. This case is a good example of a situation where the trial court was justified in applying that doctrine and concluding that the plaintiffs should now be estopped from seeking the relief they ask against their mother (the brothers constituting the Searle Brothers (P) were Edlean's (D) sons).

Analysis:

In *Searle*, the court states that collateral estoppel, or issue preclusion, prevents parties or their privies from relitigating acts and issues in a second suit that were fully litigated in a prior suit. The most important aspect of *Searle* is its discussion on the meaning of the word "privity" (which applies to both claim and issue preclusion). A person is in privity with another when he is so identified in interest with that other person that he represents the same legal right. This includes a mutual or successive relationship to rights in property. The general rule is that agents and principles do not have any mutual or successive relationship to rights of property and are not, as a consequence, in privity with each other. This means that a principal is, in the usual case, not bound by any judgment obtained against an agent, though this is not the case when the principal becomes a party or privy thereto by actually and openly defending the action.

■ **CASE VOCABULARY**

COLLATERAL ESTOPPEL: An affirmative defense that precludes a party in a prior suit from relitigating an issue that was decided in the prior suit (such as a finding of negligence in the first suit stemming from a multi-car accident). The doctrine applies even when the second action differs significantly from the first.

FULLY LITIGATED: A case is fully litigated when there no longer exist any issues that need to be decided at the trial level, but all have been resolved.

ISSUE PRECLUSION: Another name or term for collateral estoppel (not to be confused with res judicata or estoppel by judgment, both of which are names of the separate doctrine of claim preclusion).

PRIVIES: Persons in privity with another.

PRIVITY: People are in privity with another when they are so identified in interest with each other that they represent the same legal right.

(Antique Aircraft Enthusiast) v. (Administrator, Federal Aviation Administration)

553 U.S. 880 (2008)

NONPARTIES ARE RARELY BOUND BY EARLIER JUDGMENTS IN SIMILAR CASES

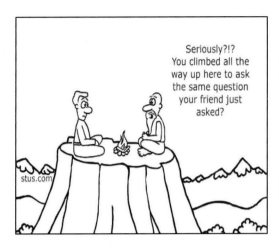

■ **INSTANT FACTS** Taylor (P) brought a Freedom of Information Act suit against the Federal Aviation Administration (D), and the suit was dismissed on the grounds of claim preclusion because a nearly identical suit brought by a close associate of Taylor's (P) had been dismissed earlier.

■ **BLACK LETTER RULE** Claim preclusion by virtual representation will not bar a suit by nonparties unless the facts of the virtual representation bring the suit within one of the existing rules that bar suits by nonparties.

■ **PROCEDURAL BASIS**

Appeal from an order of the District of Columbia Circuit Court of Appeals affirming dismissal of Taylor's (P) suit.

■ **FACTS**

Herrick filed a Freedom of Information Act (FOIA) request with the Federal Aviation Administration (FAA) (D). The request asked for technical information filed in the 1930s by Fairchild (D), the manufacturer of an antique airplane Herrick was restoring. The FOIA requires agencies to disclose requested information upon request, unless that information falls within an exception set out in the Act. Requestors are not required to state the reason for a request. The FAA (D) refused Herrick's request, stating that the requested information fell within an exception to the FOIA for trade secrets and commercial or financial information. Herrick brought suit against the FAA (D) and the District Court granted summary judgment to the defendant. The court rejected Herrick's argument that the manufacturer of the airplane waived trade secret or commercial information protection by a letter sent in 1955. The Tenth Circuit affirmed.

Less than a month later, Taylor (P), a friend of Herrick's and also an antique aircraft enthusiast, filed an FOIA request for the same information as that requested by Herrick. The FAA (D) did not reply, and Taylor (P) filed suit in the U.S. District Court for the District of Columbia. Taylor (P) argued that Fairchild (D) waived protection of the information, but also raised two issues regarding recapture of protected status that Herrick did not raise on appeal. Fairchild (D) intervened, and the District Court held that Taylor's (P) suit was barred by claim preclusion. The court granted summary judgment to Fairchild (D) and the FAA (D). The record before the court showed that Herrick was a member of the Antique Aircraft Association, an organization of which Taylor (P) was president. Herrick and Taylor were close associates. Herrick asked for Taylor's (P) help restoring the airplane, but there was no contract or agreement for Taylor (P) to do so. The same attorney represented Taylor (P) and Herrick, and Herrick gave Taylor (P) documents that had been obtained by discovery from the FAA (D) in the earlier suit. The court held that the conditions for virtual representation had been met, so that Taylor's (P) suit was precluded.

◾ ISSUE

Did virtual representation by Herrick preclude Taylor's (P) suit?

◾ DECISION AND RATIONALE

(Ginsburg, J.) No. Claim preclusion by virtual representation will not bar a suit by nonparties unless the facts of the virtual representation bring the suit within one of the existing rules that bar suits by nonparties. A person who was not a party to an earlier suit has not had a full and fair opportunity to litigate the claims and issues of the earlier suit. As a general rule, a nonparty is not precluded by an earlier suit except in six situations: 1. Agreement by the parties to be bound by a prior action; 2. A preexisting substantive legal relationship, such as preceding and succeeding owners of property; 3. Adequate representation by a party with the same interests, such as a trustee or guardian; 4. A party assuming control over prior litigation; 5. A party who loses an individual suit and then brings the suit again as representative of a class; and 6. Special statutory schemes, such as bankruptcy and probate proceedings, provided those proceedings comport with due process. Fairchild (D) and the FAA (D) urge the creation of a new category of preclusion for situations in which the nonparty is "close enough" to the party to bring the second litigant within the judgment. The "close enough" determination would be made by the courts through a "heavily fact-driven" and "equitable" inquiry.

The argument of Fairchild (D) and the FAA (D) is rejected for three reasons. First, it is a fundamental rule that a litigant is not bound by a judgment to which she was not a party. Second, adequacy of representation will limit nonparty preclusion. Representation of a nonparty will be "adequate" if the interests of the nonparty and her representative are aligned, and if either party understood herself to be acting in a representative capacity or the original court took care to protect the interests of the nonparty. Adequate representation may also require notice of the original suit. In the context of a class action, Rule 23 of the Federal Rules of Civil procedure implements these limitations. Virtual representation would, in effect, create a "common-law kind of class action" that would circumvent the existing protections of nonparties. The third reason to reject the arguments of Fairchild (D) and the FAA (D) is that a balancing approach to nonparty preclusion would create more headaches than it relieves. It could significantly complicate the task of courts faced with preclusion questions. An all-things-considered balancing approach could spark wide-ranging, time-consuming, and expensive discovery tracking potentially relevant factors.

The FAA (D) also argues for broad nonparty preclusion in "public law" litigation. First, the FAA (D) argues that the Court's holding in *Richards v. Jefferson County*, 517 U.S. 793 (1996), acknowledges a plaintiff's reduced interest in controlling the litigation because of the "public nature" of the right at issue. The Court's opinion in *Richards* merely noted that state and federal legislatures are free to adopt procedures limiting repetitive litigation in cases involving public rights. It does not follow that successive FOIA suits by different requestors should be proscribed or confined. Second, the FAA (D) argues that the threat of vexatious litigation is heightened in public law cases because of the potentially limitless number of plaintiffs with standing. This risk does not justify departure from the usual rules regarding nonparty standing. *Stare decisis* will allow courts to dispose of repetitive suits. Even when *stare decisis* is not dispositive, the human tendency not to waste money will deter suits brought on claims that have already been adversely determined against others.

In the instant case, however, Taylor's (P) suit *could* be precluded if he was acting as Herrick's agent. Accordingly, the case is remanded to determine whether Taylor (P) was in fact Herrick's undisclosed agent. Reversed and remanded.

Analysis:

The most-stated justification for the doctrine of claim preclusion is the promotion of judicial economy. As Justice Ginsburg noted, however, a rule allowing claim preclusion by virtual representation that comported with due process could bring about a separate round of litigation, as parties engaged in discovery to determine whether a suit may be brought. Judicial economy is best served by clear-cut procedural and jurisdictional rules that minimize the effort spent in pre-trial jousting.

■ CASE VOCABULARY

FREEDOM OF INFORMATION ACT (FOIA): The federal statute establishing guidelines for the public disclosure of documents and materials created and held by federal agencies, located at 5 U.S.C. § 552.

ADEQUATE REPRESENTATION: The close alignment of interests between actual parties and potential parties in a lawsuit, so that the interests of potential parties are sufficiently protected by the actual parties.

STARE DECISIS: The doctrine of precedent under which a court must follow earlier judicial decisions when the same points arise again in later litigation.

VIRTUAL REPRESENTATION: The maintenance of an action by one on behalf of others with similar interests, as by a class representative in a class action.

VIRTUAL-REPRESENTATION DOCTRINE: The principle providing that a judgment binds a person who is not a party to litigation if one of the actual parties is so closely aligned with that nonparty's interests that the nonparty was adequately represented in court.

Gargallo v. Merrill Lynch, Pierce, Fenner & Smith

(Investor) v. (Broker)

918 F.2d 658 (6th Cir.1990)

UNDER OHIO LAW A COURT MUST HAVE JURISDICTION OVER A MATTER TO RENDER A FINAL JUDGMENT ON THE MERITS FOR THE PURPOSE OF CLAIM PRECLUSION

■ **INSTANT FACTS** A disgruntled investor brought suit against his broker on grounds of violations of federal securities law.

■ **BLACK LETTER RULE** A final judgment by a state court upon a cause of action over which the adjudicating court had no subject matter jurisdiction does not have claim preclusive effect in any subsequent proceedings.

■ **PROCEDURAL BASIS**

Certification to the Sixth Circuit Court of Appeals of a federal district court decision barring a securities law claim based on grounds of res judicata.

■ **FACTS**

Miguel Gargallo (P) opened an account with Merrill Lynch (D) in 1976. He maintained that account until 1980, when his investments went awry and losses occurred, resulting in a debt of $17,000.00 owed to Merrill Lynch (D). When Gargallo (P) refused to pay, Merrill Lynch (D) brought suit for collection in Ohio state court. In response, Gargallo (P) filed a counterclaim alleging, among other things, violations of federal securities laws. The state court eventually dismissed the claim with prejudice for Gargallo's (P) refusal to comply with discovery requests and orders. Gargallo (P) then filed suit in federal district court, charging Merrill Lynch (D) with violations of various securities laws. The district court dismissed the suit on res judicata grounds, finding that the issues, facts, and evidence to sustain Gargallo's (P) action were identical to the claims asserted in his counterclaim, which was dismissed with prejudice. Gargallo (P) appealed.

■ **ISSUE**

Does a federal court have to apply state claim preclusion law in deciding whether a prior state court judgment on subject matter over which only a federal court has exclusive jurisdiction is a bar to a subsequent federal court claim upon the identical cause of action?

■ **DECISION AND RATIONALE**

(Ryan, J.) Yes. The securities law claims asserted against Merrill Lynch (D) in this case are the same as those Gargallo (P) previously asserted in the counterclaim he filed in state court. As will be explained later, Ohio law governs this situation. Consequently, we must decide whether the state judgment dismissing Gargallo's (P) first lawsuit would operate as a bar, under Ohio law, to the action now brought in this federal court. In Ohio, the requirements for claim preclusion are as follows: "The doctrine of res judicata is that an existing final judgment rendered upon the merits, without fraud or collusion, by a court of competent jurisdiction, is conclusive of rights, questions and facts in issue, as to the parties and their privies, in all other actions in the same or any other judicial tribunal of concurrent jurisdiction." Under Ohio law, the dismissal with prejudice of Gargallo's (P) state court counterclaim was a final judgment on

---

the merits. Whether a final judgment on one claim precludes the filing of another depends on whether the second embodies the same cause of action as the first. Here, Gargallo's (P) suit against Merrill Lynch (D) complains of the same transactions and alleged violations. We agree that the issues, facts, and evidence to sustain this action are identical to the claims asserted in the counterclaim, and we are satisfied that the federal claim giving rise to this appeal is the same claim or cause of action asserted in prior litigation. It is clear to us that Ohio claim preclusion law would bar Gargallo's (P) federal claim. However, the district court is not an Ohio court, but a federal tribunal. Consequently, we must decide whether a federal district court may give claim preclusive effect to an Ohio judgment regarding federal securities laws that are within the exclusive jurisdiction of the federal courts. In *Marrese v. Academy of Orthopaedic Surgeons*, the Supreme Court held that under the full faith and credit statute, federal courts are required to determine the preclusive effect of prior state court judgments, pursuant to the law of the state in which the judgment was entered, even as to claims within the exclusive jurisdiction of the federal courts. That is what we must do here. Ohio takes the position that a judgment rendered by a court lacking subject matter jurisdiction ought not to be given preclusive effect. It seems clear, then, that in Ohio, a final judgment by a court of that state, upon a cause of action over which the adjudicating court had no subject matter jurisdiction, does not have claim preclusive effect in any subsequent proceedings. In sum, we hold that the Ohio court judgment dismissing Gargallo's (P) securities law claims against Merrill Lynch (D) may not be given claim preclusive effect in a subsequent federal court action asserting those same claims because Ohio courts would not give claim preclusive effect to a prior final judgment upon a cause of action over which the Ohio court had no subject matter jurisdiction. Reversed.

Analysis:

A judgment must be "on the merits" in order for claim preclusion to apply. In this case, which applies Ohio law, Gargallo's (P) second claim, filed in federal district court, alleged violations of federal securities laws by Merrill Lynch (D). His first suit, adjudicated in state court, made the same allegations. Normally, an adjudication in state court would bar a litigant from bringing a similar suit in federal court (under the issue of claim preclusion), but in Gargallo's (P) case, there was no preclusion because, under the law, federal securities law violations can only be adjudicated in federal court (i.e., state courts are not of competent jurisdiction to address federal securities law issues as they have no subject matter jurisdiction over such issues). As such, the state court's decision was deemed to not be a "decision on the merits." Only when subject matter jurisdiction is proper (along with personal jurisdiction and venue) can issue or claim preclusion apply. This rule, however, is not absolute.

■ CASE VOCABULARY

COLLUSION: A secret agreement made to further a deceitful or illegal purpose.

CONCURRENT JURISDICTION: Concurrent jurisdiction exists when more than one tribunal has both personal and subject matter jurisdiction over an issue. For instance, when a claim can be brought in both federal and state court (at the party's choice), there exists concurrent jurisdiction.

COURT OF COMPETENT JURISDICTION: A court of competent jurisdiction is one in which jurisdiction, both personal and subject matter, is proper.

DISMISSAL WITH PREJUDICE: A dismissal with prejudice is a dismissal which bars a party from bringing suit again on the same issue or claim. In contrast, a dismissal is "without prejudice" if the party whose suit is being dismissed has leave of the court to re-file a similar action.

EXCLUSIVE JURISDICTION: A court has exclusive jurisdiction when no other court has jurisdiction over a particular case. In *Gargallo*, the court mentions that the federal courts have exclusive jurisdiction over violations of federal securities laws, meaning a state court is not competent to adjudicate such claims.

FULL FAITH AND CREDIT: A principle of law, embodied both in the federal constitution and federal statutory law, that requires one state to enforce the judicial decisions of another state.

Illinois Central Gulf Railroad v. Parks

(Railroad Company) v. (Accident Victim)

181 Ind.App. 141, 390 N.E.2d 1078 (1979)

ISSUE PRECLUSION PROHIBITS A PARTY FROM PUTTING IN ISSUE IN A SUBSEQUENT SUIT FACTS OR QUESTIONS DETERMINED AND ADJUDICATED IN AN EARLIER CASE

■ **INSTANT FACTS** An accident victim brought a second suit against the railroad company that crashed into his car, after having not been successful in a first suit.

■ **BLACK LETTER RULE** Where a judgment may have been based upon either or any of two or more distinct facts, a party desiring to plead the judgment as an estoppel by verdict or finding upon the particular fact involved in a subsequent suit must show that it was previously decided upon that fact, or else the question will be open to a new contention.

■ **PROCEDURAL BASIS**

Certification to the Indiana Court of Appeals of a trial court decision rejecting a railroad company's defense of claim preclusion in a suit for accident injuries.

■ **FACTS**

Jessie Parks (P) and his wife Bertha were injured when their car, driven by Jessie (P), collided with an Illinois Central Gulf Railroad (D) train. Both sued Illinois Central Gulf (D), and Bertha received $30,000.00 for injuries. Jessie (P) sued for loss of services and consortium, and received nothing. He then, in a separate suit, sued Illinois Central Gulf (D) for his own injuries. On a motion for summary judgment by the railroad (D), the trial court held that Park's (P) claim was not barred by the doctrine of claim preclusion. The trial court also held that the prior suit did not establish that Park (P) was contributorily negligent. The trial court held as it did on the theory that it was not possible to determine if Jessie (P) lost because he was contributorily negligent or because he could not prove damages. Illinois Central Gulf (D) appealed.

■ **ISSUE**

When a prior case was determined on one of two separate issues, and it is not clear which issue it was decided on, can issue preclusion be used to prohibit a suit that will raise one of the two issues?

■ **DECISION AND RATIONALE**

(Lybrook, J.) No. Claim preclusion does not apply in this case, but issue preclusion does. The causes of action in this suit and Park's (P) prior suit are not the same, but if the case at bar were to go to trial on all the issues raised in the pleadings and answer, some facts or questions determined and adjudicated in the earlier case would again be put in issue in this subsequent suit between the same parties. To protect the integrity of the prior judgment by precluding the possibility of opposite results by two different juries on the same set of facts, the doctrine of issue preclusion allows the judgment in the prior action to operate as an estoppel as to those facts or questions actually litigated and determined by the prior action.

[The problem at hand, then, is to determine what facts or questions were actually litigated in the prior case.] In this respect, we agree with Illinois Central Gulf (D) that because the prior case established that the railroad (D) was negligent, in order for the jury to have returned a verdict against Park (P) it had to have decided that he either sustained no damages or that his own negligence was a proximate cause of his damages. This places upon Illinois Central Gulf (D) the heavy burden outlined by Judge Shake in *Flora v. Indiana Service Co.*: "[W]here a judgment may have been based upon either or any of two or more distinct facts, a party desiring to plead the judgment as an estoppel by verdict or finding upon the particular fact involved in a subsequent suit must show that it went upon that fact, or else the question will be open to a new contention. The estoppel of a judgment is only presumptively conclusive, when it appears that the judgment could not have been rendered without deciding the particular matter brought in question. It is necessary to look to the complete record to ascertain what was the question in issue." The railroad (D) argues that, because Park's (P) evidence as to his loss was uncontroverted, the jury's verdict had to be based upon a finding of contributory negligence. Park (P) counters with a contention that, ⟨although the evidence was uncontroverted, it was minimal and, thus, could have caused the jury to find no compensable damages. We reviewed the complete record in the companion case and hold that the jury verdict against Park (P) in that case could mean that he had failed in his burden of proving compensable damages. We hold that Illinois Central Gulf (D) has failed its burden of showing that the judgment against Park (P) in the prior action could not have been rendered without deciding that he was contributorily negligent in the accident which precipitated the two lawsuits. Consequently, the trial court was correct in granting partial summary judgment estopping the railroad from denying its negligence and in limiting the issues at trial to whether Park (P) was contributorily negligent, whether any such contributory negligence was a proximate cause of the accident, and whether Park (P) sustained personal injuries and compensable damages. Affirmed.

Analysis:

Park (P) brought two suits against the railroad (D). The first, in state court, resulted in his receiving nothing in the way of compensation. However, the basis or reasoning behind that decision was not made clear. As far as the second court knew, the decision could have been based on one of two issues or reasons: (1) the jury found that Park (P) had sustained no compensable injuries, or (2) Park (P) was contributorily negligent to the degree that he deserved no compensation. After Park (P) brought suit a second time, the railroad tried to raise the defense of issue preclusion. The court held, however, that because there was no clear evidence as to the basis of the first court's decision, it would be improper to allow the railroad to raise the defense. In order for the railroad to preclude the litigation of one of the two issues, it had to prove that the prior court made its decision based on that particular issue, and therefore it had already been litigated.

■ **CASE VOCABULARY**

ESTOPPEL BY VERDICT: Another name or term, used by the *Park* court, to refer to issue preclusion.

THE SUPREME COURT OF THE UNITED STATES GIVES COURTS BROAD DISCRETION IN DETERMINING WHEN AND WHERE OFFENSIVE COLLATERAL ESTOPPEL SHOULD BE APPLIED

■ **INSTANT FACTS** Shore (P), a stockholder in Parklane Hosiery Co. (D) ("Parklane") brought a class action against the latter alleging that Parklane (D) had issued a materially false and misleading proxy statement in connection with a merger.

■ **BLACK LETTER RULE** Trial courts have broad discretion to apply the doctrine of offensive collateral estoppel, even in cases where the defendant will be deprived of a jury trial.

■ **PROCEDURAL BASIS**

Certiorari to the United States Court of Appeals for the Second Circuit in stockholder class action suit.

■ **FACTS**

Shore (P), a stockholder, brought a class action suit against Parklane (D) alleging that the latter had issued a materially false and misleading proxy statement in connection with a merger. Before, the instant case reached trial, the SEC filed suit against Parklane (D) based on the same allegations as Shore (P). In that action, the District Court ruled in favor of the SEC, and entered a declaratory judgment to that effect. The Court of Appeals for the Second Circuit affirmed. Subsequently, Shore (P) moved for summary judgment, asserting that Parklane (D) was collaterally estopped from litigating the same issues which had been resolved against it in the suit by the SEC. The District Court denied the motion on the ground that the estoppel would deny Parklane (D) its Seventh Amendment Right to a jury trial. The Court of Appeals for the Second Circuit reversed. The Supreme Court of the United States granted certiorari.

■ **ISSUE**

1) Can a party be precluded from re-litigating facts resolved adversely to the party in prior equitable proceedings where the court determines that the party has had full and fair opportunity to litigate the facts? 2) Would the use of offensive collateral estoppel violate such party's Seventh Amendment right to a jury trial?

■ **DECISION AND RATIONALE**

(Stewart, J.) (1) Yes. A party can be precluded from re-litigating facts resolved adversely to the party in prior equitable proceedings where a court has determined that the party has had a fair and full opportunity to litigate the facts. This case involves offensive collateral estoppel, where a plaintiff is seeking to estop a defendant from re-litigating the issues which the defendant previously litigated and lost in an earlier action. This court resolved that the *Blonder-Tongue* case involved defensive collateral estoppel. Contrary to defensive collateral estoppel, offensive collateral estoppel does not promote judicial economy. Since the plaintiff will be able to rely on a previous judgment against a defendant but will not be bound by that judgment if the defendant wins, the plaintiff has every incentive to wait before bringing an action against the defendant, in the hope that the first action by another plaintiff will result in a favorable judgment. Also, offensive collateral estoppel may be unfair to the defendant if the defendant had little incentive to defend vigorously in the first action. However, the preferable approach is not to rule out offensive collateral estoppel altogether, but to allow judges broad discretion to determine when it should be applied. Thus, where a plaintiff could have easily joined the earlier action, where for other reasons the application of offensive collateral estoppel would be unfair to the defendant, a trial judge should not allow its use to the plaintiff. In this case, the use of offensive collateral estoppel should be allowed because the plaintiff most probably could not have joined in the injunctive action brought by the SEC. Also, there is no unfairness to Parklane (D) because the latter had every incentive to litigate the SEC lawsuit fully and vigorously in light of the gravity of the charges and the foreseeability of private lawsuits which could follow. Additionally, there are no procedural opportunities in this action that were not available in the SEC action. (2) No. The use of offensive collateral estoppel would not violate the party's Seventh Amendment right to a jury trial. Parklane (D) argues that the Seventh Amendment should be interpreted based on its scope in 1791, and that since the common law at that time permitted collateral estoppel only where there was mutuality, collateral estoppel cannot be applied where there is no mutuality. There is no persuasive reason however, why the meaning of the Seventh Amendment should depend on the existence of mutuality. A litigant who has lost in an equity action is equally deprived of a jury trial whether he is estopped from re-litigating the same facts and issues against the same or a different party. In either case, there are no more factual issues to be decided by the jury because the facts were already resolved in the previous action. The development of collateral estoppel is not repugnant to the Seventh Amendment simply because they did not exist in 1791. (Affirmed.)

■ DISSENT

(Rehnquist, J.) The contents of the Seventh Amendment right to jury trial should be judged based on historical standards. If a jury would have been impaneled in a particular case in 1791, the Seventh Amendment requires a jury trial today. No one can doubt that at common law, as it existed in 1791, Parklane would have been entitled to a jury trial to determine whether the proxy statement was false and misleading as alleged. The development of non-mutual collateral estoppel is a substantial departure from the common law and its use in this case completely deprives Parklane of its right to have a jury determine contested issues of fact.

Analysis:

Traditionally, collateral estoppel could be asserted by a party only if that party was bound by the earlier judgment. However, in this case, the party seeking to assert collateral estoppel against the other party was not even involved in the earlier action. This case involves offensive collateral estoppel. The plaintiff in the instant action is asserting the judgment of the court against the defendant in the earlier action. Because the party asserting the estoppel was not involved in the earlier action, the doctrine is called "non-mutual" collateral estoppel.

■ CASE VOCABULARY

IN PERSONAM: "Into or against the person"; in pleading, the term refers to an action against a person or persons founded on personal liability, and requiring jurisdiction over the person sought to be held liable.

NON-MUTUAL COLLATERAL ESTOPPEL: Where a party who is not bound by an earlier judgment may use the judgment against a party who is bound by the judgment.

OFFENSIVE COLLATERAL ESTOPPEL: Offensive collateral estoppel refers to a situation where a plaintiff is seeking to estop a defendant from re-litigating the issues which the defendant previously litigated and lost in an earlier action.

State Farm Fire & Casualty Co. v. Century Home Components
(Neighboring Warehouse Owner) v. (Warehouse Owner)

275 Or. 97, 550 P.2d 1185 (1976)

IF THE CIRCUMSTANCES ARE SUCH THAT A COURT'S CONFIDENCE IN THE INTEGRITY OF A PRIOR JUDICIAL DETERMINATION IS SEVERELY UNDERMINED, OR THAT THE RESULT WOULD LIKELY BE DIFFERENT IN A SECOND TRIAL, IT WOULD WORK AN INJUSTICE TO DENY THE LITIGANT ANOTHER OPPORTUNITY TO PRESENT HIS CASE

■ **INSTANT FACTS** Suit regarding the propriety of employing issue preclusion where three cases regarding the negligence of a house builder in starting a fire reached inconsistent results.

■ **BLACK LETTER RULE** Where, in a prior case, there are extant determinations that are inconsistent on the matter in issue with those made in a subsequent case, it is a strong indication that the application of collateral estoppel would work an injustice.

■ **PROCEDURAL BASIS**

Certification to the Oregon Supreme Court of a state trial court decision finding that collateral estoppel barred Century Home (D) from contesting liability in suits following one in which it was held liable for negligence.

■ **FACTS**

Century Home (D) was in the business of constructing prefabricated housing, which it did primarily in a large shed. State Farm (P) stored some of its property in a warehouse about sixty feet from Century Home's (D) shed. On a Sunday morning in the summer of 1968, a fire started in Century Home's shed, which spread to engulf and destroy State Farm's (P) warehouse. The cause of the fire was disputed, but potentially the result of the actions of Century Home's janitor. Eventually, more than 50 lawsuits were filed against Century Home (D). In the first three, two resulted in judgment for the plaintiffs (i.e., Century Home (D) was found negligent) (*Pacific N. W. Bell* and *Hesse*), and one resulted in a judgment for Century Home (D) (i.e., they were not negligent) (*Sylwester*). Following the entry of judgment in *Pacific N. W. Bell* and *Hesse*, State Farm (P) and a number of other plaintiffs filed amended complaints to match those cases, and asserted that the judgments therein should preclude Century Home (D) from again litigating the question of liability. Century Home (D) relied on the verdict in *Sylwester* to argue that it was not negligent and should not have to re-litigate negligence.

■ **ISSUE**

When prior cases are inconsistent in their verdicts, can a court refuse to apply collateral estoppel in a third suit?

■ **DECISION AND RATIONALE**

(Holman, J.) Yes. There is no foundation in either experience or policy for accepting the suggestion that a decision rendered after a full and fair presentation of the evidence and issues should be considered either substantially suspect or infected with variables indicating the question might be decided differently in another go-around. However, we are not free to disregard incongruous results when they are looking us in the eye. If the circumstances are such that our confidence in the integrity of the determination is severely undermined, or that the result would likely be different in a second trial, it would work an injustice to deny the litigant another chance. Thus, where it is apparent that the verdict was the result of a jury compromise, the losing party should not be precluded by the judgment. It has also been held that if the prior determination was manifestly erroneous the judgment should not be given preclusive effect. And the existence of newly discovered or crucial evidence that was not available to the litigant at the first trial would provide a basis for denying preclusion where it appears the evidence would have a significant effect on the outcome. Further, where outstanding determinations are actually inconsistent on the matter sought to be precluded, it would be patently unfair to estop a party by the judgment it lost. We agree that, where there are extant determinations that are inconsistent on the matter in issue, it is a strong indication that the application of collateral estoppel would work an injustice. There seems to be something fundamentally offensive about depriving a party of the opportunity to litigate the issue again when he has shown beyond a doubt that on another day he prevailed. State Farm (P) contends that the determinations are not inconsistent because the issues in *Hesse* and *Pacific N.W. Bell* were not identical with the issues in *Sylwester*. It is true that the phrasing of the allegations of negligence differed and that certain specifications of negligence were not submitted to the jury in *Sylwester*. We do not give much weight to variations in the working of the pleadings, however, where essentially the same acts and omissions are alleged. The thrust of State Farm's (P) argument must be that the jury in *Hesse* and the court in *Pacific N.W. Bell* adjudicated Century Home (D) negligent in respects which were not considered by the jury in *Sylwester*. The records of these cases, however, do not permit such a conclusion. Since the jury in *Hesse* returned a general verdict, we do not know in which respects it found Century Home (D) negligent and, given the similarity of some of the allegations and the basic thrust of negligence alleged, we are unable to conclude that it found Century Home (D) negligent on the basis of conduct not submitted to the jury in *Sylwester*. We conclude that the prior determinations are basically inconsistent and that the circumstances are such that it would be unfair to preclude Century Home (D) from relitigating the issue of liability. Reversed.

Analysis:

State Farm demonstrates the importance of fairness in the application of issue preclusion. One of the most significant reasons supporting the doctrine of issue preclusion is that to allow a party to re-litigate issues that have already been decided would work an unfairness in that it would produce potentially conflicting results and decisions. However, this case demonstrates that fairness goes the other way as well. The Supreme Court of Oregon makes it clear that when it would be unfair to apply issue preclusion, such as when a prior decision was reached through jury compromise, preclusive effect should be denied to prior judgments. Additionally, when an issue has been tried more than once and the cases have rendered inconsistent verdicts, it would be similarly unfair to apply issue preclusion. In sum, fairness is key.

■ **CASE VOCABULARY**

COMPROMISE VERDICT: A verdict that is reached when some jurors concede on certain issues so other issues can be settled in the way they would like them to be.

GENERAL VERDICT: A verdict in which a jury simply finds in favor of one side or the other, as opposed to resolving particular specified questions of fact.

Kovach v. District of Columbia

(Ticketed Motorist) v. (Red-Light Camera Installer)

805 A.2d 957 (D.C. Ct. App. 2002)

COLLATERAL ESTOPPEL MAY APPLY WHERE RES JUDICATA DOES NOT

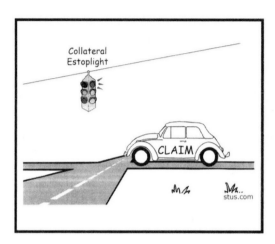

Collateral Estoplight

CLAIM

stus.com

■ **INSTANT FACTS** A motorist "caught" by a red-light camera brought suit after the District of Columbia realized that the intersection where the camera was installed was confusing to motorists and forgave all unpaid fines, but refused to issue refunds for fines already paid.

■ **BLACK LETTER RULE** Under the doctrine of res judicata, or claim preclusion, a final judgment on the merits precludes relitigation between the same parties concerning the same factual transaction not only as to every ground of recovery or defense actually presented in the action, but also as to every ground that might have been presented.

■ **PROCEDURAL BASIS**

Appellate court review of a trial court judgment dismissing the plaintiff's complaint.

■ **FACTS**

The District of Columbia (D) installed a camera at a traffic-controlled intersection in the District (D) that recorded motorists going through red lights. The violators were then issued traffic tickets. The District (D) disconnected the camera when it realized that motorists found the intersection confusing, which resulted in an inordinate number of tickets and fines. It agreed to dismiss all outstanding fines, but not to reimburse those drivers who had already paid their fines as a result of being "caught" by the camera. Kovach (P), one such violator who had already paid his seventy-five-dollar fine, sued on behalf of himself and others similarly situated, arguing that the District's (D) decision to forgive some violators and not others was unfairly discriminatory. The trial court held that Kovach's (P) previous payment of the fine precluded him from contesting the District's (D) subsequent decision on the ground of res judicata, and the plaintiff appealed.

■ **ISSUE**

Was the plaintiff barred from contesting the District's (D) decision to forgive only those violators who had not paid their fines by the fact that he had already paid his?

■ **DECISION AND RATIONALE**

(Ruiz, J.) Yes. Under the doctrine of res judicata, or claim preclusion, a final judgment on the merits precludes relitigation between the same parties concerning the same factual transaction not only as to every ground of recovery or defense actually presented in the action, but also as to every ground that might have been presented. The arguments in Kovach's (P) complaint, however—statutory and constitutional challenges to the District's (D) decision to forgive outstanding tickets but refuse to refund those already paid—could not have been raised before the Bureau of Traffic Adjudication, because the District's decision occurred after the fine was paid. Thus, res judicata does not bar Kovach's (P) claims. We affirm the trial court's dismissal nonetheless, but on other grounds.

Even when res judicata is inapplicable, collateral estoppel may bar relitigation of the issues determined in a prior action. Collateral estoppel restricts a party in certain circumstances from relitigating issues or facts that were actually litigated or necessarily decided in an earlier proceeding, including agency determinations. The Traffic Adjudication Act provided Kovach (P) with the opportunity to contest his fine, but he chose not to do so. By admitting liability, he has taken himself out of the class of persons he claims have been unfairly prejudiced by the District's (D) decision. Kovach's (P) claim that he was confused by the traffic light comes too late. His payment of the fine and failure to raise any defense at the time leads us to conclude that there was no manifest error in the prior proceeding, nor was there any manifest injustice that calls for an exception to the collateral estoppel doctrine. Affirmed.

Analysis:

This case concerns the difference between *res judicata*, or *claim preclusion*, and *collateral estoppel*, or *issue preclusion*. The principal distinction is that the former doctrine forecloses litigation of matters that have never been litigated, as long as they could have—or should have—been advanced in an earlier suit. Res judicata is sometimes used as a general term referring to all of the ways in which one judgment will have a binding effect on another, but that usage is inaccurate, lumping under a single name two quite different effects of judgments. In reality, collateral estoppel has the effect of foreclosing relitigation of facts or issues that have already been litigated and decided. Although the terms "res judicata" and "collateral estoppel" continue to be routinely employed, some have long argued that, for the sake of clarity, the terms "claim preclusion" and "issue preclusion" should be used, and this usage is increasingly employed by the courts, as it is by Restatement (Second) of Judgments.

■ CASE VOCABULARY

COLLATERAL ESTOPPEL: The binding effect of a judgment as to matters actually litigated and determined in one action on later controversies between the parties involving a different claim from that on which the original judgment was based; a doctrine barring a party from relitigating an issue determined against that party in an earlier action, even if the second action differs significantly from the first one.

RES JUDICATA: An issue that has been definitively settled by judicial decision; an affirmative defense barring the same parties from litigating a second lawsuit on the same claim, or any other claim arising from the same transaction or series of transactions and that could have been—but was not—raised in the first suit. The three essential elements are (1) an earlier decision on the issue, (2) a final judgment on the merits, and (3) the involvement of the same parties, or parties in privity with the original parties.

FULL FAITH AND CREDIT GENERALLY REQUIRES EVERY STATE TO GIVE TO A JUDGMENT AT LEAST THE RES JUDICATA EFFECT WHICH THE JUDGMENT WOULD BE ACCORDED IN THE STATE WHICH RENDERED IT

■ **INSTANT FACTS** Suit regarding the preclusive effect of a prior decision as to the ownership of certain bottom land on the Missouri River.

■ **BLACK LETTER RULE** A judgment is entitled to full faith and credit, even as to the question of jurisdiction, when the second court's inquiry disclosed that those questions have been fully and fairly litigated and finally decided in the court which rendered the original judgment.

■ **PROCEDURAL BASIS**

Certification to the United States Supreme Court of a federal appellate court decision not to give res judicata effect to a Nebraska Supreme Court judgment regarding the title to a certain piece of land.

■ **FACTS**

In 1956, the petitioners brought a quiet title action against the respondent in Nebraska state court seeking title to certain bottom land situated on the Missouri River. The main channel of that river forms the boundary between Missouri and Nebraska. The Nebraska court had jurisdiction over the subject matter of the controversy only if the land in question was in Nebraska. Whether the land was in Nebraska depended on whether a shift in the river's course had been caused by avulsion or accretion. The respondent appeared in Nebraska court and fully litigated the issues of the case, all the while contesting subject matter jurisdiction. The court found in favor of the petitioners and quieted title to them. The respondent appealed, and the Supreme Court of Nebraska affirmed. Two months later, the respondent filed suit against the petitioners in a Missouri court to quiet title to the same land, alleging that the land in question was in Missouri. The suit was removed to federal district court, which held that the land was in fact in Missouri, but that all the issues had been litigated and determined in the Nebraska litigation, and that the judgment of the Nebraska Supreme Court was res judicata and "binding on this court." The Court of Appeals reversed, holding that the district court was not required to give full faith and credit to the Nebraska judgment, and that normal res judicata principles did not apply because the controversy involved land and a court in Missouri was therefore free to retry the question of Nebraska's subject matter jurisdiction. This appeal followed.

■ **ISSUE**

When an issue has been fully and fairly litigated and finally decided in a particular court, must other courts give full faith and credit to that judgment?

■ DECISION AND RATIONALE

(Stewart, J.) Yes. The constitutional command of full faith and credit requires that "judicial proceedings . . . shall have the same full faith and credit in every court within the United States . . . as they have by law or usage in the courts of such State . . . from which they are taken." Full faith and credit thus generally requires every State to give to a judgment at least the res judicata effect which the judgment would be accorded in the State which rendered it. By the Constitutional provision for full faith and credit, the local doctrines of res judicata become part of the national jurisprudence, and therefore the federal questions cognizable here. It is not questioned that the Nebraska courts would give full res judicata effect to the Nebraska judgment quieting title in the petitioners. It is the respondents' position, however, that whatever effect the Nebraska courts might give to the Nebraska judgment, the federal court in Missouri was free independently to determine whether the Nebraska court in fact had jurisdiction over the subject matter, i.e., whether the land in question was actually in Nebraska. In support of this position, the respondent relies on the many decisions of this Court which have held that a judgment of a court in one State is conclusive upon the merits in a court in another State only if the court in the first State had jurisdiction to render the judgment. However, while it is established that a court in one State, when asked to give effect to the judgment of a court in another State, may constitutionally inquire into the foreign court's jurisdiction to render that judgment, the modern decisions of this Court have carefully delineated the permissible scope of such an inquiry. From these decisions there emerges the general rule that a judgment is entitled to full faith and credit, even as to the question of subject matter jurisdiction, when the second court's inquiry disclosed that those questions have been fully and fairly litigated and finally decided in the court which rendered the original judgment. One trial of an issue is enough. It is just as important that there should be a place to end as that there should be a place to begin litigation. After a party has his day in court, with opportunity to present his evidence and his view of the law, a collateral attack upon the decision as to jurisdiction there rendered merely retries the issue previously determined. To be sure, the general rule of finality or jurisdictional determinations is not without exceptions. Doctrines of federal preemption or sovereign immunity may in some contexts be controlling, but no such overriding considerations are present here. In sum, for the reasons stated, we hold that the federal court in Missouri had the power and, upon proper averments, the duty to inquire into the jurisdiction of the Nebraska courts to render the decree quieting title to the land in the petitioners. We further hold that when that inquiry disclosed, as it did, that the jurisdictional issues had been fully and fairly litigated by the parties and finally determined in the Nebraska courts, the federal court in Missouri was correct in ruling that further inquiry was precluded. The Court of Appeals is reversed.

■ CONCURRENCE

(Black, J.) I concur in today's reversal of the Court of Appeal's judgment, but with the understanding that we are not deciding the question whether the respondent would continue to be bound by the Nebraska judgment should it later be authoritatively decided, either in an original proceeding between the States in this Court or by a compact between the two States that the disputed tract is in Missouri.

Analysis:

Courts must give preclusive effect to the decisions of other courts in the same state. Under the Full Faith and Credit Clause (Article IV) and the Full Faith and Credit Act (28 U.S.C. §1738), this requirement is extended to the United States as a whole. Under the clause, courts in one state must give preclusive effect to the decisions of courts in other states or the federal government. This makes the United States as a whole a single unit for the purpose of issue and claim preclusion. *Durfee* is one of the first cases to deal with this issue, holding that when jurisdiction, along with the other issues in the case, has been fully and fairly litigated, subsequent courts will be required to accept decisions as to jurisdiction made by the prior court.

■ CASE VOCABULARY

ACCRETION: The increase, growth, or enlargement of land caused by the action of natural forces.

AVERMENTS: A declaration or affirmation that a particular fact is true, such as an allegation in a legal pleading.

AVULSION: A separation or cutting-off of land by the change in course of a river or other body of water.

BOTTOM LAND: A piece of low-lying land near a river or other watercourse.

COLLATERAL ATTACK: An attack on a judgment outside of the proceeding in which it was entered. The usual intent of a collateral attack is to have the prior judgment overturned or impeached.

FEDERAL PREEMPTION: A principle of constitutional law holding that, under the Supremacy Clause, federal law supersedes state law that is inconsistent with federal law.

SOVEREIGN IMMUNITY: The principle that a sovereign cannot be sued in its own courts without its prior consent.

TRIAL DE NOVO: A new trial of a particular case, addressing both questions of fact and issues of law, that is conducted as if the original trial had never taken place.

(Federal Government) v. (Land Owner)

524 U.S. 38, 118 S.Ct. 1862 (1998)

A NEW AND INDEPENDENT ACTION SHOULD BE AVAILABLE AFTER A PRIOR TRIAL
ONLY TO PREVENT A GRAVE MISCARRIAGE OF JUSTICE

■ **INSTANT FACTS** A purported land owner sought to reopen a suit over the ownership of a particular piece of land.

■ **BLACK LETTER RULE** Independent actions must be reserved for those cases of injustices which, in certain circumstances, are deemed sufficiently gross to demand a departure from the rigid adherence to the doctrine of res judicata.

■ **PROCEDURAL BASIS**

Certification to the United States Supreme Court of a federal appellate court decision to allow the reopening of a prior judgment.

■ **FACTS**

In 1979, as a part of creating a National Seashore, the federal government (D) brought a quiet title action (the *Adams* litigation) against Beggerly (P) in the Southern District of Mississippi. The issue in that case was the ownership of certain beach-front property. More specifically, the case turned on whether, before the Louisiana Purchase in 1803, the land in question had been deeded to a private individual. If so, Beggerly (P) owned the land. If not, the U.S. government (D) already owned it, and would not have to purchase it from Beggerly (P). On the eve of trial, the case settled, and a small sum was provided to Beggerly (P) by the government (D); Beggerly (P) agreed to settle because there was not strong proof of his claim. Judgment was entered based on the settlement agreement. Twelve years later in 1994, however, Beggerly (P) brought suit in the same court, seeking to have the settlement agreement set aside. Beggerly (P) also sought a damage award. The new suit was based on a document found by a genealogical record specialist in the National Archives in Washington, D.C. The specialist found materials that, according to her, showed that on August 1, 1781, Bernardo de Galvez, then the Governor General of Spanish Louisiana, granted Hom Island to a private party, meaning that Beggerly (P) had been the owner of the land. The District Court found that it was without jurisdiction to hear Beggerly's (P) new suit and dismissed the complaint. The Court of Appeals, however, reversed, concluding that the suit satisfied the elements of an "independent action," and was therefore proper under Federal Rule of Civil Procedure 60(b). The United States (D) appealed.

■ **ISSUE**

Can completed litigation be reopened when new evidence is found?

■ **DECISION AND RATIONALE**

(Rehnquist, J.) Yes, but only in special circumstances. The Government's (D) primary contention is that the Court of Appeals erred in concluding that it had jurisdiction over Beggerly's (P) 1994 suit. The Government (D) argues that there was no statutory basis for

---

the Beggerlys' (P) 1994 action, and the District Court was therefore correct to have dismissed it. We think the Government's (D) position is inconsistent with the history and language of Rule 60(b) [allowing a new trial to be granted in certain circumstances]. The 1946 Amendment to the rule made clear that nearly all of the old forms of obtaining relief from a judgment, i.e., coram nobis, coram vobis, audita querela, bills of review, and bills in the nature of review, had been abolished. The revision make equally clear, however, that one of the old forms, i.e., the "independent action," or the "original action," still survived. The Advisory Committee notes confirm this view. The Government (D) is therefore wrong to suggest that an independent action brought in the same court as the original lawsuit requires an independent basis for jurisdiction. This is not to say, however, that the requirements for a meritorious independent action have been met here. If relief may be obtained through an independent action in a case such as this, where the most that may be charged against the Government is a failure to furnish relevant information that would at best form the basis for a Rule 60(b)(3) motion, the strict one-year limit on such motions would be set at naught. Independent actions must, if Rule 60(b) is to be interpreted as a coherent whole, be reserved for those cases of injustices which, in certain circumstances, are deemed sufficiently gross to demand a departure from the rigid adherence to the doctrine of res judicata. Under the Rule, an independent action should be available only to prevent a grave miscarriage of justice. In this case, it should be obvious that the Beggerlys' (P) allegations do not nearly approach this demanding standard. It surely would work no "grave miscarriage of justice," and perhaps no miscarriage of justice at all, to allow the judgment to stand. We therefore hold that the Court of Appeals erred in concluding that this was a sufficient basis to justify the reopening of the judgment in the *Adams* litigation. Reversed.

Analysis:

Sometimes, restricting an attack on a judgment to the appeals process may work an injustice. For instance, in a case in which one side hides evidence from the other, in contravention of a proper discovery request, and that hiding of evidence is not discovered until after the appeals process is complete, there is no chance for further appeal. In cases such as this, litigants are given the opportunity to reopen a judgment, which is the subject of *Beggerly*. When justice requires it, a court may relieve a party from a final judgment, order, or proceeding because of mistake, inadvertence, surprise, newly discovered evidence that could not have been brought to light in time for trial, fraud, or a number of other reasons.

■ CASE VOCABULARY

AUDITA QUERELA: A common law writ in which a party brought an action seeking relief against a judgment already entered on the ground that some defense has arisen since the entry of judgment that could not be taken advantage of unless the judgment is re-opened.

BILL IN THE NATURE OF REVIEW: A common law bill brought in equity to cancel judicial proceedings before the entry of judgment.

BILL OF REVIEW: A common law bill brought to have a decree of a court reviewed, altered, set aside, or reversed.

CORAM NOBIS: A writ of error used to correct errors of fact, and to bring before a court which has entered judgment matters of fact which, if known at the time the judgment was entered, would have prevented its entry.

CORAM VOBIS: A writ of error entered by an appellate court instructing a trial court to correct an error of fact.

"GRAVE MISCARRIAGE OF JUSTICE": An action creates a "grave miscarriage of justice" when it results in a decision that is inconsistent with or prejudicial to the substantial rights of one of the parties.

INDEPENDENT ACTION: As used in this case, an independent action is an action independent and separate from a prior action (i.e., not an appeal) that is brought to set aside the prior action.

ORIGINAL ACTION: Used in this case as another name for "independent action."

CHAPTER 12

Joinder

Plant v. Blazer Financial Services

Instant Facts: Plant (P) borrowed $2,520 from Blazer Financial (D), made no payments for eight months, then sued Blazer Financial (D) under the Truth-in-Lending Act.

Black Letter Rule: An action on an underlying debt in default is a compulsory counterclaim that must be asserted in a suit by the debtor on a truth-in-lending cause of action.

Mosley v. General Motors Corp.

Instant Facts: Mosely (P) and nine others joined together to bring suit against General Motors (D) for discrimination against blacks and women.

Black Letter Rule: The difficulties in ultimately adjudicating damages to various plaintiffs in a class are not so overwhelming as to require severance of the plaintiffs' causes of action.

Price v. CTB, Inc.

Instant Facts: After Price (P) sued Latco (D) for negligence, Latco (D) filed a third-party complaint against ITW (D) seeking implied indemnity.

Black Letter Rule: A defendant may assert a claim against anyone not a party to the original action if that third party's liability is in some way dependent upon the outcome of the original action.

Kroger v. Omaha Public Power District

Instant Facts: Steel worker was killed when the crane he was working with came too close to power lines and he was electrocuted.

Black Letter Rule: Summary judgment may be granted on the issue of duty if the court concludes that, as a matter of law, the defendant owed no duty.

Owen Equipment & Erection Co. v. Kroger

Instant Facts: In a wrongful death suit for the electrocution of her husband, Mrs. Kroger (P) attempted to obtain federal diversity jurisdiction over Owen Equipment and Erection Company (D), a nondiverse party, by alleging pendent party jurisdiction.

Black Letter Rule: A federal court does not retain jurisdiction over an action, based on diversity of citizenship, when the plaintiff adds a pendent party defendant who destroys complete diversity.

Temple v. Synthes Corp.

Instant Facts: The federal district court dismissed Temple's (P) suit against Synthes Corp. (D) for failure to join all necessary parties.

Black Letter Rule: It is not necessary to join all potential joint tortfeasors in a single action.

Helzberg's Diamond Shops v. Valley West Des Moines Shopping Center

Instant Facts: A jewelry store sued the shopping mall for violating its lease agreement and allowing four full line jewelry stores lease spaces in the mall.

Black Letter Rule: It is generally recognized that a person does not become indispensable to an action to determine rights under a contract simply because that person's rights or obligations under an entirely separate contract will be affected by the result of the action.

Natural Resources Defense Council v. United States Nuclear Regulatory Commission

Instant Facts: A complaint was filed to prevent NRC (D) from issuing licenses for the operation of uranium mills without first preparing environmental impact statements.

Black Letter Rule: Applicants satisfying their burden of the three requirements of Rule 24(a)(2) should be allowed to intervene in an action.

Martin v. Wilks

Instant Facts: Pursuant to consent judgments between the City of Birmingham ("City") and the Jefferson County Personnel Board ("Board") with black firefighters, the white firefighters filed a suit against the City and the Board alleging reverse discrimination.

Black Letter Rule: A party seeking a judgment binding on another cannot obligate the latter to intervene in the action without mandatorily joining that person in the action.

Paragon Molding Ltd. v. Safeco Insurance Company

Instant Facts: Paragon's (P) real estate and inventory were damaged by a fire, and different parties made claims on the proceeds of an insurance policy.

Black Letter Rule: The function of interpleader is to resolve inconsistent claims against designated assets based on mutually exclusive theories, rather than to adjudicate rival claims that are mutually exclusive only because of the limited size of the assets.

Hansberry v. Lee

Instant Facts: Hansberry (D), the black purchaser of land that was subject to a racially restrictive sales covenant, sought to avoid a prior class action holding that the covenant was valid.

Black Letter Rule: Granting res judicata effect to a class action judgment, in which the prerequisites and procedures for class action were not satisfied, violates due process.

Phillips Petroleum Co. v. Shutts

Instant Facts: Shutts (P) and several other holders of royalty interests brought a class action against Phillips Petroleum (D) to recover royalty payments. The Kansas court obtained personal jurisdiction over all parties and applied Kansas law to all claims.

Black Letter Rule: In class actions, personal jurisdiction does not require that each class member have minimum contacts with the forum state, but the forum state must have sufficient interests in the claims to assert its state law to all claims.

Wal-Mart Stores, Inc. v. Dukes

Instant Facts: The District Court certified a class of approximately 1.5 million current and former female employees of Wal-Mart (D) in an employment discrimination case, and the Ninth Circuit affirmed the certification.

Black Letter Rule: Certification of a class action is appropriate only when the common contention of the class members is capable of a class-wide resolution.

Amchem Products, Inc. v. Windsor

Instant Facts: People exposed to asbestos products created a settlement-only class to settle current and future asbestos-related claims.

Black Letter Rule: In determining the propriety of a settlement only class certification, the requirements of Rule 23(a) and (b)(3) Fed. R. Civ. P. must be satisfied, and the settlement must be taken into account as well.

(Debtor) v. (Lender)

598 F.2d 1357 (5th Cir.1979)

DEBT COUNTERCLAIMS IN TRUTH-IN-LENDING ACTIONS ARE COMPULSORY

■ **INSTANT FACTS** Plant (P) borrowed $2,520 from Blazer Financial (D), made no payments for eight months, then sued Blazer Financial (D) under the Truth-in-Lending Act.

■ **BLACK LETTER RULE** An action on an underlying debt in default is a compulsory counterclaim that must be asserted in a suit by the debtor on a truth-in-lending cause of action.

■ **PROCEDURAL BASIS**

Plaintiff's appeal from the trial court's ruling that the defendant's counterclaim on the underlying debt was compulsory.

■ **FACTS**

Theresa Plant (P) executed a note in favor of Blazer Financial Services, Inc. (D) for $2,520 to be paid in monthly installments of $105. No payments were made on the note. Eight months later, Plant (P) commenced a civil action under the Truth-in-Lending Act for failure to make disclosures required by the Act. Blazer Financial (D), counterclaimed on the note for the unpaid balance. Based on Blazer Financial's (D) failure to disclose a limitation on an after-acquired security interest, the trial court held the disclosures inadequate and awarded Plant (P) the statutory penalty of $944.76 and $700 in attorney's fees.

■ **ISSUE**

Is an action on an underlying debt in default a compulsory counterclaim? *required by law*

■ **DECISION AND RATIONALE**

(Roney, J.) Yes. Plant (P) challenges the trial court's ruling that Blazer Financial's (D) counterclaim on the underlying debt was compulsory. The issue of whether a state debt counterclaim in a truth-in-lending action is compulsory or permissive is one of first impression in this Circuit, has never, to our knowledge, been decided by a court of appeals, and has received diverse treatment from a great number of district courts. Rule 13(a), Federal Rules of Civil Procedure, provides that a counterclaim is compulsory if it "arises out of the transaction or occurrence" that is the subject matter of the plaintiff's claim. The test which has commended itself to most courts, including our own, is the logical relation test. This test is a loose standard which permits "a broad realistic interpretation in the interest of avoiding a multiplicity of suits." The hallmark of this approach is its flexibility. Applying the logical relationship test literally to the counterclaim in this case suggests its compulsory character because a single aggregate of operative facts, the loan transaction, gave rise to both Plant's (P) and Blazer Financial's (D) claims. Because a tallying of the results from the district courts which have decided this question, however, shows that a greater number have found such a counterclaim merely permissive, we subject the relationship between the claims to further analysis. The purpose of the Truth-in-Lending Act is to assure a meaningful disclosure of credit terms so that the consumer will be able to compare more readily the various credit terms available to him and avoid the uninformed use of credit. It has been argued that this purpose would be frustrated if federal courts were entangled in the myriad factual and legal questions essential to a decision on the debt claims but unrelated to the truth-in-lending violation. Additionally, courts have predicted a flood of debt counterclaims, greatly increasing the federal court workload. Other courts have suggested that regarding such debt counterclaims as compulsory would infringe on the power of states to adjudicate disputes grounded in state law. After careful consideration of these factors relied upon to find counterclaims permissive, we opt for the analysis applied by courts in several states in determining debt counterclaims to be compulsory. Emphasizing the goal of judicial economy furthered by a single presentation of facts, one court observed that suits on notes will inevitably deal with the circumstance of the execution of the notes and any representation made to induce the borrowing. We add to these arguments the observation that one of the purposes of the compulsory counterclaim rule is to provide complete relief to the defendant who has been brought involuntarily into the federal court. Absent the opportunity to bring a counterclaim, this party could be forced to satisfy the debtor's truth-in-lending claim without any assurance that his claims against the defaulting debtor arising from the same transaction will be taken into account or even that the funds he has been required to pay will still be available should he obtain a state court judgment in excess of the judgment on the truth-in-lending claim. In addition, a determination that the underlying debt was invalid may have a material effect on the amount of damages a debtor could recover on a truth-in-lending claim. To permit the debtor to recover from the creditor without taking the original loan into account would be a serious departure from the evenhanded treatment afforded both parties under the Act. Truth-in-lending claims can be brought in either state or federal court. To the extent this dual jurisdiction was intended to permit litigation of truth-in-lending claims in actions on the debt, it reflects a purpose that the debt claim and the truth-in-lending claims be handled together. We conclude that the obvious interrelationship of the claims and rights of the parties, coupled with the common factual basis of the claims, demonstrates a logical relationship between the claim and counterclaim under the logical relation test. We affirm the trial court's determination that the debt counterclaim is compulsory.

Analysis:

A permissive counterclaim must have an independent jurisdictional basis, while it is generally accepted that a compulsory counterclaim fails within the ancillary jurisdiction of the federal courts even if it would ordinarily be a matter for state court consideration. In this case, there is no independent basis, since neither federal question nor diversity jurisdiction is available for the counterclaim. Consequently, if the counterclaim were treated as permissive, Blazer Financial's (D) action on the underlying debt would have to be pursued in state court. The split of opinion on the nature of debt counterclaims in truth-in-lending actions appears to be, in large part, the product of competing policy considerations between the objectives of Rule 13(a) and the policies of the Truth-in-Lending Act, and disagreement over the extent to which federal courts should be involved in state causes of action for debt. While Rule 13(a) is intended to avoid multiple litigation by consolidating all controversies between the parties, several courts and commentators have observed that accepting creditors' debt counterclaims may obstruct the goals of the Truth-in-Lending Act. Courts that have concluded that debt counterclaims are to be permissive have found the nexus between the truth-in-lending violation and debt obligation too abstract or tenuous to regard the claims as logically related.

■ CASE VOCABULARY

ANCILLARY JURISDICTION: the federal court acquires jurisdiction over the entire case, even though some of the matters would not independently be subject to federal jurisdiction.

COMPULSORY COUNTERCLAIM: Arises out of the same transaction or occurrence as the present claim.

DIVERSITY JURISDICTION: The federal courts have jurisdiction over cases involving citizens of different states.

FEDERAL QUESTION JURISDICTION: The federal courts have jurisdiction over all cases arising under the U.S. Constitution and certain federal statutes.

PERMISSIVE COUNTERCLAIM: Does not arise out of the present claim.

TRUTH-IN-LENDING ACT: A federal law requiring that persons applying for commercial credit be provided with accurate and understandable information relating to the cost of credit.

Mosley v. General Motors Corp.

(Black Employee) v. (Discriminating Employer)

497 F.2d 1330 (8th Cir.1974)

TEN PLAINTIFFS SUING THE DEFENDANT FOR DISCRIMINATION MAY BE JOINED TOGETHER IN A SINGLE ACTION

■ **INSTANT FACTS** Mosely (P) and nine others joined together to bring suit against General Motors (D) for discrimination against blacks and women.

■ **BLACK LETTER RULE** The difficulties in ultimately adjudicating damages to various plaintiffs in a class are not so overwhelming as to require severance of the plaintiffs' causes of action.

■ **PROCEDURAL BASIS**

Application to permit an interlocutory appeal after district court ordered each plaintiff to bring separate causes of actions.

■ **FACTS**

Nathaniel Mosely (P) and nine others joined in bringing this action individually and as class representatives alleging that their rights guaranteed under 42 U.S.C. Sec. 2000 et seq. and 42 U.S.C. Sec. 1981 were denied by General Motors (D) and the local Union by reason of their color and race. Each of the ten had, prior to the filing of the complaint, filed a charge with the Equal Employment Opportunity Commission (EEOC) asserting the facts underlying these claims. Pursuant thereto, the EEOC made a reasonable cause finding that General Motors (D) and the Union had engaged in unlawful employment practices in violation of Title VII of the Civil Rights Act of 1964. Accordingly, the charging parties were notified by EEOC of their right to institute a civil action in the appropriate federal district court. All of the individual plaintiffs requested injunctive relief, back pay, attorneys' fees and costs [dig deep]. The class counts of the complaint also sought declaratory and injunctive relief, back pay, attorneys' fees and costs. The district court ordered that "insofar as the first ten counts are concerned, those ten counts shall be severed into ten separate causes of action," and each plaintiff was directed to bring a separate action based upon his complaint, duly and separately filed. Upon entering the order, and upon application of the plaintiffs, the district court found that its decision involved a controlling question of law as to which there is a substantial ground for difference of opinion and that any of the parties might make application for appeal under 28 U.S.C. Section 1292(b). This court granted the application to permit this interlocutory appeal.

■ **ISSUE**

Are the issues of ten plaintiffs claiming unlawful employment sufficient to sustain joinder under Federal Rules of Civil Procedure 20(a)?

■ **DECISION AND RATIONALE**

(Ross, J.) Yes. To determine whether the district court's order was proper herein, we must look to the policy and law that have developed around the operation of Rule 20. The Supreme Court has said that under the Rules, the impulse is toward entertaining the broadest possible scope of action consistent with fairness to the parties. Joinder of claims, parties and remedies is strongly encouraged. Permissive joinder is not, however, applicable in all cases. The rule

---

imposes two specific requisites to the joinder of parties: (1) a right to relief must be asserted by, or against, each plaintiff or defendant relating to or arising out of the same transaction or occurrence, or series of transactions or occurrences; and (2) some question of law or fact common to all the parties must arise in the action. Here, Mosely (P) and the other plaintiffs have asserted a right to relief arising out of the same transactions or occurrences. Each of the ten plaintiffs alleged that he had been injured by the same general policy of discrimination on the part of General Motors (D) and the Union. We conclude that a company-wide policy purportedly designed to discriminate against blacks in employment similarly arises out of the same series of transactions or occurrences. Thus Mosely (P) and the others meet the first requisite for joinder under Rule 20(a). The second requisite necessary to sustain a permissive joinder under the rule is that a question of law or fact common to all the parties will arise in the action. The rule does not require that *all* questions of law and fact raised by the dispute be common. Yet, neither does it establish any qualitative or quantitative test of commonality. With respect to employment discrimination cases under Title VII, courts have found that the discriminatory character of a defendant's conduct is basic to the class, and the fact that the individual class members may have suffered different effects from the alleged discrimination is immaterial for the purposes of the prerequisite. The right to relief here depends on the ability to demonstrate that each of the plaintiffs was wronged by racially discriminatory policies on the part of General Motors (D) and the Union. The discriminatory character of General Motors' (D) and the Union's conduct is thus basic to each plaintiff's recovery. The fact that each plaintiff may have different effects from the alleged discrimination is immaterial for the purposes of determining the common question of law or fact. Thus we conclude that the second requisite for joinder under Rule 20(a) is also met by the complaint. For the reasons set forth above, we conclude that the district court abused its discretion in severing the joined actions. The difficulties in ultimately adjudicating damages to the various plaintiffs are not so overwhelming as to require such severance. If appropriate, separate trials may be granted as to any particular issue after the determination of common questions. The judgment of the district court disallowing joinder of the plaintiffs' individual actions is reversed and remanded with directions to permit Mosely (P) and the other plaintiffs to proceed jointly.

Analysis:

Rule 20(a) of the Federal Rules of Civil Procedure provides that "all persons may join in one action as plaintiffs if they assert any right to relief jointly, severally, or in the alternative in respect of or arising out of the same transaction, occurrence, or series of transactions or occurrences and if any question of law or fact common to all these persons will arise in the action." Rule 20(b) and Rule 42(b) vest in the district court the discretion to order separate trials or make such other orders as will prevent delay or prejudice. In this manner, the scope of the civil action is made a matter for the discretion of the district court, and a determination on the question of joinder of parties will be reversed on appeal only upon a showing of abuse of that discretion. The purpose of Rule 20 is to promote trial convenience and expedite the final determination of disputes, thereby preventing multiple lawsuits. Single trials generally tend to lessen the delay, expense and inconvenience to all concerned. In ascertaining whether a particular factual situation constitutes a single transaction or occurrence for purposes of Rule 20, a case-by-case approach is generally pursued.

■ CASE VOCABULARY

DECLARATORY RELIEF: A judgment of the court to express an opinion of the court on a question of law without ordering anything to be done.

ET SEQ.: "Et sequentia"; and the following; used in denominating page reference and statutory section numbers.

INJUNCTIVE RELIEF: Requires a party to refrain from doing or continuing to do a particular action.

INTERLOCUTORY APPEAL: Provisional, temporary.

JOINDER: Uniting of several causes of action or parties in a single unit.

Price v. CTB, Inc.

(Consumer) v. (Poultry House Builder)

168 F.Supp.2d 1299 (M.D. Ala. 2001)

A THIRD PARTY MAY BE IMPLEADED INTO AN ACTION IF IT COULD FACE LIABILITY
THROUGH INDEMNITY

■ **INSTANT FACTS** After Price (P) sued Latco (D) for negligence, Latco (D) filed a third-party complaint against ITW (D) seeking implied indemnity.

■ **BLACK LETTER RULE** A defendant may assert a claim against anyone not a party to the original action if that third party's liability is in some way dependent upon the outcome of the original action.

■ **PROCEDURAL BASIS**

On consideration of ITW's (D) motion to dismiss for improper impleader and on the doctrine of laches.

■ **FACTS**

Price (P) sued CTB, Inc. (D) and Latco (D) for breach of contract, fraudulent misrepresentation, negligence, and wantonness in the construction of a chicken house constructed by Latco (D). Six months after the complaint was filed, Latco (D) moved to file a third-party complaint against ITW (D), a nail manufacturer that allegedly negligently designed the nails used to construct the chicken house, seeking indemnity. ITW (D) moved to dismiss for improper impleader.

■ **ISSUE**

Was ITW (D) properly impleaded into the action?

■ **DECISION AND RATIONALE**

(De Ment, J.) Yes. Under Federal Rule of Civil Procedure 14(a), "a defendant may assert a claim against anyone not a party to the original action if that third party's liability is in some way dependent upon the outcome of the original action." The third-party claim, however, may not be based on a separate and independent claim, even though both claims share common underlying facts. Impleader is proper only when a defendant asserts that the liability for the original action is properly placed upon the third party. Although Alabama law does not recognize a right of contribution among joint tortfeasors, which would preserve Latco's (D) liability, if any, Alabama does recognize implied contractual indemnity running from a manufacturer to a seller of its products. Under this doctrine, a manufacturer is bound to indemnify the seller if the seller is not at fault, the manufacturer is responsible, and the seller has been bound by a monetary judgment. Accordingly, ITW (D) has been properly impleaded into the action, since Latco (D) may have a right of indemnity against ITW (D). Motion denied.

Analysis:

Because impleader requires the potential liability of a third party, the appropriateness of impleader in a federal diversity case necessarily depends on the applicable substantive state law. Because ITW (D) would be potentially liable to Latco (D) if the action were brought in

---

state court, impleader in federal court is proper. If, however, a state does not recognize any right of contribution or indemnification, impleader is inappropriate.

■ **CASE VOCABULARY**

IMPLEADER: A procedure by which a third party is brought into a lawsuit, especially by a defendant who seeks to shift liability to someone not sued by the plaintiff.

THIRD-PARTY COMPLAINT: A complaint filed by the defendant against a third party, alleging that the third party may be liable for some or all of the damages that the plaintiff is trying to recover from the defendant.

Kroger v. Omaha Public Power District

(Administratrix) v. (Original Owner of Transmission Lines)

523 F.2d 161 (8th Cir.1975)

SUMMARY JUDGMENT CAN BE GRANTED IN WRONGFUL DEATH ACTION WHEN THE DEFENDANT HAS NO DUTY TOWARD THE DECEDENT

■ **INSTANT FACTS** Steel worker was killed when the crane he was working with came too close to power lines and he was electrocuted.

■ **BLACK LETTER RULE** Summary judgment may be granted on the issue of duty if the court concludes that, as a matter of law, the defendant owed no duty.

■ **PROCEDURAL BASIS**

Appeal from the district court's granting of the defendant's motion for summary judgment.

■ **FACTS**

James Kroger was employed by Paxton & Vierling Steel Company at one of its factories. James was involved in the movement of a large steel tank by means of a crane with a 60-foot boom. While one man drove the crane and another operated the boom, James walked alongside the tank to steady it. During this maneuver, the boom came close enough to high-tension lines that electricity from those lines arced over to the boom. Another are of electricity arced from the tank over to James and killed him [shocking!]. Omaha Public Power District (OPPD) (D), a public corporation of the state of Nebraska, had at one time owned the transmission lines involved. Six years prior to the accident which killed James, OPPD (D) sold the lines and equipment to Paxton & Vierling. OPPD (D) thereafter sold electricity to Paxton & Vierling, and when so requested, made repairs upon the lines and equipment. Geraldine Kroger (P), as administratrix of the estate of James Kroger, brought suit based on diversity jurisdiction for damages resulting from the decedent's wrongful death by electrocution. The district court found that OPPD (D) owed no duty to James, and granted OPPD's (D) motion for summary judgment.

■ **ISSUE**

Does OPPD (D) owe a duty to James Kroger, the breach of which would give rise to liability?

■ **DECISION AND RATIONALE**

(Nangle, J.) No. The District Court based its order of summary judgment on the fact that ownership of the transmission lines lay indisputably with Paxton & Vierling, that OPPD (D) had no duty to maintain the lines, that OPPD (D) had not been requested to discontinue the flow of electricity on the date of the accident and that OPPD (D) had not been put on notice that a crane was being operated in the vicinity of the lines. As a result, there was no duty owed by OPPD (D) to James Kroger, the breach of which would give rise to liability. We agree with the findings of the District Court and thus affirm the order of summary judgment.

Analysis:

The Court found that OPPD (D) could not have been held liable in a wrongful death action in this case because it owed no duty to James Kroger. OPPD (D) was far enough removed from

---

the circumstances surrounding the accident that liability could not attach. OPPD (D) had not owned the transmission lines for six years and, although it did occasionally perform maintenance on the lines and equipment, it was under no obligation to do so. Finally, since OPPD (D) had not been requested to cut off the electricity, nor was it given notice of crane work in the area, there was no opportunity for OPPD (D) to take steps to prevent the accident. There was no cause for holding OPPD (D) responsible for the accident that claimed James Kroger's life, so the Court granted OPPD's (D) motion for summary judgment.

■ CASE VOCABULARY

SUMMARY JUDGMENT: Preverdict judgment rendered by the court because there is no real factual dispute as a matter of law.

WRONGFUL DEATH ACTION: Cause of action for any wrongful act, neglect, or default which causes death.

Owen Equipment & Erection Co. v. Kroger

(Crane Company) v. (Wife)

437 U.S. 365, 98 S.Ct. 2396 (1978)

THE COMPLETE DIVERSITY REQUIREMENT CANNOT BE CIRCUMVENTED BY WAITING
FOR A DEFENDANT TO IMPLEAD A NONDIVERSE PARTY

■ **INSTANT FACTS** In a wrongful death suit for the electrocution of her husband, Mrs. Kroger (P) attempted to obtain federal diversity jurisdiction over Owen Equipment and Erection Company (D), a nondiverse party, by alleging pendent party jurisdiction.

■ **BLACK LETTER RULE** A federal court does not retain jurisdiction over an action, based on diversity of citizenship, when the plaintiff adds a pendent party defendant who destroys complete diversity.

■ **PROCEDURAL BASIS**

Writ of certiorari from affirmation of denial of motion to dismiss, for lack of subject matter jurisdiction, an action for damages for wrongful death.

■ **FACTS**

Mrs. Kroger's (P) husband was electrocuted while walking next to a steel crane which came too close to a high tension electric line. Mrs. Kroger (P), a citizen of Iowa, sued the Omaha Public Power District (OPPD) (D), a Nebraska corporation which allegedly negligently operated the power line [how do you negligently operate a power line?], for wrongful death. Kroger (P) brought the suit in federal court based on diversity of citizenship. OPPD (D) filed a third-party complaint against Owen Equipment and Erection Company (Owen) (D), alleging that Owen's (D) negligence proximately caused the death [this certainly seems more reasonable]. Mrs. Kroger (P) then amended her complaint to name Owen (D) as a defendant, alleging that Owen (D) was a Nebraska corporation with its principal place of business in Nebraska. However, as revealed at trial, Owen's (D) principal place of business was actually Iowa [surprise, surprise!]. Thus, complete diversity of citizenship was lacking. After OPPD (D) was granted summary judgment, Owen (D) moved to dismiss based on a lack of subject-matter jurisdiction. The District Court denied the motion, the Court of Appeals affirmed, and the Supreme Court granted certiorari.

■ **ISSUE**

Does a federal court retain jurisdiction over an action, based on diversity of citizenship, when the plaintiff adds a pendent party defendant who destroys complete diversity?

■ **DECISION AND RATIONALE**

(Stewart, J.) No. If a plaintiff obtains jurisdiction based on diversity of citizenship, the plaintiff cannot later add a defendant, who would destroy the complete diversity, as a pendent party. The jurisdiction of federal courts is limited both by the Constitution and by Acts of Congress. Pursuant to the *Gibbs* test, the constitution allows for pendent jurisdiction provided that the federal and nonfederal claims arise from a common nucleus of operative fact. However, as noted in *Aldinger*, congressional intent underlying the jurisdictional statute must be examined when pendent party jurisdiction is attempted. With regards to the relevant statute in this case, 28 U.S.C. §1332(a)(1), Congress has consistently required complete diversity of citizenship. Thus, no plaintiff can be a citizen of the same state as any defendant. Mrs. Kroger (P) could

---

not have originally brought suit against both Owen (D) and OPPD (D) based on diversity jurisdiction, since Owen's (D) principal place of business is the same state in which Mrs. Kroger (P) lives [don't you think she probably knew this?]. Likewise, Mrs. Kroger (P) should not be allowed to obtain federal jurisdiction by naming only the diverse party, OPPD (D), in her original suit, and by waiting for OPPD (D) to implead the nondiverse party, Owen (D). This procedure, if allowed, would permit plaintiffs to circumvent the complete diversity requirement of §1332(a)(1). Furthermore, considerations of convenience and judicial economy do not suffice to extend pendent or ancillary jurisdiction over Owen (D) in this case.

Analysis:

The Supreme Court decided that Mrs. Kroger's (D) attempt at circumventing the complete diversity requirement for federal jurisdiction—whether disingenuous or forthright—should not succeed. An alternative holding would conflict with the complete diversity requirement of §1332(a)(1). Certainly Mrs. Kroger (D) knew, or should have known, that Owen (D) was at least partially responsible for negligently operating the crane and proximately causing Mr. Kroger's electrocution. Even if OPPD (D) negligently operated the power line—the court obviously disagreed by granting summary judgment in OPPD's (D) favor—Mrs. Kroger should have known that OPPD (D) would want Owen (D) in the suit in order to reduce OPPD's (D) negligence.

■ **CASE VOCABULARY**

ANCILLARY JURISDICTION: Jurisdiction obtained when a party injects a claim lacking an independent basis for jurisdiction by way of a counterclaim, cross-claim, or third party complaint.

IMPLEAD: The act of bringing a new party, who is part of the subject matter of a claim, into an action.

THIRD-PARTY COMPLAINT: Complaint brought against a person or entity who was not formerly a party to the lawsuit.

Temple v. Synthes Corp.

(Patient) v. (Medical Manufacturer)

498 U.S. 5, 111 S.Ct. 315, *reh'g denied*, 498 U.S. 1042, 111 S.Ct. 715 (1990)

THE SURGEON AND HOSPITAL WERE NOT INDISPENSIBLE PARTIES IN A PRODUCT LIABILITY SUIT

■ **INSTANT FACTS** The federal district court dismissed Temple's (P) suit against Synthes Corp. (D) for failure to join all necessary parties.

■ **BLACK LETTER RULE** It is not necessary to join all potential joint tortfeasors in a single action.

■ **PROCEDURAL BASIS**

Certiorari to review a decision of the Fifth Circuit Court of Appeals, affirming a decision of the federal district court dismissing the plaintiff's action.

■ **FACTS**

After a "plate and screw device" surgically placed on Temple's (P) spine by Dr. LaRocca broke, Temple (P) sued Synthes Corp. (D), the manufacturer of the device, in federal court. Temple (P) simultaneously filed a state administrative proceeding for malpractice against Dr. LaRocca and the hospital in which the surgery was performed. When the administrative proceeding was completed, Temple (P) sued Dr. LaRocca and the hospital in state court. Rather than implead Dr. LaRocca and the hospital, Synthes (D) filed a motion to dismiss the federal suit for failure to properly join all necessary parties. The federal court ruled that Temple (P) must promptly join Dr. LaRocca and the hospital or the action would be dismissed. After Temple (P) failed to join Dr. LaRocca and the hospital, the action was dismissed with prejudice. Temple (P) appealed to the Fifth Circuit Court of Appeals. Determining that the defendant was prejudiced by Temple's (P) failure to join all parties, the Fifth Circuit affirmed. Temple (P) petitioned for review to the Supreme Court.

■ **ISSUE**

Did the court err in concluding that Dr. LaRocca and the hospital were indispensable parties necessary to the litigation?

■ **DECISION AND RATIONALE**

(Per curiam) Yes. It is not necessary to join all potential joint tortfeasors in a single action. The Advisory Committee to the Federal Rules of Civil Procedure clearly stated that "a tortfeasor with the usual 'joint-and-several' liability is merely a permissive party to an action against another with like liability." Although Rule 19(b) does indicate that all parties should be joined if "feasible," that section is inapplicable here because the plaintiff may obtain complete relief against Synthes (D) without the other defendants' involvement. Because the threshold requirements of Rule 19 have not been met, Dr. LaRocca and the hospital are not indispensable parties. Reversed and remanded.

Analysis:

Joint and several liability is a legal principle that benefits injured plaintiffs. In order to recover for the whole of a plaintiff's injuries, he or she need only establish one defendant's liability and the amount of damages sustained. It is immaterial whether other tortfeasors contributed to the cause of the injuries. From a practical standpoint, however, it would benefit a plaintiff to name all potentially liable joint tortfeasors as defendants to open the avenues of recovering on a judgment.

■ **CASE VOCABULARY**

COMPULSORY JOINDER: The necessary joinder of a party if either of the following is true: (1) in that party's absence, those already involved in the lawsuit cannot receive complete relief; or (2) the absence of such a party, claiming an interest in the subject of an action, might either impair the protection of that interest or leave some other party subject to multiple or inconsistent obligations.

INDISPENSIBLE PARTY: A party who, having interests that would inevitably be affected by a court's judgment, must be included in the case.

JOINDER: The uniting of parties or claims in a single lawsuit.

JOINT AND SEVERAL LIABILITY: Liability that may be apportioned either among two or more parties or to only one of a few select members of the group, at the adversary's discretion.

NECESSARY PARTY: A party who, being closely connected to a lawsuit, should be included in the case if feasible, but whose absence will not require dismissal of the proceedings.

THE FACT THAT A PERSON'S RIGHTS UNDER A SEPARATE CONTRACT WILL BE
AFFECTED BY THE RESULT OF AN ACTION DOES NOT MAKE THAT PERSON
INDISPENSABLE TO THE ACTION DETERMINING CONTRACT RIGHTS

■ **INSTANT FACTS** A jewelry store sued
the shopping mall for violating its lease
agreement and allowing four full line
jewelry stores lease spaces in the mall.

■ **BLACK LETTER RULE** It is generally
recognized that a person does not become
indispensable to an action to determine
rights under a contract simply because
that person's rights or obligations under an
entirely separate contract will be affected
by the result of the action.

■ **PROCEDURAL BASIS**

Appeal from the district court's order denying the defendant's motion to dismiss pursuant to
Rule 19, Federal Rules of Civil Procedure.

■ **FACTS**

On February 3, 1975, Helzberg's Diamond Shops, Inc. (P) and Valley West Des Moines
Shopping Center (D) entered into a written lease agreement. The lease agreement granted
Helzberg (P) the right to operate a full line jewelry store at space 254 in the Valley West Mall.
Section 6 of Article V of the lease agreement provided that Valley West (D) "agrees it will not
lease premises in the shopping center for use as a catalog jewelry store nor lease premises
for more than two full line jewelry stores in the shopping center in addition to the leased
premises." Subsequently, Helzberg (P) commenced operation of a full-time jewelry store in the
Valley West Mall. During the next twenty one months, Valley West (D) and two other
corporations entered into leases for spaces in the Valley West Mall for use as full line jewelry
stores. Pursuant to those leases, the two corporations also initiated actual operation of full line
jewelry stores. On November 2, 1976, Valley West (D) and Kirk's Incorporated, doing
business as Lord's Jewelers, entered into a written lease agreement granting Lord's the right to
occupy space in Valley West Mall "only as a retail specialty jewelry store (and not as a
catalogue or full line jewelry store)." However, Lord's intended to open and operate what
constituted a full line jewelry store at space 261 [surely just a small misunderstanding]. In an
attempt to avoid the opening of a fourth full line jewelry store in the Valley West Mall and the
resulting breach of the Helzberg (P)-Valley West (D) lease agreement, Helzberg (P) instituted
suit seeking preliminary and permanent injunctive relief restraining Valley West's (D) breach of
the lease agreement. The suit was filed in the United States District Court for the Western
District of Missouri. Subject matter jurisdiction was invoked pursuant to 28 U.S.C. Sec. 1332
based upon diversity of citizenship between the parties and an amount in controversy which
exceeds $10,000. Personal jurisdiction was established by service of process on Valley West
(D) pursuant to the Missouri "long arm" statute. Valley West (D) moved to dismiss pursuant to
Rule 19 because Helzberg (P) had failed to join Lord's as a party defendant [always looking
for the easy way out]. The motion was denied. The district court went on to order (in part) that
pending the determination of the action on the merits, Valley West (D) is enjoined and

restrained from allowing, and shall take all necessary steps to prevent, any other tenant in its Valley West Mall (including but not limited to Lord's Jewelers) to open and operate a fourth full line jewelry store. From this order Valley West (D) appeals.

■ ISSUE

Did the district court properly deny the motion to dismiss for failure to join an indispensable party?

■ DECISION AND RATIONALE

(Alsop, J.) Yes. Because Helzberg (P) was seeking and the District Court ordered injunctive relief which may prevent Lord's from operating its jewelry store in the Valley West Mall in the manner in which Lord's originally intended, the District Court correctly concluded that Lord's was a party to be joined if feasible. Therefore, because Lord's was not and is not subject to personal jurisdiction in the Western District of Missouri, the District Court was required to determine whether or not Lord's should be regarded as indispensable. After considering the factors which Rule 19(b) mandates be considered, the District Court concluded that Lord's was not to be regarded as indispensable. We agree. We think that Lord's absence will not prejudice Valley West (D) in a way contemplated by Rule 19(b). Valley West (D) contends that it may be subjected to inconsistent obligations as a result of a determination in this action and a determination in another forum that Valley West (D) should proceed in a fashion contrary to what has been ordered in these proceedings. It is true that the obligations of Valley West (D) to Helzberg (P), as determined in these proceedings, may be inconsistent with Valley West's (D) obligations to Lord's. However, we are of the opinion that any inconsistency in those obligations will result from Valley West's (D) voluntary execution of two lease agreements which impose inconsistent obligations rather than from Lord's absence from the present proceedings. Valley West's (D) contention that it may be subjected to inconsistent judgments if Lord's should choose to file suit elsewhere and be awarded judgment is speculative at best. In the first place, Lord's has not filed such a suit. Secondly, there is no showing that another court is likely to interpret the language of the two lease agreements differently from the way in which the District Court would. Therefore, we also conclude that Valley West (D) will suffer no prejudice as a result of the District Court's proceeding in Lord's absence. Rule 19(b) also requires the court to consider ways in which prejudice to the absent party can be lessened or avoided. The District Court afforded Lord's the opportunity to intervene in order to protect any interest it might have in the outcome of this litigation. Lord's chose not to do so. In light of Lord's decision not to intervene we conclude that the District Court acted in such a way as to sufficiently protect Lord's interests. Similarly, we also conclude that the District Court's determinations that a judgment rendered in Lord's absence would be adequate and that there is no controlling significance to the fact that Helzberg (P) would have an adequate remedy in the Iowa courts were not erroneous. It follows that the District Court's conclusion that in equity and good conscience the action should be allowed to proceed was a correct one. In sum, it is generally recognized that a person does not become indispensable to an action to determine rights under a contract simply because that person's rights or obligations under an entirely separate contract will be affected by the result of the action. We conclude that the district court properly denied the motion to dismiss for failure to join an indispensable party. The judgment of the District Court is affirmed.

Analysis:

Rule 19(b) requires the court to look to the extent to which a judgment rendered in Lord's absence might be prejudicial to Lord's or to Valley West (D). It seems axiomatic that none of Lord's rights or obligations will be ultimately determined in a suit to which it is not a party. Even if, as a result of the district court's granting of the preliminary injunction, Valley West (D) should attempt to terminate Lord's leasehold interest in its space in the Valley West Mall, Lord's will retain all of its rights under its lease agreement with Valley West (D). None of its rights or obligations will have been adjudicated as a result of the present proceedings,

proceedings to which it is not a party. Therefore, Lord's would not be prejudiced under Rule 19(b) as a result of this action. Additionally, Helzberg seeks only to restrain Valley West's (D) breach of the lease agreement to which Helzberg (P) and Valley West (D) were the sole parties. Certainly, all of the rights and obligations arising under a lease can be adjudicated where all of the parties to the lease are before the court. Thus, in the context of these proceedings, the District Court can determine all of the rights and obligations of both Helzberg (P) and Valley West (D) based upon the lease agreement between them, even though Lord's is not a party to the proceedings.

■ **CASE VOCABULARY**

ADJUDICATED: Final judgment of the court.

ENJOINED: Legally prevented from doing a certain act.

"LONG ARM" STATUTE: Allows local courts to obtain jurisdiction over nonresident defendants.

PERSONAL JURISDICTION: Refers to the court's power over the parties involved in a particular lawsuit.

SUBJECT MATTER JURISDICTION: Refers to the competency of the court to hear and determine a particular category of cases.

INTERVENTION WILL BE ALLOWED IF THE APPLICANT HAS ANY SIGNIFICANT INTEREST IN THE TRANSACTION AT ISSUE

■ **INSTANT FACTS** A complaint was filed to prevent NRC (D) from issuing licenses for the operation of uranium mills without first preparing environmental impact statements.

■ **BLACK LETTER RULE** Applicants satisfying their burden of the three requirements of Rule 24(a)(2) should be allowed to intervene in an action.

■ **PROCEDURAL BASIS**

Appeal from the district court's denial of the applicants' motion to intervene.

■ **FACTS**

The American Mining Congress and Kerr-McGee Nuclear Corporation seek review of the district court's order denying their motions to intervene as a matter of right or on a permissive basis, pursuant to Rule 24(a)(2) [applicant claims interest relating to the property or transaction, and disposition of the action may impair or impede ability to protect that interest, unless interests are adequately protected] and (b), Fed. Rules Civil Proc. The underlying action in which the movants requested intervention was instituted by the Natural Resources Defense Council (P) and others. In the action, declaratory and injunctive relief is directed to the United States Nuclear Regulatory Commission (NRC) (D) and the New Mexico Environmental Improvement Agency (NMEIA), prohibiting those agencies from issuing licenses for the operation of uranium mills in New Mexico without first preparing environmental impact statements. Kerr-McGee and United Nuclear are potential recipients of the licenses. Congress, in the Atomic Energy Act of 1954, has authorized the NRC (D) to issue such licenses. NMEIA is involved because under Sec. 274(b) of the Act, the NRC (D) is authorized to enter into such agreements with the states allowing the states to issue licenses. Thus the action in effect seeks to prevent the use of Sec. 274(b) of the Act so as to avoid the requirement of an impact statement for which provision is made in the National Environmental Policy Act. The complaint alleges that such statements are now prepared by the NRC (D) in states that have not entered into agreements with the NRC (D), but that the NRC (D) does not prepare such statements where there is an agreement with a state such as New Mexico. The relief sought by the National Resources Defense Council's (P) complaint is, first, that NRC's (D) involvement in the licensing procedure in New Mexico is, notwithstanding the delegation to the state, sufficient to constitute major federal action, whereby the impact statement requirement is not eliminated. Second, that if an impact statement is not required in connection with the granting of licenses, the New Mexico program is in conflict with Sec. 274(d)(2) of the Atomic Energy Act. The motion of United Nuclear Corporation to intervene was not opposed by the parties and it was granted. On the date the complaint was filed, NMEIA granted a license to United Nuclear to operate a uranium mill. The complaint seeks to enjoin the issuance of the license thus granted. It was after that, that Kerr-McGee, American Mining Congress, and others filed motions to intervene. These motions, insofar as they sought intervention as of right, were denied on the ground that the interests of the parties or movants would be adequately represented by United Nuclear [too many cooks]. Permissive intervention was also denied. Kerr-McGee and American Mining Congress both appeal denial of both intervention as of right and permissive intervention.

■ **ISSUE**

Was the Court's denial of intervention correct under Rule 24(a) of the Federal Rules of Civil Procedure?

■ **DECISION AND RATIONALE**

(Doyle, J.) No. Our issue is a limited one. We merely construe and weigh Rule 24(a) of the Fed. R. Civ. P. (intervention as of right) and decide in light of the facts and considerations presented whether the denial of intervention was correct. The position adopted by the trial court that Kerr-McGee was adequately represented dispensed with the need for the court to consider the question whether Kerr-McGee had an interest in the litigation before the court. The question then is whether the contention made is a correct concept of interest. Strictly to require that the movant in intervention have a *direct* interest in the outcome of the lawsuit strikes us as being too narrow a construction of Rule 24(a)(2). Thus we are asked to interpret interest in relationship to the second criterion in Rule 24(a)(2), impairment or impeding ability to protect the interest. The Supreme Court has said that the interest must be a significantly protectable interest. The matter of immediate interest is the issuance and delivery of the license sought by United Nuclear. However, the consequence of the litigation could well be the imposition of the requirement that an environmental impact statement be prepared before granting any uranium mill license in New Mexico, or, secondly, it could result in an injunction terminating or suspending the agreement between NRC (D) and NMEIA. Either consequence would be felt by United Nuclear and to some degree, of course, by Kerr-McGee, which is said to be one of the largest holders of uranium properties in New Mexico. A decision in favor of the Natural Resources Defense Council (P), which is not unlikely, could have a profound effect upon Kerr-McGee. Hence, it does have an interest within the meaning of Rule 24(a)(2). The next question is whether, assuming the existence of an interest, the chance of impairment is sufficient to fulfill the requirement of Rule 24(a)(2). The question of impairment is not separate from the question of existence of an interest. The Natural Resources Defense Council (P) contend that Kerr-McGee and the American Mining Congress would not be bound by the results of the case if they are not participants, therefore their interests are not impaired. Kerr-McGee points out that even though it may not be res judicata, still it would have a stare decisis effect. Moreover, with NRC (D) and NMEIA as parties, the result might be more profound than stare decisis. The Rule refers to impairment "as a practical matter," thus the court may consider any significant legal effect in Kerr-McGee's and the American Mining Congress' interest and is not restricted to a rigid res judicata test. Hence, the stare decisis effect might be sufficient to satisfy the requirement. We are of the opinion, therefore, that Kerr-McGee and the American Mining Congress have satisfied the impairment criterion. The final question is whether the trial court was correct in its conclusion that United Nuclear would adequately represent Kerr-McGee and the American Mining Congress. United Nuclear has already been granted its license, thus Kerr-McGee urges that United Nuclear may be ready to compromise the case by obtaining a mere declaration that while environmental impact statements should be issued, this requirement need be prospective only, whereby it would not affect them. While we see this as a remote possibility, we gravely doubt that United Nuclear would opt for such a result. It is true, however, that United Nuclear has a defense of laches that is not available to Kerr-McGee or the others. There are other reasons for allowing intervention. There is some value in having the parties before the court so that they will be bound by the result. American Mining Congress represents a number of companies having a wide variety of interests. This can, therefore, provide a useful supplement to the defense of the case. The same can be said of Kerr-McGee. Thus Kerr-McGee and the American Mining Congress have satisfied their burden of the three requirements of Rule 24(A)(2). Consequently, they should be and they are hereby allowed to intervene. The order of the district court is reversed and the cause is remanded with instructions to the trial court to grant Kerr-McGee's and the American Mining Congress' motions to intervene.

Analysis:

The district court's order denying intervention by the several corporations focused on whether the interest of the party seeking to intervene was adequately represented by a fellow member of the industry. The court decided that the interests of Kerr-McGee and the American Mining Congress were adequately protected by United Nuclear, which possessed the necessary experience and knowledge in a complex area of business. The district court thought that to allow the intervention would engender delay and produce unwieldy procedure, and that the Kerr-McGee and the American Mining Congress requirements were met by allowing the filing of amicus curiae briefs. This court, however, found that the interests of Kerr-McGee and the American Mining Congress in the subject matter were sufficient to satisfy the requirements of Rule 24 and that the threat of loss of their interest and inability to participate is of such magnitude as to impair their ability to advance their interest.

■ CASE VOCABULARY

AMICUS CURIAE BRIEF: Submitted by one not a party to the lawsuit on behalf of third parties who will be affected by the resolution of the dispute.

FRCP 24(a): " . . . [A]nyone shall be permitted to intervene in an action: . . . . (2) when the applicant claims an interest relating to the property or transaction which is the subject of the action and the applicant is so situated that the disposition of the action may as a practical matter impair or impede the applicant's ability to protect that interest, unless the applicant's interest is adequately represented by existing parties."

INTERVENTION: A proceeding allowing a person to enter into a lawsuit already in progress.

LACHES: Doctrine providing a party an equitable defense where long-neglected rights are sought to be enforced against the party.

RES JUDICATA: Final judgment has been made in a court.

STARE DECISIS: Principles announced in former decisions will be upheld.

(City) v. (Firefighters)

490 U.S. 755, 109 S.Ct. 2180, 104 L.Ed.2d 835 (1989)

A PARTY SEEKING A JUDGMENT BINDING ON ANOTHER CANNOT OBLIGATE THE
LATTER TO INTERVENE IN A SUIT TO WHICH THAT PERSON IS NOT A PARTY

■ **INSTANT FACTS** Pursuant to consent judgments between the City of Birmingham ("City") and the Jefferson County Personnel Board ("Board") with black firefighters, the white firefighters filed a suit against the City and the Board alleging reverse discrimination.

■ **BLACK LETTER RULE** A party seeking a judgment binding on another cannot obligate the latter to intervene in the action without mandatorily joining that person in the action.

■ **PROCEDURAL BASIS**

Certiorari to the United States Court of Appeals for the Eleventh District in discrimination suit.

■ **FACTS**

The City of Birmingham ("City") and the Jefferson County Personnel Board ("Board") entered into a consent judgment with black firefighters for discrimination in hiring and promotion of the latter. Subsequently, white firefighters ("Martin") (P) brought an action against the City and the Board (D), alleging that the promotions were in violation of federal law because they were based on race. The City and the Board (D) defended on the ground that the consent judgment precluded the current suit. The District Court, holding in favor of the City and the Board (D), declared that the consent judgment was a defense to the reverse discrimination alleged by the white firefighters (P). The Court of Appeals reversed on the ground that the consent judgment did not preclude the current suit because the white firefighters (P) were not parties to the previous judgment. In the Supreme Court, the City and the Board (D) argued that the white firefighters could have intervened in the first suit.

■ **ISSUE**

May a party seeking a judgment binding another obligate the latter to intervene in the action without mandatorily joining that party in the action?

■ **DECISION AND RATIONALE**

(Rehnquist, C.J.) No. A party seeking a judgment binding on another cannot obligate the latter to intervene in the action without mandatorily joining that person in the action. Generally, one is not bound by a judgment in which he was not a party, or was not made a party by service of process. The City and the Board (D) argue that because the white firefighters (P) failed to voluntarily intervene in the earlier action, their suit is impermissible, especially in light of their knowledge that the consent judgment would affect them. This court, however, is in agreement with Justice Brandeis' view in *Chase National Bank v. Norwalk*, that a person entitled to a hearing does not have the burden of voluntary intervention in a suit in which he is not a party. The drafters of the Federal Rules of Civil Procedure have determined that the concern for finality and completion of a judgment is better served by mandatory joinder procedure and not by permissive intervention. FRCP 19(a) provides for mandatory joinder in circumstances where a judgment rendered in the absence of a person may impose a risk of incurring inconsistent obligations in a party. Joinder as a party, rather than knowledge of a lawsuit and an opportunity to intervene, is the method by which potential parties are subjected to the jurisdiction of the court and bound by a judgment or decree. The parties in a suit know better the nature and scope of the relief sought in the action, and at whose expense the relief might be granted. Thus, the burden should be on these parties to bring additional parties where such a step is indicated, rather than potential additional parties to intervene upon gaining knowledge of the suit. The City and the Board (D) argue that mandatory joinder will be burdensome because the potential claimants may be numerous and difficult to identify, and that if they are not joined, there is potential for inconsistent judgments. Such difficulties, although possible, are not alleviated by allowing voluntary intervention. Again, plaintiffs who seek the aid of the courts to alter existing employment opportunities, or the employer who might be subject to conflicting decrees, are best able to bear the burden of designating those who would be adversely affected if the plaintiffs prevail. (Affirmed.)

■ **DISSENT**

(Stevens, J., Brennan, J., Marshall, J., Blackmun, J.) While the consent decree in this case could not deprive the white firefighters of their contractual rights, such as seniority or other legal rights, there is no reason why the consent judgment might not produce changes in conditions at the white firefighters' place of employment that may have a serious effect on their opportunities for employment or promotion. The fact that one of the effects of the decree is to curtail the opportunities of nonparties does not mean that the nonparties have been deprived of legal rights or that they have standing to appeal from that decree without becoming parties. A person who can foresee that a lawsuit is likely to have an impact on his interests may pay a heavy price if he elects to sit on the sidelines instead of intervening in the action. In this case, the District Court, after conducting a trial and carefully considering the firefighters' arguments, concluded that the effort of the City and the Board to eradicate discrimination through a consent decree was lawful. Thus, the firefighters have already had their day in court and have failed to carry their burden.

Analysis:

This case was subsequently overruled by an act of Congress that prohibits challenges to employment consent decrees by individuals who had actual notice and reasonable opportunity to intervene, or those whose interests were adequately represented. In this case, the court distinguishes between a voluntary intervention and mandatory joinder. As the word itself suggests, voluntary intervention is "voluntary"; a party whose interests are at stake may choose to join in the action. Mandatory joinder, on the other hand, is when a party to the case seeks to join other parties as plaintiffs or defendants. The decision of the court in this case indicates that even if a party's rights may be affected, the party is not obligated to intervene. However, when a party in a case wants to make the judgment binding on a nonparty, that party must join the nonparty in the action under the mandatory joinder rules of the Federal Rules of Civil Procedure.

■ **CASE VOCABULARY**

INTERVENTION: A proceeding permitting a person to enter into a lawsuit already in progress. This term refers to admission of a person not an original party to the suit, so that the person can protect some right or interest which is allegedly affected by the proceeding.

JOINDER: Uniting of several causes of action or parties in a single suit. Mandatory joinder refers to the mandatory joining of certain parties which are required for the just adjudication of a controversy.

Paragon Molding Ltd. v. Safeco Insurance Company

(Manufacturer) v. (Insurer)

2010 WL 2386355 (S.D. Ohio 2010)

INTERPLEADER EXISTS TO RESOLVE DIFFERENT CLAIMS TO THE SAME FUNDS

Wow, that's terrible--just imagine the litigation.

■ **INSTANT FACTS** Paragon's (P) real estate and inventory were damaged by a fire, and different parties made claims on the proceeds of an insurance policy.

■ **BLACK LETTER RULE** The function of interpleader is to resolve inconsistent claims against designated assets based on mutually exclusive theories, rather than to adjudicate rival claims that are mutually exclusive only because of the limited size of the assets.

■ **PROCEDURAL BASIS**

Order directing the parties to brief the issues.

■ **FACTS**

Paragon Molding (P) had a fire at its facility and sustained damage to the real estate and inventory for its business. Paragon (P) filed suit against its insurer, AEIC (D), claiming that AEIC (D) wrongfully withheld proceeds from an insurance policy. Before AEIC (D) could remit the funds, other parties came forward to present claims against the insurance proceeds. The parties filed a motion to deposit the funds with the court. The proceeds of the policy were then filed with the court. Besides Paragon (P), the parties who intervened in the suit to make claims were:

1. Miller Industries, LLC (D), the owner of the real estate occupied by Paragon (P), represented by Don Little, the attorney who also represented Paragon (P);

2. Paragon (P) and Miller (D) jointly, for attorney fees for Attorney Little;

3. Alex N. Sill Company (D), loss consultants and appraisers, for fees allegedly owed for assisting Paragon (P) in preparing the insurance claim;

4. Roy Rhodes (D), part owner of a business purchased by Paragon (P), who alleged that most of the non-realty assets destroyed or damaged by the fire belonged to that business (Roy Rhodes (D) also held a state court judgment against Paragon (P) for breach of contract);

5. Jimmie Rhodes (D), holder of a promissory note from Paragon (P); and

6. JPMorgan Chase Bank, NA (D), holder of state court judgments against Paragon (P) based on promissory notes and a mortgage guaranty.

■ **ISSUE**

Should the suit proceed as an interpleader action?

■ **DECISION AND RATIONALE**

(Rice, J.) Yes. The function of interpleader is to resolve inconsistent claims against designated assets based on mutually exclusive theories, rather than to adjudicate rival claims that are mutually exclusive only because of the limited size of the assets. Historically, strict interpleader actions were available when the same debt or duty was demanded by all of the defendants, all of the defendants' claims were derived from or dependent upon a common source, the plaintiff was a neutral stakeholder with no claim to the fund or property, and the plaintiff had no independent liability to any of the defendants. Interpleader actions are governed by strict equitable principles.

The court suggested here that the insurance proceeds be deposited with the court, and that the action proceed in the nature of an interpleader. AEIC (D) should be dismissed, as it has no further interest in the action. Paragon (P) should proceed as the only proper plaintiff. All of the other parties are defendants. The court foresees no problem, except for the representation of Paragon (P) and Miller (D) by the same attorney. All parties must waive this potential conflict of interest before Attorney Little may proceed in his dual role. The priority of distribution will go to claimants who have a claim in the specific *res* held by the court, rather than general, unrelated claims against Paragon (P). This approach is especially apt in this case, as the court has no information regarding the funds that may be available to Paragon (P) to satisfy general liabilities unrelated to the fire insurance proceeds. Parties must specify whether they have a claim in the *res* or, if not, what, if anything, entitles them to priority of payments over other claimants.

Finally, the federal interpleader statute, 28 U.S.C. § 1335, requires the participation of at least two adverse claimants of diverse citizenship. According to the pleadings, Paragon (P) is a citizen of Ohio. The other parties are directed to submit a short amendment to their pleadings regarding diversity of citizenship. The parties are also directed to submit the following:

1. Confirmation of agreement that the suit should proceed as an interpleader, or an explanation of the basis of the party's disagreement;

2. Confirmation of agreement with the dismissal of AEIC (D), or an explanation of the party's disagreement;

3. Waiver of the conflict of interest between Paragon (P) and Miller (D) regarding representation by Attorney Little, or an explanation of the party's disagreement;

4. Explanation of the party's claim on the *res* of the fire insurance proceeds, or an explanation of why the party claims priority over other claimants;

5. Paragon (P) is directed to submit a copy of the fire insurance policy, and a discussion of any arrangement regarding why Paragon (P), as tenant, insured the property on behalf of Miller (D), the owner of the property; and

6. Sill (D) is required to file a statement of why it is entitled to additional payment by Paragon (P), along with how much it previously received from Paragon (P), and why Sill (D) failed to disclose that amount before.

The court will entertain no further summary judgment motions, but will allow the parties to submit one responsive memorandum to respond to any new memoranda submitted by the parties. So ordered.

Analysis:

Paragon (P), as the insured under the policy, is not a neutral stakeholder here, as it presumably wants to retain as much of the insurance proceeds as possible. The two claimants who would seem to have the lowest priority for payment are JP Morgan Chase (D), whose claim is for various notes and guaranties, and Jimmie Rhodes (D), whose claim is based solely on a promissory note. Roy Rhodes (D) may have some claim, based on the destruction of the assets of the division of Paragon (P) of which he was a part-owner, but he also has a large claim based on an unrelated state court judgment. The court's impatience with Sill (D), for not stating how much it was already paid for services rendered, is apparent.

■ CASE VOCABULARY

RES: A "thing." The subject matter or object of an action "in rem," which is an action against a thing and not a person.

Hansberry v. Lee
(Buyer) v. (Covenantor)

311 U.S. 32, 61 S.Ct. 115 (1940)

IN A CLASS ACTION SUIT, WHERE A CLASS MEMBER WAS NOT ADEQUATELY REPRESENTED, GIVING RES JUDICATA EFFECT TO THE JUDGMENT VIOLATES DUE PROCESS

■ **INSTANT FACTS** Hansberry (D), the black purchaser of land that was subject to a racially restrictive sales covenant, sought to avoid a prior class action holding that the covenant was valid.

■ **BLACK LETTER RULE** Granting res judicata effect to a class action judgment, in which the prerequisites and procedures for class action were not satisfied, violates due process.

■ **PROCEDURAL BASIS**

Writ of certiorari from order affirming res judicata effect of prior decree.

■ **FACTS**

This class action suit was brought in an Illinois state court to enforce a racially restrictive covenant involving some land in Chicago. The covenant provided that it was not effective unless signed by 95% of the landowners. In the complaint. Lee (P), a white person, sought to enjoin the purchase of some restricted land by Hansberry (D), a black. Lee (P) alleged that the seller had signed the covenant, and that an earlier state court decision had held that the covenant was effective, since 95% of the landowners had signed the agreement. Hansberry (D) and other defendants argued that they were not bound by the res judicata effect of the earlier judgment, since they had not been parties to the suit. Thus, Hansberry (D) and the others argued that their due process rights were being violated. The Illinois Circuit Court and Supreme Court held that the original action was a class suit, and therefore that the holding was binding on all class members, including Hansberry (D) and the sellers. The United States Supreme Court granted certiorari.

■ **ISSUE**

Where the procedural requirements for class action have not been satisfied, is the judgment res judicata and therefore binding on absent parties?

■ **DECISION AND RATIONALE**

(Stone, J.) No. Where the procedure and course of litigation in a class action do not insure the protection of absent parties, a judgment entered in the action is not binding on those absent parties. An alternative holding would violate the due process rights of the absent members. In a typical litigation, notice and an opportunity to be heard are requisite to due process, and a judgment in which a person is not designated as a party does not have a res judicata effect on that person. An exception exists, however, in the class action context [Just when you thought you understood due process, class actions confuse the issue!]. Judgments entered in class or representative suits may bind members of the class or those represented who were not made parties to it. However, there is a failure of due process where the procedure adopted does not fairly insure the protection of the interest of absent parties who are to be bound by it. In the original case at hand, which found the covenant effective, the procedure did not adequately

---

protect the interests of Hansberry (D) and the sellers. First, the restrictive agreement did not purport to create a joint obligation or liability. Rather, the racially restrictive covenant was a series of several obligations of the signers. Second, the signers seeking to enforce the agreement cannot be considered members of the same class as those signers seeking to challenge the validity of the agreement or to resist its performance. The signers such as Lee (P) attempting to enforce the agreement have conflicting interests with the parties such as Hansberry (D) and the sellers attempting to challenge the agreement. Thus, the mere fact that all of the parties had signed the agreement does not make them the same class, and the absent parties in the original litigation were not provided due process protections in asserting their interests. Reversed.

Analysis:

While due process in the jurisdictional context typically focused on the adequacy of notice and opportunity to be heard, the Supreme Court here focuses on the adequacy of class representation. This makes sense in the class action context, given the potentially severe res judicata effects of a judgment on an absent class member. In effect, the Court is saying that people such as Hansberry (D) and the sellers were not adequately represented in the original litigation. Thus, they are not to be considered members of the original class. Conversely, if they were class members, the Court asserts, then the original judgment would be binding. The U.S. Supreme Court apparently assumed that the adequacy of representation in an original action could be analyzed in a later action. The logic of this approach is sound, since a final determination of the adequacy of representation could only be made through subsequent challenges to the res judicata effect of the suit. As Rule 23(c)(3) states, a class action decree should define the members of the class, presumably to aid in future determinations of the judgment's binding effect. The original court hearing the class action cannot predetermine the binding effect of its judgment, since this construction of Rule 23 would arguably be substantive in nature and thus violate the Rules Enabling Act, 28 U.S.C. §2072.

■ CASE VOCABULARY

CLASS SUIT: An action brought, on behalf of a large number of people, by a representative who is similarly situated and who purports to represent the interests of the absent parties.

MINIMUM CONTACTS ARE NOT REQUIRED FOR PERSONAL JURISDICTION IN CLASS ACTIONS, BUT THE FORUM STATE MAY NOT NECESSARILY APPLY ITS OWN LAW TO ALL CLAIMS

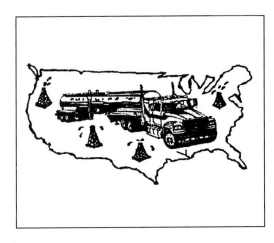

■ **INSTANT FACTS** Shutts (P) and several other holders of royalty interests brought a class action against Phillips Petroleum (D) to recover royalty payments. The Kansas court obtained personal jurisdiction over all parties and applied Kansas law to all claims.

■ **BLACK LETTER RULE** In class actions, personal jurisdiction does not require that each class member have minimum contacts with the forum state, but the forum state must have sufficient interests in the claims to assert its state law to all claims.

■ **PROCEDURAL BASIS**

Writ of certiorari reviewing affirmance of class action judgment in favor of class for damages for contractual violations.

■ **FACTS**

Phillips Petroleum (D) obtained natural gas from leased land in eleven different states. Shutts (P) and several other lessors brought an action against Phillips Petroleum (D) in a Kansas state court, seeking to recover interest on royalty payments due under the leases. The Kansas trial court certified a class consisting of 33,000 royalty owners, and the class representatives provided each class member with notice by mail and with an opportunity to opt out of the class action. [Don't worry, the $100,000 in postage could later be recovered by the representatives!] The final class consisted of 28,100 class members residing in all fifty states and in foreign countries. Nevertheless, the trial court asserted personal jurisdiction and applied only Kansas contract law, finding Phillips Petroleum (D) liable for interest on suspended royalties to all class members. Phillips Petroleum (D) argued that the Due Process Clause prevented the Kansas court from adjudicating the claims of the non-resident class members, and that the Full Faith and Credit Clause prohibited the application of Kansas law to all of the claims. The Kansas Supreme Court affirmed the trial court's ruling, and the U.S. Supreme Court granted certiorari.

■ **ISSUE**

(1) May a court exercise personal jurisdiction over absent class members even if the members do not possess the minimum contacts with the forum which would support personal jurisdiction over a defendant? (2) Does a mailed notice and opt out provision satisfy the notice requirements for due process purposes? (3) May a forum state apply that state's law to every claim in a class action where the state does not have a significant contact and interest in every claim asserted by each member of the class?

■ **DECISION AND RATIONALE**

(Rehnquist, J.) (1) Yes. A court may exercise personal jurisdiction over absent class members even if the members do not possess the minimum contacts with the forum which would

---

support personal jurisdiction over a defendant. As this Court has held in several cases, due process requires that a defendant have sufficient minimum contacts with the forum state in order for a court to obtain personal jurisdiction over a defendant. Phillips Petroleum (D) argues that, likewise, the Kansas courts may not assert personal jurisdiction over class members who neither affirmatively consent to jurisdiction nor have sufficient minimum contacts with Kansas. However, there are significant differences between jurisdiction over a defendant and jurisdiction over a class of plaintiffs. While defendants deserve due process protections from being haled into a distant state with which the defendants have no contacts, plaintiffs in class actions are not haled anywhere to defend themselves upon threat of default judgments. In class actions, both the court and the class representatives protect the interests of absent class members. Moreover, absent class members do not have to hire counsel or appear, are not subject to coercive or punitive remedies, and are not bound by adverse judgments for damages. Thus, the due process rights afforded to defendants, who should not be forced to travel to and appear in distant states with which they have no minimum contacts, do not apply equally to plaintiff class members. (2) Yes. A mailed notice including an opt out provision satisfies the due process requirements to provide notice to all interested litigants. This notice must be reasonably calculated to apprise the interested parties of the pendency of the actions and present them an opportunity to be heard. In the case at hand, the class representatives reasonably used first class mail to notify all 33,000 royalty owners of the pending action. Moreover, this notice provided the parties an opportunity to opt out of the litigation so as to avoid the binding effect of any judgment, allowing such members to bring separate claims. Phillips Petroleum (D) maintains that notice in class actions must provide an "opt in" provision, and that jurisdiction is improper over all distant plaintiffs who do not voluntarily opt in to the litigation. We do not think that the Constitution requires the State to sacrifice the obvious advantages in judicial efficiency resulting from the opt out approach for the protection of the onerous opt in approach. (3) No. Where a forum state does not have a significant contact and interest in every claim asserted by each member of the class, the state may not apply that state's law to every claim in a class action. In the case at hand, the Kansas state court applied Kansas contract law to every claim, notwithstanding that over 99% of the leases and 97% of the plaintiffs had no apparent connection to Kansas. Phillips Petroleum (D) contends that the application of Kansas substantive law in this situation violates the Due Process Clause and the Full Faith and Credit Clause, and we agree. Kansas must have a significant contact to the claims asserted by each member of the plaintiff class, creating sufficient state interests, in order to ensure that the application of Kansas law is not arbitrary or unfair. However, Kansas did not have a sufficient interests in claims unrelated to the state. Moreover, the Kansas laws conflict with laws of jurisdictions such as Texas, in which many class members reside. In addition, there is no indication that the leases contemplated an application of Kansas law to all claims arising out of the leases. Therefore, the application of Kansas law to every claim in this case is sufficiently arbitrary and unfair as to exceed constitutional limits. In conclusion, we affirm the judgment of the Supreme Court of Kansas insofar as it upheld Kansas jurisdiction over all claims, but we reverse its judgment insofar as it held that Kansas law was applicable to all of the transactions. Remanded for further proceedings not inconsistent with this opinion.

Analysis:

The due process protections afforded to defendants in ordinary civil actions simply do not parallel the protections necessary for plaintiffs in class actions, since class action plaintiffs do not suffer similar hardships and are adequately protected by the court and by the class representatives. Phillips Petroleum's (D) arguments, that every class member must "opt in" to class actions and must have minimum contacts with the forum state, would obliterate class actions involving numerous plaintiffs residing in several different states and countries. Clearly, the efficiencies provided by class actions outweigh the minimal needs to obtain consent or for the forum to have minimum contacts with each class member. The instant case justifies jurisdiction despite a lack of minimum contacts on one of two grounds: either consent to jurisdiction is inferred by the members' failure to opt out, or class action plaintiffs are not entitled to (and do not need) the same due process protections. In all likelihood, the latter interpretation is the most probable.

■ CASE VOCABULARY

PRO FORMA: A required format with which procedures must comply.

RARA AVIS: Literally "a rare bird"; a unique person or thing.

FEDERAL RULE 23(b) SETS THE STANDARD FOR CLASS CERTIFICATION

■ **INSTANT FACTS** The District Court certified a class of approximately 1.5 million current and former female employees of Wal-Mart (D) in an employment discrimination case, and the Ninth Circuit affirmed the certification.

■ **BLACK LETTER RULE** Certification of a class action is appropriate only when the common contention of the class members is capable of a class-wide resolution.

■ **PROCEDURAL BASIS**

Appeal from an order of the Ninth Circuit Court of Appeals affirming certification of a class.

■ **FACTS**

Wal-Mart (D) employs more than one million people in 3400 stores nationwide. Pay and promotion decisions are generally committed to the discretion of local managers, who exercise that discretion in a largely subjective manner. Although there are some objective standards for promotions, the ultimate decision is left to the discretion of an employee's superiors. Dukes (P) and the other plaintiffs brought a class action suit on behalf of all current and former female employees of Wal-Mart (D), alleging sex discrimination. Dukes (P) claimed that the local managers' discretion over pay and promotion decisions was exercised disproportionately in favor of men, leading to a disparate impact on women. Dukes (P) did not allege that Wal-Mart (D) had an express policy against the advancement of women, but claimed that Wal-Mart (D) was aware of the disparate impact of the local managers' decisions and refused to limit their discretion. Dukes (P) claimed that all women who worked at Wal-Mart (D) were subject to discrimination, by virtue of a strong and uniform corporate culture that permitted bias to infect, perhaps subconsciously, the discretionary decisions of each of Wal-Mart's (D) managers. The complaint requested injunctive and declaratory relief, punitive damages, and backpay.

Dukes (P) moved for certification of her suit as a class action, relying on Rule 23(b)(2) of the Federal Rules of Civil Procedure. That rule states that a class may be certified when "the party opposing the class has acted or refused to act on grounds that apply generally to the class, so that final injunctive relief or declaratory relief is appropriate respecting the class as a whole." As evidence that there were questions of law and fact common to all class members, Dukes (P) relied on statistical evidence regarding pay and promotion disparities, anecdotal reports of discrimination from about 120 female employees of Wal-Mart (D), and the testimony of a sociologist who conducted an analysis of Wal-Mart's (D) culture and personnel practices, concluding that Wal-Mart (D) was vulnerable to gender discrimination. The district court granted the certification motion, and the Ninth Circuit Court of Appeals affirmed. The Ninth Circuit determined that the case could be manageably tried as a class action by taking a random selection of class members' claims, referring them to a special master, and extrapolating the validity and value of the claims of all class members from that sample.

■ **ISSUE**

Was the case properly certified as a class action?

■ **DECISION AND RATIONALE**

(Scalia, J.) No. Certification of a class action is appropriate only when the common contention of the class members is capable of a class-wide resolution. Commonality does not mean merely the assertion of common allegations of fact, or even allegations of violation of the same law. Instead, commonality requires a plaintiff to demonstrate that the class members have suffered the same injury. Class certification questions will sometimes overlap with the merits of the underlying claim. In this case, proof of commonality overlaps with the contention that Wal-Mart (D) engaged in a pattern or practice of discrimination. The crux of the inquiry is the reason for the employment decisions. Without something holding the reasons for all of the claims together, it will be impossible to say that examination of all of the class members' claims will produce a common answer to the question, "Why was I disfavored?" In employment discrimination cases, commonality may be addressed by showing that an employer used a biased testing procedure, or by significant proof that an employer operated under a general policy of discrimination. Since Wal-Mart (D) uses no company-wide testing or evaluation policy, Dukes (P) must present significant proof of a general policy of discrimination. There is no such proof here. Wal-Mart (D) has an announced policy that forbids sex discrimination and imposes penalties for denying equal employment opportunities. The only evidence produced by Dukes (P) of a company policy was the expert testimony that Wal-Mart (D) is "vulnerable" to gender bias. The expert could not, however, determine how regularly stereotypes played a meaningful role in employment decisions at Wal-Mart (D).

The only corporate policy Dukes (P) established is the discretion given to local supervisors. On its face, this is the opposite of a uniform employment practice. In appropriate cases, giving discretion to lower-level supervisors can be the basis of Title VII liability under a disparate impact theory. But the recognition that such liability can exist does not lead to a conclusion that every employee in a company with such a policy has a claim in common. Dukes (P) has not demonstrated a common mode of exercising discretion that pervades the entire company. It is unbelievable that all of the managers in a company the size of Wal-Mart (D) would exercise their discretion in a common way without some common direction. The statistical and anecdotal evidence offered by Dukes (P) is insufficient. The anecdotal evidence was provided by 120 current or former employees and related to employees at 235 of Wal-Mart's 3400 stores. Even if every affidavit were true, that would not demonstrate that the entire company operates under a general policy of discrimination.

The claims for backpay were also improperly certified. Claims for monetary relief may not be certified under Fed. R. Civ. P. 23(b)(2), at least when the monetary relief is not incidental to the injunctive or declaratory relief. The key to class certification under Rule 23(b)(2) is the indivisible nature of the injunctive or declaratory remedy warranted. The Rule applies only when a single injunction or declaratory judgment would provide relief to each member of the class. Claims for individualized relief do not satisfy commonality requirements. Historically, Rule 23(b)(2) has been used for civil rights cases against parties charged with class-based discrimination, but not claims for individualized relief. Permitting the combination of individualized and class-wide relief would also be inconsistent with the structure of Rule 23(b). Classes certified under (b)(1) and (b)(2) share the traditional justifications for class treatment, namely, for a (b)(1) class, that individual adjudications would be impossible or unworkable, or, for a (b)(2) class, that the relief would affect the entire class at once. There is no opportunity to opt out of one of these classes. Rule 23(b)(3), however, allows class action certification in a broader set of circumstances. The only prerequisites are questions of law or fact common to class members that predominate over individual questions, and a showing that a class action is superior to other methods of adjudicating the controversy. A class member can opt out of a (b)(3) class. Given the structure of the Rule, it is clear that individualized monetary claims belong in Rule 23(b)(3) cases. The procedural protections of (b)(3) cases are missing from (b)(2) not because they are unnecessary, but because they are unnecessary to a (b)(2) class. Dukes (P) argues that the backpay claims were properly certified, because those claims do not predominate over the requests for injunctive and declaratory relief, but the "predominance" test runs the risk of putting potentially valid claims for monetary relief at risk. Individual claims could be precluded by litigation from which individuals could not opt out.

The Court of Appeals would have replaced individual proceedings with trial by formula. The Rules Enabling Act, 28 U.S.C. § 2072(b), states that Rule 23 may not be used to "abridge, enlarge or modify any substantive right." A class cannot be certified on the premise that Wal-Mart (D) will not be entitled to litigate its statutory defenses to individual claims. Reversed.

■ CONCURRENCE IN PART, DISSENT IN PART

(Ginsburg, J.) The class should not have been certified under Rule 23(b)(2). The monetary relief is not merely incidental to declaratory or injunctive relief. The class could be certified under Rule 23(b)(3) if Dukes (P) showed that the common class questions predominated over individual questions. Whether the class meets the requirements of Rule 23(b)(3) is not before the Court, however, and should have been decided on remand.

Analysis:

Justice Scalia was not too impressed with Dukes' (P) statistical evidence. In a portion of her concurring and dissenting opinion not reproduced in the casebook, Justice Ginsburg points out that women fill seventy percent of the hourly jobs in Wal-Mart's (D) stores, but make up only thirty-three percent of the management employees. Statistical evidence also showed wide disparities in the pay of male and female employees. A number of commentators on this case have pointed out that, if the statistics and anecdotal evidence are ignored, the only class actions allowed would be against employers foolish enough not to make a formulaic written statement that they disapprove of discrimination.

■ CASE VOCABULARY

DECLARATORY JUDGMENT: A binding adjudication establishing the rights of the parties without providing for or ordering enforcement.

DISPARATE IMPACT: The adverse effect of a facially neutral practice (esp. an employment practice) that nonetheless discriminates against persons because of their race, sex, national origin, age, or disability and that is not justified by business necessity. Discriminatory intent is irrelevant in a disparate-impact claim.

PUNITIVE DAMAGES: A damages award not related to the actual harm caused by the plaintiff, but intended to punish the defendant and deter future wrongdoing.

Amchem Products, Inc. v. Windsor

(Asbestos Producer) v. *(Exposed Class)*

521 U.S. 591, 117 S.Ct. 2231 (1997)

SETTLEMENT IS RELEVANT TO A CLASS CERTIFICATION

■ **INSTANT FACTS** People exposed to asbestos products created a settlement-only class to settle current and future asbestos-related claims.

■ **BLACK LETTER RULE** In determining the propriety of a settlement-only class certification, the requirements of Rule 23(a) and (b)(3) Fed. R. Civ. P. must be satisfied, and the settlement must be taken into account as well.

■ **PROCEDURAL BASIS**

Appeal from the Court of Appeals' reversal of the trial court, thus denying the class certification.

■ **FACTS**

This case concerns the legitimacy under Rule 23 of the Federal Rules of Civil Procedure of a class-action certification sought to achieve global settlement of current and future asbestos-related claims. The class proposed for certification potentially encompasses hundreds of thousands, perhaps millions, of individuals [is that all?] tied together by this commonality: each was, or someday will be, adversely affected by past exposure to asbestos products manufactured by one or more of 20 companies (D). The class action thus instituted was not intended to be litigated [no courtroom big enough?]. Rather, within the space of a single day, the settling parties presented to the District Court a complaint, and answer, a proposed settlement agreement, and a joint motion for conditional class certification. As requested by the settling parties, the District Court conditionally certified, under Fed. R. Civ. P. Rule 23(b)(3), an encompassing opt-out class. Various class members raised objections to the settlement stipulation, and the Judge granted the objectors full rights to participate in the subsequent proceedings. Objectors urged that the settlement unfairly disadvantaged those without currently compensable conditions in that it failed to adjust for inflation or to account for changes, over time, in medical understanding. Strenuous objections had also been asserted regarding the adequacy of representation, a Rule 23(a)(4) requirement. Objectors maintained that class counsel and class representatives had disqualifying conflicts of interest. In particular, objectors urged, claimants whose injuries had become manifest and claimants without manifest injuries should not have common counsel and should not be aggregated in a single class. Declaring the class certification appropriate and the settlement fair, the District Court preliminarily enjoined all class members from commencing any asbestos-related suit against Amchem (D) in any state or federal court. The Court of Appeals reversed, finding that "serious intra-class conflicts precluded the class from meeting the adequacy of representation requirement" of Rule 23(a)(4). The objectors maintain in this Court an array of jurisdictional barriers. Most fundamentally, they maintain that the settlement proceeding is not a justiciable case or controversy within the confines of Article III of the Federal Constitution. In the main, they say the proceeding is a nonadversarial endeavor to impose on countless individuals without currently ripe claims and administrative compensation regime binding on those individuals if

---

and when they manifest injuries. Like the Third Circuit, the Supreme Court declined to reach these issues because they "would not exist but for the class action certification."

■ ISSUE

Does settlement play a role when determining the propriety of a settlement-only class certification?

■ DECISION AND RATIONALE

(Ginsburg, J.) Yes. Among current applications of Rule 23(b)(3), the "settlement only" class has become a stock device. Although all Federal Circuits recognize the utility of Rule 23(b)(3) settlement classes, courts have divided on the extent to which a proffered settlement affects court surveillance under Rule 23's certification criteria. We granted review to decide the role settlement may play, under existing Rule 23, in determining the propriety of class certification. Contrary to the Third Circuit's opinion, we hold that settlement is relevant to a class certification. Confronted with a request for settlement-only class certification, a district court need not inquire whether the case, if tried, would present intractable management problems, for the proposal is that there be no trial. But other specifications of the rule—those designed to protect absentees by blocking unwarranted or overbroad class definitions—demand undiluted, even heightened, attention in the settlement context. Such attention is of vital importance, for a court asked to certify a settlement class will lack the opportunity, present when a case is litigated, to adjust the class, informed by the proceedings as they unfold. The safeguards provided by the Rule 23(a) and (b) class-qualifying criteria, we emphasize, are not impractical impediments—checks shorn of utility—in the settlement class context. Federal courts, in any case, lack authority to substitute for Rule 23's certification criteria a standard never adopted—that if a settlement is "fair," then certification is proper. Applying to this case criteria the rulemakers set, we conclude that the Third Circuit's appraisal is essentially correct. Although the court should have acknowledged that settlement is a factor in the calculus, a remand is not warranted on that account. The Court of Appeals' opinion amply demonstrates why—with or without a settlement on the table—that sprawling class the District Court certified does not satisfy Rule 23's requirements. We address first the requirement of Rule 23(b)(3) that "common questions of law or fact predominate over any questions affecting only individual members." We hold that the predominance requirement is not met by the factors on which the District Court relied. The benefits asbestos-exposed persons might gain from the establishment of a grand-scale compensation scheme is a matter fit for legislative consideration, but it is not pertinent to the predominance inquiry. Nor can the class approved by the District Court satisfy Rule 23(a)(4)'s requirement that the named parties "will fairly and adequately protect the interests of the class." As the Third Circuit pointed out, named parties with diverse medical conditions sought to act on behalf of a single giant class rather than on behalf of discrete subclasses. Because we have concluded that the class in this case cannot satisfy the requirements of common issue predominance and adequacy of representation, we need not rule, definitively, on the notice given here. The argument is sensibly made that a nationwide administrative claims processing regime would provide the most secure, fair, and efficient means of compensating victims of asbestos exposure. Congress, however, has not adopted such a solution. And Rule 23, which must be interpreted with fidelity to the Rules Enabling Act and applied with the interests of absent class members in close view, cannot carry the large load Amchem (D), class counsel, and the District Court heaped upon it.

■ CONCURRENCE AND DISSENT

(Breyer, J.) The issues in this case are complicated and difficult. The District Court might have been correct. Or not. Subclasses might be appropriate. Or not. I cannot tell. And I do not believe that this Court should be in the business of trying to make these fact-based determinations. That is a job suited to the district courts in the first instance, and the courts of appeal on review.

Analysis:

The settling parties, in sum, achieved a global compromise with no structural assurance of fair and adequate representation for the diverse groups and individuals affected. Although the named parties alleged a range of complaints, each served generally as representative for the whole, not for a separate constituency. The Court found no assurance here, however, either in the terms of the settlement or in the structure of the negotiations, that the named plaintiffs operated under a proper understanding of their representational responsibilities. As a result, the class could not satisfy the requirements under Rule 23 and, as such, the Court was required to deny the motion.

■ CASE VOCABULARY

JUSTICIABLE: Capable of being tried in a court of law or equity.

OPT-OUT CLASS: Those potential plaintiffs who choose to not be part of the class action.

RIPE CLAIM: A case which is ready to be adjudicated.

SETTLEMENT-CLASS CERTIFICATION: A class action not intended to be litigated, but merely for settlement purposes.

STIPULATION: An agreement made by the parties relating to the matter before the court.